LAW
ENFORCEMENT
TRAINING

Dynamic Leadership Strategies

Thomas E. Baker
Lt. Col. MP USAR (Ret.)

Looseleaf Law Publications, Inc.

43-08 162nd Street
Flushing, NY 11358
www.LooseleafLaw.com
800-647-5547

This publication is not intended to replace nor be a substitute for any official procedural material issued by your agency of employment nor other official source. Looseleaf Law Publications, Inc., the author and any associated advisors have made all possible efforts to ensure the accuracy and thoroughness of the information provided herein but accept no liability whatsoever for injury, legal action or other adverse results following the application or adoption of the information contained in this book.

Baker, Thomas E., 1941-
  Law enforcement training : dynamic leadership strategies / by Thomas E. Baker.
      pages cm
  Includes bibliographical references and index.
  ISBN 978-1-60885-126-3
  1. Police training--United States. 2. Police administration--United States. 3. Police--Supervision of--United States.. I. Title.
  HV8142.B35 2015
  363.2068'3--dc23

                                        2015013861

Digital ISBN 978-1-60885-127-0

Cover by *Tin Box Studio*, Cincinnati, Ohio

TABLE OF CONTENTS

Many of the best leaders who ascend to high law enforcement command positions gained their leadership foundation as trainers. These instructors and managers learned their communication, speaking, and social skills in a training capacity. The opportunities to grow, develop, and exceed their grasp offered pathways to successful career transitions.

Law enforcement personnel who aspire to achieve leadership and command positions should not miss opportunities to participate in the training experience. The enhancement of content knowledge is only part of the training environment. The opportunity to help others is gratifying, and offers special insight into management and leadership strategies.

If you take this learning journey chapter-by-chapter and follow the learning pathways, you will apply your training management system successfully. Take advantage of the case studies, reflective exercises, and self-testing opportunities.

Read **Law Enforcement Training: Dynamic Leadership Strategies** as if I were a friend writing to you. This book is for all who seek to assist others in pursuit of law enforcement knowledge.

Read this book carefully. The pages provide evidence for dynamic instructional strategies. The training content is your instructional power at work. Make it work for you! Your potential is unlimited. How far do you want to go?

Tom Baker

Personal Acknowledgments

To the staff at Looseleaf Law Publications: Mary Loughrey, Editorial Vice President; Maria Felten, Production Editor; Mike Loughrey, President and CEO. Jane Piland-Baker's contribution as an editor and graphic designer for this book required considerable dedication.

About the Author

Thomas E. Baker served as a university associate professor of criminal justice and taught criminal justice/law enforcement courses for many years. In addition, he served as a police officer with Henrico County, Virginia and an undercover/intelligence officer with the Organized Crime, Vice Intelligence Unit, Montgomery County Police Department, Maryland.

He also served as a Lieutenant Colonel, United States Military Police Corps, USAR (Ret.). Lt. Col. Baker is a graduate of the Basic Military Police Officer's Course, Advanced Infantry Officer's Course, Advanced Military Police Officer's Course, Criminal Investigation Course, Advanced Criminal Investigation, Management Course, Psychological Operations Course, Field Grade Infantry Course, and the United States Army Command and General Staff College.

He served in the regular Army for three years, and then he joined the Reserve Component as a Special Agent/Warrant Officer with United States Army Criminal Investigation Command. Furthermore, he served as a Captain, Major, Lieutenant Colonel, Staff Officer, and CID Commander.

Lt. Col. Baker's military assignments included special agent, detachment commander, battalion level commander, and a Command Headquarters assignment with the United States Army Criminal Investigation Command. His additional assignments included provost marshal, military police investigations, staff officer for Training and Doctrine Command, and instructor for the United States Army Command and General Staff College.

His academic degrees include: A.A. Law Enforcement, B.S. Social Welfare and M.S. Counseling from Virginia Commonwealth University; M.Ed. Sports Science, M.S. Health Education and Educational Administration, East Stroudsburg University; CAGS Psychology and Counseling, Marywood University; and

Advanced Study Education, Pennsylvania State University and Temple University.

Tom's service also includes teaching physical education at the Diagnostic Center for Children in Virginia. He taught numerous criminal justice courses in the Virginia Community College System curriculum and served as the Program Head for Law Enforcement. Professor Baker taught Introduction to Criminal Justice, Organized Crime Patterns, Criminal Investigation, Introductory Criminal Analysis, Crime Prevention, Public Safety Administration, and Criminal Justice Management for many years at the university level.

He is the author of 8 books and over 170 publications, which have appeared in professional and peer-reviewed journals; he has written encyclopedia articles and presented research at national meetings. Professor Baker is the author of *Intelligence-Led Policing: Leadership, Strategies and Tactics; Effective Police Leadership: Moving Beyond Management; Positive Police Leadership: Problem-solving Planning; Police Suicide: Prevention, Assessment, and Intervention,* and *Organized Crime Conspiracies: Investigator Strategies and Tactics* with Looseleaf Law Publications.

DEDICATION

To Jane Piland Baker, Shannon Baker Swing, and the family members of those who serve in American law enforcement. Family members understand the sacrifices and dangerous risks law enforcement officers take every day. They wait for their safe return home and may stand in harm's way.

PREFACE

The aim of education is not knowledge, but action.
— Herbert Spencer

Focus

The Preface introduces the book and discusses learner support items. *Law Enforcement Training: Dynamic Leadership Strategies* assists instructors in promoting instructional goals, performance objectives, and lesson planning. Instructors develop methods that direct learners toward desired educational/training outcomes and to successfully assess and evaluate the learning process. The foremost purpose of this text is to prepare instructors and support training applications.

Overview

Law Enforcement Training: Dynamic Leadership Strategies serves the needs of readers interested in pursuing instructional and training careers. The author seeks to serve the needs of law enforcement agencies and trainers by addressing instructional skills. This book integrates many progressive educational practices, principles, and concepts. It serves an expanding textbook market for excellent training. Training continues to evolve, and this book addresses those requirements. University, community college, military, and agency libraries will find this book to be an asset to their collections.

Distance Training and Technology

Law Enforcement Training: Dynamic Leadership Strategies supports multidimensional training progressions and transitions. Themes address diverse training experiences and the application of modern technology. Law enforcement practitioners and *distance education (on-line)* participants benefit from the book's reader-friendly design. The future of law enforcement in-service training will include *on-line training, e-books,* and *independent learning.* There is a shift from the captive instructor audience approach to a more learner-centered active learning approach.

Virtual Reality **3D Training Systems** provide dynamic law enforcement programmed instruction. Opportunities for engaging high-risk training activities that offer innovative applications represent the future. Now, *virtual reality training* serves the needs of military, first responders, and other agency training applications.

Law Enforcement Training Applications

Law Enforcement Training: Dynamic Leadership Strategies supports training programming. It serves as a source of dialogue and planning information for law enforcement agencies at the local, state, and federal levels. This general format is open to modification and original instructor applications.

Law Enforcement Training: Dynamic Leadership Strategies supports training managers and instructors. Successful law enforcement instructors vary their instructional methods to meet target audience requirements. This text specializes in sustaining training certification and accreditation requirements.

Structure and Organization

Law Enforcement Training: Dynamic Leadership Strategies emphasizes interactive and active learning strategies. The pursuit of knowledge is a lifetime quest and a worthy goal for those who desire to serve in the field of law enforcement.

Law Enforcement Training: Dynamic Leadership Strategies emphasizes critical thinking and problem-solving strategies. Critical thinking requires organizing information and applying concepts to new and unique situations. The author seeks to educate readers who can appraise, think beyond mere facts, and eventually discover untapped boundaries concerning self and trainee potential.

Law Enforcement Training: Dynamic Leadership Strategies is multifaceted; consequently, the text and illustrations enhance learner understanding and retention. The paragraphs and sentences are deliberately short and concise. The book addresses diverse learning styles—numerous illustrations and concrete examples clarify concepts and maintain reader interest. The author has made every attempt to integrate an active voice writing style. Sentences in the active voice have energy and directness, both of which will keep the reader turning the pages.

Training Support

Law Enforcement Training: Dynamic Leadership Strategies incorporates an extensive variety of illustrative materials:

- This text presents considerable analytical concepts; therefore, numerous graphics, models, charts, and tables supplement the text.
- Visual components assist in active explanation of text concepts.
- Subheadings and short paragraphs enhance transition, coherence, and clarity for the learner.
- Large fonts assist those who read for speed and accuracy.

Assessment and evaluation are necessary to determine instructor effectiveness, participant learning, and course design revisions. This systematic educational design offers critical thinking and incorporates problem-solving concepts. Classroom critical thinking activities offer additional opportunities for learner participation and personal development.

Focus Points

Law Enforcement Training: Dynamic Leadership Strategies is reader friendly. Instructor organization and planning assures teaching effectiveness. The text follows these principles of curriculum and learning instruction:

Learning organizing centers include:

- Active learning goals and objectives
- Curriculum planning
- Lesson planning
- Lecture planning

- Active leaning strategies
- Critical thinking
- Problem-solving
- Decision-making
- Group case study exercises
- Practical exercises
- Learning simulations
- Performance feedback
- Peak performance training
- Counseling and advising
- Training management: pulling it all together
- Assessment and course evaluation procedures
- Self-inventory assessments

This text introduces analytical training concepts, strategies, and practical training applications. Effective training enhances law enforcement performance as well as personal competencies with such issues as coping with stress, thinking when exhausted, and maintaining self-control.

Conclusion

Law enforcement training is one of the most significant leadership/management functions. Training supports the mission and, at the same time, cultivates motivation and morale. Crucial to *Law Enforcement Training: Dynamic Leadership Strategies* is the development of training content into a meaningful format for decision-making applications.

PART I: THE LEADERSHIP JOURNEY BEGINS

"Obstacles in the pathway of the weak become stepping stones in the pathway of the strong."
— Thomas Carlyle

Figure Part I-A: The Leadership Journey Begins!

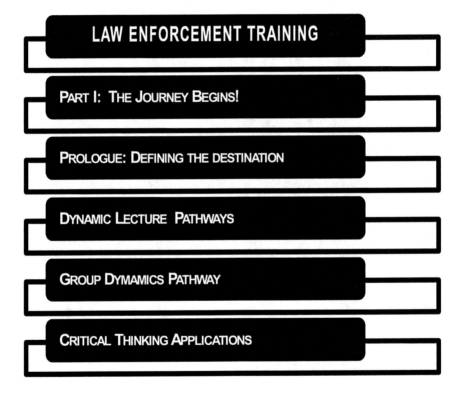

LAW ENFORCEMENT TRAINING

PART I: THE JOURNEY BEGINS!

PROLOGUE: DEFINING THE DESTINATION

DYNAMIC LECTURE PATHWAYS

GROUP DYNAMICS PATHWAY

CRITICAL THINKING APPLICATIONS

2

Figure Part I-B: The Leadership Journey Begins!

Connecting Instructional Dots	Guidepost Pathways
Prologue: Defining The Destination • Ten Basic Pathways • Training Mandates • Training Excellence • Cyberspace Applications	• Think Outside Box • Connect Training Dots • Avoid Failure to Train • Apply Standards • Lead and Guide • Point Way to Destination
Dynamic Lecture Pathway: • Instructor Philosophy • Instructor Attributes • Lecture Strategies	• Role Model Attributes • Define Lecture Central Idea • Address Student Bids • Provide Student Feedback
Group Dynamics Pathway: • Active Group Learning • Group Stages • Group Feedback • Instructor Interventions • Group Leadership	• Case Study Method • Provide Case Description • Explain Rules • Appraise Group Development • Assess Group Content Dimension • Conduct Group Critique

INTRODUCTION

Defining the Leadership Destination

Traveling training pathways sets the foundation for connecting the main roads. However, you must begin by collecting the pathways. Only then do you have the ability to connect the dynamic training road map.
— Thomas E. Baker

Focus

Law Enforcement Training: Dynamic Leadership Strategies describes four dynamic themes: (1) critical thinking, (2) problem-solving, (3) decision-making, and (4) problem-solving active learning. The purpose of the Prologue is to focus on the role of dynamic learning strategies and the promotion of positive training outcomes. This book provides direction and appropriate pathways on the journey to successful training destinations.

Overview

Training personnel serve as leaders, role models, and mentors—coaches that motivate learners to resolve personal limitations and struggles to their highest measure of success. Their positive attitude mirrors integrity, optimism, and courage—leadership qualities that inspire others to follow.

Training management/leaders earn and maintain respect from those who serve under their direction. Insightful leaders, who understand human behavior, extract positive qualities from a wealth of untapped personnel resources. Positive leadership offers opportunities to unleash veiled human potential – barriers that once dismissed, encourage enlightened ideas and learning to emerge. Trained leaders recognize the untapped potential in others and motivate them to discover it.

The effort may take considerable patience and time; however, the reward for initiating positive leadership strategies reaps benefits far beyond financial compensation. Your contribution is significant and optimistically transmittable to future generations of trainers. **Your leadership legacy reflects how you made someone *feel* – more than what you *said!***

For example, anyone can look at a person and see their facade. A good training manager/instructor can look at a person and predict how they will perform on a specific task(s). An excellent manager/instructor can envision the human being. But an advanced professional manager/instructor can look at a person, portray them exactly as a unique personality, and envision what the person can be ... and more than that, they can with training insight, perceive the person, not only in the classroom, but guide the professional law enforcement field practitioner of the future.

Training Excellence

Some experts believe that there are few differences between excellent education and training. Education has the broader purpose over instruction. The former strives for human development, the latter to achieve proficiency at related professional performance tasks. Excellent training also views human development as essential to positive learning outcomes. There are overlapping instructional concepts, therefore; education and training are not mutually exclusive. The goal of excellence in education is directly connected and applied to professional law enforcement training.

Superior instructors know how to connect with learners. They encourage and motivate learners to become more than they thought possible. Excellent instruction facilitates learner knowledge. The ultimate goal of training is the development of the learner expertise and professional development. How well the instructor communicates can make a significant difference in shaping positive learning outcomes.

Learning is a process that requires adaptation, growth, and development. These behaviors require participants to exceed their grasp and not waiver when confronted with demanding tasks. People differ in their aspirations and potential; the instructor's goal is to challenge each participant within their capabilities to learn and develop. Therefore, participants are not dependent, but can pursue knowledge from the original learning experience.

Superior leaders instill successful achievement in their followers; they also accomplish the same behaviors in the training management/instructor role. Successful instructors lead by example, demonstrate courage, emotional stability, integrity, and problem-solving abilities. The instructor role demands intelligence, mature judgment, and the ability to communicate.

Training excellence requires law enforcement personnel to participate in critical thinking and field problem-solving skills. These foundation requirements are the essence of every law enforcement-training program. Federal, state, and local officers should confront real-world situations they may encounter. The emphasis must center on active learning field scenarios, role-play, learning simulations, and (on-line) **cyberspace applications.**

Cyberspace Applications

Training manager goals include leadership, guidance, and pointing the way to future destinations. A sense of vision incorporates novel technology applications and opportunities. Online courses create dramatic modifications on how trainers serve learners; active-learning applications continue to unfold. Virtual reality programmed instruction may become the norm for in-service training. Master virtual instructors address learner preferred learning styles and senses in multiple-dimensional presentations.

The quickly changing emphasis to *distance (on-line) education and in-service training* requires detailed curriculum analysis and evaluation. Furthermore, the expansion of *on-line* instruction continues to diversify learning opportunities for law enforcement training. This movement will eventually evolve into dynamic law enforcement and universal training progressions.

Distance education requires increased planning, organization, and diverse evaluation methods. Learners work alone or in groups; study materials are organized by the instructor. However, *distance education* may be combined with on-site instructors, conference calling, or local assistance.

Higher education law enforcement, criminal justice management, and leadership programs continue to expand. These academic degree programs offer career developments that contribute to lifetime learning and promotional opportunities. For example, the highly rated American Military University enrollment surpasses 64,000 students.

Virtual reality training applications offer diverse training scenarios, opportunities to practice confronting high-risk situations in controlled, safe environments. Training simulations are realistic and accurate.

Virtual reality training can create 3D models, which provide realistic representations of what the trainer is trying to achieve. The visualizations of complex theories, concepts, and data offer real world applications. Menu options offer instantaneous learner assessments and program evaluations that enhance the process.

Learners feel motivated to ask questions and accept accurate feedback in a nonthreatening *virtual reality* environment. Immersion techniques offer unique connections to real law enforcement applications. The process provides instructor monitoring on interactive practical exercises or learning simulations. Support systems offer programmed instructions and answers for frequently asked questions.

Innovative law enforcement trainers experiment, evaluate, and vary instructional approaches. They remain the ultimate driving force for positive training outcomes. Technology applications continue to unfold and are limited only by the imagination.

Training Leadership: Legal Mandates

Law Enforcement Training: Dynamic Leadership Strategies assists in preventing litigation against law enforcement agencies. Training leaders/managers follow legal issues regarding the failure to train properly. Unknown and blind spots motivate financial and political consequences. Training programs promote respect for constitutional rights and human dignity. Trainees develop an appreciation for equity, due process, fairness, and the United States Constitution.

According to Ross (2000), there is not anything as important as making sure law enforcement officers receive proper training. Not only does training increase their chances for winning field confrontations, the lack of such puts the department at risk of being held liable, according to guidelines set in the 1989 U.S. Supreme Court ruling, City of Canton, Ohio v. Geraldine Harris, 489, U.S. 378 (1989). The court made it clear in Canton that training police personnel is a critical managerial responsibility and is not a financial extravagance. Administrators may be liable if inadequate or improper training causes injury or violates a citizen's constitutional rights. The Court also made it clear that basic police academies emphasize law and discipline, but that such training alone is not enough.

Supreme Court opinion: police department liability is judged on "deliberate indifference." "We hold that the inadequacy of police training may serve as the basis for 1983 liability only where the failure-to-train amounts to deliberate indifference to the rights of persons with whom the police come into contact." The Justices articulated the fact that *deliberate indifference* would apply when judging department liability with regard to the failure-to-train officers.

Law Enforcement Training Programs

Law enforcement training programs seek to guide and prepare trainees for service in the twenty-first century. The constant reevaluation of curriculum provides participants with the knowledge, skills, and abilities to perform successfully in the future. This book supports those training opportunities. Refer to Training Table I-1: Forms of Law Enforcement Training for an illustration.

Table I-1: Forms of Law Enforcement Training

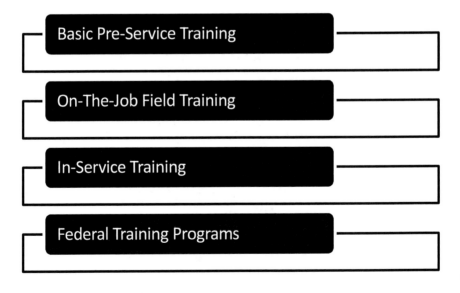

Basic Pre-Service Training

On-The-Job Field Training

In-Service Training

Federal Training Programs

Forms of Law Enforcement Training

There are many forms of law enforcement training on the local, state, and federal levels in the United States. Basic pre-service training involves recruits who pass a background investigation. Then recruits are the eligible for training academies, which introduce the candidates to basic law enforcement procedures.

After completing entry-level requirements, candidates proceed to on-the-job field training. This training agenda is generally for approximately one year in a probationary status and is under the supervision of a Field Training Officer (FTO). Recruits are evaluated and eventually assigned to patrol functions.

Law enforcement personnel attend various in-service training courses during their career. These training sessions include numerous subjects and specific time requirements. In-service training represents a career-mandated process and topics vary. However, there is an emphasis on legal content, use of force, firearms training, and other technology updates. In addition, promotions may require advanced training programs.

Federal programs follow a similar format. Many federal programs meet agency needs and specialties. State and local officers attend federal training programs. One example is the Federal Bureau of Investigation National Training Program at Quantico, Virginia.

Law enforcement agencies will be subject to additional certification requirements in the future. State and regional police academies have course certification requirements. Law enforcement agencies require professional assessment and evaluation procedures. This planning process, assessment, and evaluation support professional accreditation efforts.

Defining the Destination

What does excellent training accomplish? Excellent training procedures produce efficient law enforcement personnel who successfully perform mission requirements. Positive training provides the skills for accomplishing essential field tasks. Law enforcement training must be performance-oriented, not simply passive classroom learning. Determining positive learning outcomes requires understanding the principles of training management, curriculum planning, and performance-oriented training.

Successful learning strategies encourage insightful instruction and demand quality preparation. This text emphasizes dynamic law enforcement training and performance applications. Superior training strategies require curriculum management and lesson planning. The following **ten pathways** provide training excellence and guidance for arriving at appropriate destinations.

Pathway One

Role Modeling: Dynamic Lecture Strategies

Lectures are formal dialogues that function well when instructors present a series of facts, events, concepts, or principles. The lecture operates best when instructors explore a significant problem or explain important human relationships. This approach serves as a navigational system for learners. Lecture presentations should be dynamic and action-oriented; they must involve critical thinking and problem solving. Whatever the lecture truth-seeking position, it answers questions concerning learner destinations.

The instructor's philosophy is an individual preference that provides the learner a direction. Many instructors favor a philosophy that ensures respect for learners and their right to learn. A teaching viewpoint is necessary for behavior consistency and is a prerequisite to curriculum design.

The lecture method has several disadvantages. One example is the lack of learner participation. That lack of free interplay with the learner audience may present problems with maintaining high levels of focus and interest. Excessive reliance on instructor expertise may decrease attention span.

Instructional aides make the lecture effective, interesting, and increase efficient learning transitions; these are followed-up with field demonstrations. Demonstrations include trainee participation and interaction. Law enforcement training facilitates active, not passive learning. Refer to Figure I-1: Pathway for an overview of this Chapter.

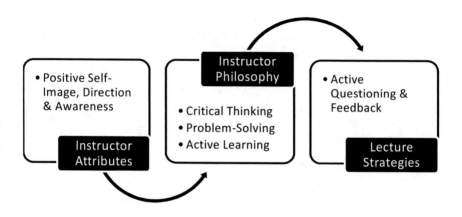

Figure I-1: Pathway One

Chapter 1: Learning Objectives

- Identify the elements of instructor attributes.
- Appraise the instructor lecture fundamentals.
- Cite the main lecture speaking points.
- Appraise the rational for questioning.
- Define lecture-questioning feedback.
- Distinguish between the purposes of communication bidding.
- Illustrate the related terms: *turning toward, turning away,* and *unrequited responses.*
- Describe the qualities of the reflection technique.
- List the purpose of the lecture's central idea.
- Identify the principle of the rhetorical question.

Instructor Applications

The lecture method permits adaptability concerning the specific needs of a particular training group. Examples address appropriate educational and experience levels. Versatility is the main advantage. It applies to a variety of subjects, at any point of the training program or with any other instructional method.

Many instructors prefer *control* to timing, content, and learning progressions.

Successful learners and instructors welcome an exchange of questions, a meaningful dialogue, and mutual communication. This interaction ensures that questioning bids and replies among class members and instructors thrive. Furthermore, it remains a compass for offering training excellence and quality instruction.

Pathway Two

Group Leadership Dynamics

Instructors need to understand the principles of small group interaction to achieve learning opportunities. Group dynamics is the principal instructional method for arriving at positive learning destination. Organize participants in learning groups and ask members to develop responses. They engage the content in an active learning and critical thinking approach. Wonderful things unfold in their intellectual potential.

One of the best ways to stimulate questions is the ***case study method***. Realistic scenarios offer opportunities for learners to analyze the problem and determine possible solutions. Preferably, there is no one right solution or answer. Instructors take full advantage of critical thinking questions, and performance objectives that correlate with the case studies.

Case study analysis opens the door for positive learner rapport with the instructor. Rapport may be defined as cooperation and understanding. Instructors require positive relationships with participants to enhance learning climates. The instructor/ trainee relationship should be one of synchronization and respect. Refer to Figure I-2: Pathway for an overview of this Chapter.

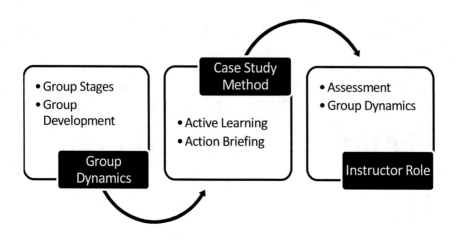

Figure I-2: Pathway Two

Chapter 2: Learning Objectives

- Appraise the group dynamics approach.
- Identify group feedback.
- Appraise the active learning process.
- Describe the three stages of group development.
- Appraise the group content dimension.
- Distinguish the group development dimension.
- Define group cohesion.
- Apply the rules of the feedback process.
- Apply the case study method.
- Define the group critique.

Instructor Applications

The case study method emphasizes the trainee's role in the learning process. The goal is to encourage learner involvement, maintain high levels of trainee activity, and connect the relevancy of real-world situations. The case study method should approximate problems participants encounter in field situations. In addition, this instructional method connects and blends well with other instructional methods: lectures, discussions, group dynamics, or brainstorming. Skills expand when learners apply critical thinking applications. Interactive group dynamics facilitate options to divide class sessions into segments: lecture, case study, and participant briefings.

Pathway Three

Dynamic Curriculum Management

Certainly, the requirement to analyze, construct curriculum, and improve the quality of instruction involves a planned effort. A training philosophy is necessary for consistency. The instructor defines goals, related performance objectives, and assessment procedures that ensure successful learning outcomes. Critical thinking serves as the philosophical foundation for law enforcement personnel.

Training philosophy, goals, and performance objectives receive special emphasis in training programs. Learning or behavioral objectives set the foundation for detailed performance objectives. Performance objectives have:

- **Specific conditions**
- **Detailed standards**
- **Task criteria**

Learner assessment and training program evaluation assists in arriving at the proper destination. Evaluation methods also help provide learners with proper training, timing, and learning progressions. The combination of program evaluation and learner assessment strategies provides the curriculum blueprint to learner destinations. Refer to Figure I-3: Pathway for an overview of this Chapter.

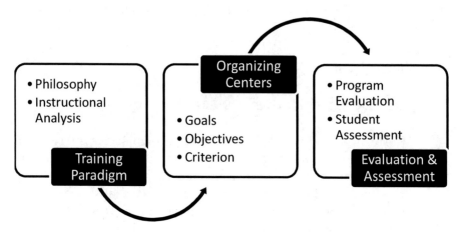

Figure I-3: Pathway Three

Chapter 3: Learning Objectives

- Define the curriculum paradigm.
- List the three parts of a performance objective.
- Appraise the concept of curriculum philosophy.
- Describe the critical thinking foundations.
- Distinguish the elements of active learning strategies.
- List the elements of an organizing center.
- Define requirements of training goals.
- Apply the Training Systems Model process.
- Appraise the role of the learner assessment process.
- Identify the elements of summative evaluation planning.

Instructor Applications

The basic principle for organizing curriculum is the organizing center. Three basic questions remain essential:

- Where are you going?
- How will you get there?
- How will you know when you have arrived?

Organizing centers frame curriculum performance objectives, tasks, conditions, and standards. Professional instructors work on a prioritized basis. They concentrate on desired learning outcomes that offer positive solutions. In addition, they initiate optimistic learning opportunities and avoid past mistakes.

Pathway Four

Dynamic Lesson Planning

The main purpose of dynamic lesson plans is to check on preparation. Planning process review ensures the lesson is complete and suggests teaching methods. Teaching points and time limitations establish content emphasis. The lesson planning process facilitates the instructor's ability to anticipate learner questions.

Lesson plans originate from specific goals and performance objectives. In addition, they define training standards and learning progressions. Positive learning outcomes demand effort and intricate lesson plans. Refer to Figure I-4: Pathway for an overview of this Chapter.

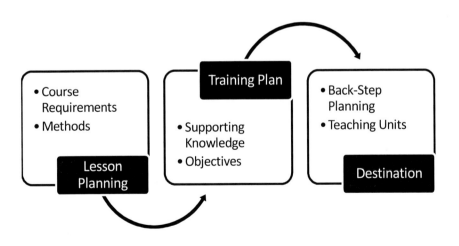

Figure I-4: Pathway Four

Chapter 4: Learning Objectives

- Describe the purpose of lesson plan checkpoints.
- Appraise the elements of the back-step lesson planning process.
- Define the "lesson hook."
- List the elements of an overview-training plan.
- Illustrate the purpose of instructional units.
- Describe the application of learning progressions.
- Describe the elements of developing a course.
- Cite principal instructional points.
- Apply the body of supporting knowledge.
- Appraise elements of the final review.

Instructor Applications

The lesson plan outlines subject matter and techniques—not instructor comments. This plan serves as the foundation for personal notes and comments. The plan is not a substitute for lecture notes. Instructor research and notes serve as the main presentation. However, the instructor keeps the lesson plan accessible to maintain lecture progressions and pertinent content. The instructor's personal notes and PowerPoint presentations serve as the foremost classroom plan.

Pathway Five

Leadership Feedback

Learner feedback is the preliminary activity for assessing trainee learning performance task(s) retention. Apply feedback during the performance-oriented task. Trainee feedback is essential in the achievement and retention of training knowledge, and typically unfolds during the training or practice sessions.

Learners perform under controlled conditions and receive immediate feedback during practical exercises. Trainees learn by doing. Apply practical exercise methods along with other instructional strategies, such as lecture presentations or demonstrations. Refer to Figure I-5: Pathway for an overview of this chapter.

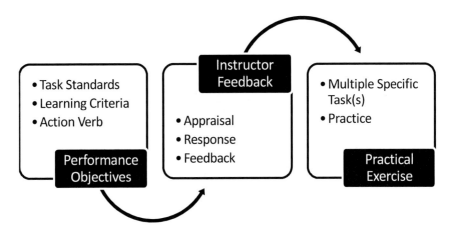

Figure I-5: Pathway Five

Chapter Five: Learning Objectives

- Appraise the three preferred learning styles.
- List the four basic feedback steps.
- Describe a performance objective.
- Illustrate the application of the elements of learner feedback.
- Name the elements of the practical exercise model.
- Identify basic components of the practical exercise feedback process.
- Distinguish the elements of task analysis.
- List appropriate performance standards.
- List the four goals of the Field Training Program (FTO).
- Outline the rational for performance training development.

Instructor Applications

Practical exercise applications permit trainees to practice and perform basic skills. Therefore, participants increase understanding of principles and procedures through application. Participants have opportunities to demonstrate their mastery of skills and feel a sense of pride through personal or group accomplishment(s).

Most important, instructors can assess the application of training skills and technical procedures.

A practical exercise lead-up activity serves the purpose of reducing emotional responses during field encounters, encourages logical decision-making, and critical thinking. Building a bridge from theory to practical application stimulates an effective learning response that creates learner curiosity.

Pathway Six

Organizing the Practical Exercise

Scientific leaps in forensic science revolutionized crime scene investigation (CSI). Moreover, the media's recent emphasis on CSI serves as a visual demonstration of its importance—not necessarily an accurate representation. The gravesite excavation exercise contributes to our understanding of how crime scene reconstruction plays a role in the exoneration of the innocent and identifying the guilty. In addition, the gravesite excavation practical exercise explores training techniques and strategies that permit crime scene investigators to link criminals with their crimes. Refer to Figure I-6: Pathway for an overview of this chapter.

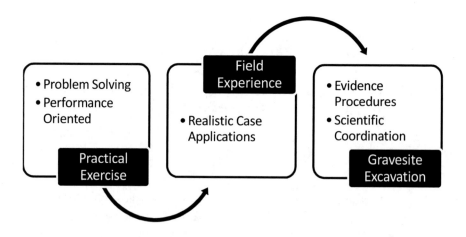

Figure I-6: Pathway Six

Chapter 6: Learning Objectives

- Appraise three essential elements of an organizing center.
- Identify three essential elements of the gravesite practical exercise.
- Identify gravesite practical exercise goals.
- List elements of the PREPARE training model acronym.
- Distinguish the principles of comparison and victim identification.
- Explain gravesite practical exercise procedures.
- Identify gravesite practical exercise support measures.
- Describe gravesite excavation checkpoints.
- Appraise elements of the monitoring and feedback process.
- Appraise gravesite coordination requirements.

Instructor Applications

The instructor provides feedback opportunities during case study and practice laboratories. Short, practical exercises provide learning foundations for the gravesite excavation exercise. Preparatory rehearsals and critiques ***prepare*** trainees for the right level of proficiency to excel independently.

Organize groups in teams and encourage group leaders to attend to feedback on gravesite excavation tasks. In addition, class leaders refer participants who demonstrate performance problems to the instructor.

Pathway Seven

Organizing the Learning Simulation

The application of learning simulations originated in civil emergency preparedness, aviation, business, and medicine. Learning simulations offer an ideal venue for critical thinking and application of newly acquired skills. Instructors interested in meeting diverse learning needs, encourage and stimulate learning through a variety of simulation techniques.

The combination of effective instructional strategies motivates learners, enhances retention, and helps maintain a creative learning environment. In addition, the simulation method offers opportunities for trainees to explore their own learning styles. Diverse learning domains are engaged in role-play: (1) affective (interests), (2) cognitive (knowledge), (3) social (self-fulfillment), and (4) tactile (motor learning). Refer to Figure I-7: Pathway for an overview of this chapter.

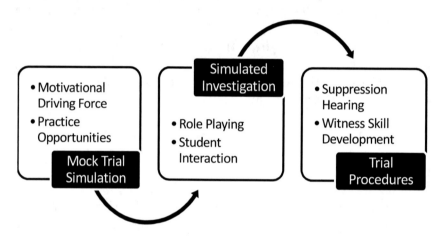

Training Figure I-7: Pathway Seven

Chapter 7: Learning Objectives

- Appraise mock trial learning simulation strategies.
- List five basic learning progressions.
- Identify witness preparation progressions.
- Appraise Suppression Hearing rehearsal strategies.
- Identify mock trial active learning strategies.
- List learning benefits when learners engage in role-play.
- Describe the requirement for rules and procedures during simulations.
- Describe role requirements for the judge and magistrate (district justice) during the mock trial simulation.
- Define the need for practice exercises and case study applications.

- **Appraise the necessity for an evaluation survey questionnaire.**

Instructor Applications

Simulations create opportunities for learners to practice complex skills in positions of responsibility. Excellent critical thinking and active learning methods assist learners in acquiring knowledge from the mock trial simulation. This mock trial case scenario has realistic applications that parallel law enforcement investigations and encourage opportunities to apply knowledge. Many critical thinking concepts unfold during the simulation exercise: (1) focusing on a question; (2) analyzing argument; (3) judging the credibility of a source; (4) deducing and judging deduction; and (5) interaction with others (Ennis, 1985).

Pathway Eight

Peak Performance Training

Training for peak performance is a long-range goal ideally suited for personal achievement. Privette (1983) describes peak performance as those moments when we perform at a level that is beyond our normal level of functioning. Peak performance is described as behavior that is "more efficient, more creative, more productive, or in some ways better than [the person's] ordinary behavior ... and may occur in any facet of human activity: intellectual, emotional, or physical" (Privette & Landsman, 1983 p. 195).

Being in a creative flow generally occurs during peak performance events. The feeling of achievement is exhilarating and rewarding. The peak performance experience is unforgettable; however, reaching for peak performance makes the effort worth it. Refer to Figure I-8: Pathway for an overview of this chapter.

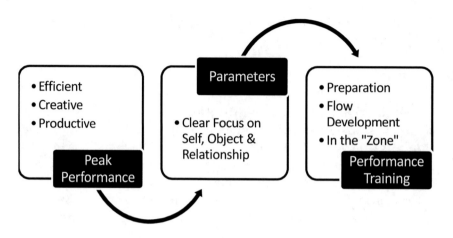

Figure I-8: Pathway Eight

Chapter 8: Learning Objectives

- Define peak performance.
- List four parameters of peak performance.
- Illustrate level one: peak performance.
- Illustrate level two: peak performance.
- Appraise peak performance applications.
- Distinguish the elements of "flow."
- Appraise elements of creativity.
- Identify criteria for the Resonance Performance Model (RPM).
- Define the brainstorming problem-solving process.
- Appraise the main argument for peak performance training.

Instructor Applications

Listen to your dreams! When you imagine a creative instructional process, implement it. Take calculated risks; the results may surprise you. Trust the inspirational and creative process and do not compromise. Apply what you have learned and pursue the struggle for peak performance. Engage learners to uncover their own level of peak performance. Seek the necessary support to accomplish the peak performance-training mission.

Pathway Nine

Leadership Counseling

Understanding what interferes with the guidance process increases positive trainee opportunities. Responding requires an objective assessment of the situation and decisive execution of a mutual agreement. In addition, instructor perceptions must be accurate and have a sense of vision concerning consequences. Several guidance/instructor support skills unfold during the learner problem-solving phase.

Effective advisement can improve trainee performance and remove training obstacles. Law enforcement instructors prepare to advise participants when the need unfolds. The definition of counseling or guidance in the training environment concerns directing learners to an improved or change in behavior. This process emphasizes developing a helping relationship and a consensus for achieving positive outcomes. Refer to Figure I-9: Pathway for an overview of this Chapter.

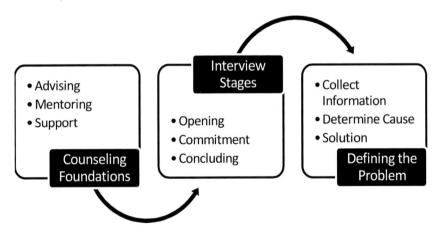

Figure I-9: Pathway Nine

Chapter 9: Learning Objectives

- List three basic parts of the counseling/advising process.
- Identify basic phases of the counseling process.

- Appraise ideal instructor/counseling attitudes.
- Identify basic learner attitude patterns.
- Describe foundations for helping learners gain self-understanding.
- Appraise learner confidentiality concerns.
- List three counseling overlapping phases.
- Cite basic counseling advising skills.
- Appraise counseling theories.
- Identify basic criteria for professional referral.

Instructor Applications

Instructors may encounter learners who do not take responsibility for their behaviors. Certain participants consistently seek instructor opinions on how to handle problem situations. Establishing a supportive and helping relationship can assist in successful learner transitions. Guide trainees into accepting responsibility for making effective decisions.

Pathway Ten

Dynamic Leadership: Pulling it All Together

Curriculum managers/training staff members are accountable for supervisory and coordination of learning opportunities. They guide the training mission, mentor, and eliminate learning obstacles. This requires being aware and understanding individual differences in Emotional Command Systems. Therefore, this insight presents the opportunity to reduce conflict and allow individuals opportunities to operate in their "comfort zone." Refer to Training Figure I-10: Pathway for an overview of this chapter.

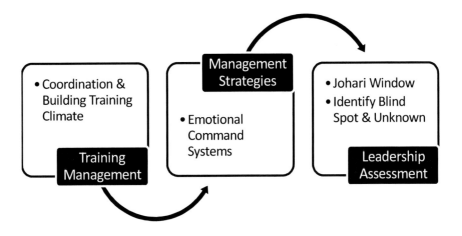

Figure I-10: Pathway Ten

Chapter 10: Learning Objectives

- Distinguish elements of curriculum leadership/management.
- Appraise emotional command systems.
- Define the Commander-Chief System.
- Define the Explorer System.
- Define the Energy Czar System.
- Define the Nest-Builder System.
- Define the Jester System.
- Define the Sentry System.
- Describe feedback bid-busting behaviors.
- Distinguish elements of the Johari Window.

Instructor Applications

Instructors have a basic source of power on which they depend. When looking at instructor influence, examine the *source*. The instructional *center of gravity* that binds the entire staff and learners together is the primary goal of the curriculum leader/manager. The *center of gravity* must be respect, competence, and expertise. Avoid negative reactions. Take control and conduct effective instructional strategies. Strategic curriculum planning and instructional applications require on-going assessment, evaluation, and addressing staff and trainee needs. Understanding preferred emotional staff and learner mind-sets can encourage the acceptance of others.

Epilogue: Self-assessment Review

This chapter serves a summary review of theories, concepts, and instructional strategies. The final learning experience includes a chapter, Self-Inventory Rating Scale, for the learning content. The Training Self-Rating Inventory represents an author-created, training self-assessment questionnaire. The goal: to explore areas that may offer opportunities for improvement and future skill development.

Instructor Applications

Readers who do not hold training positions may visualize how they may apply training strategies. Training Self-Rating Inventories represent non-scientific personal assessment opportunities. Scale graphics are rated one to ten, with ten being the *high* and one the *low*. Readers take opportunities to self-test their training knowledge and skills, and evaluate the learning process.

Focus Points: Computer Applications

Gradually, the content and methods of instruction within the law enforcement community have changed. Computer technology is now an essential component. Instructors need information on how to implement computer technology to their area of specialization. The addition of law enforcement websites diversifies the learning process and extends instructor influence beyond the classroom.

The combination of effective computer strategies motivates learners, enhances retention, and helps maintain a creative learning environment. Additional active learning assignments diversify the learning process. For example, on-line practice testing builds confidence and creates opportunities for learners to become familiar with testing expectations.

The computer is now an integral component of the instructional and lesson planning process. Computer technology offers opportunities for law enforcement participants to think critically and enhances the learning environment. Computer instructional strategies offer opportunities to explore and apply problem-solving skills. Search engines and external links assist in retrieving information on the Internet. Listed below are possible instructional strategies:

- **External Links:** Posted external links on the website provide guideposts for learners. Learning experiences can be coordinated with external links on the website. For example, trainees are required to use the website to participate in classroom instruction.
- **Flashcards:** Provide additional support for learners. This system reviews major theories and concepts in a sequential manner for individual teaching units. The key advantage is that flashcards require more recollection than recognition like true/false and multiple-choice questions. This learning exercise requires trainees to fill-in-the-blanks from memory.
- **Practice Quizzes:** The quiz format requires that learners answer ten multiple-choice questions on each teaching unit or lesson plan. Flashcards and true/false quizzes are available twenty-four hours a day on the website. The testing reinforcement assists participants in identifying major research, concepts, and vocabulary.
- **Pre-examinations:** Non-credit multiple-choice questions provide insight into the kind of questions learners may encounter on examinations. Post pre-examinations prior to graded exams.
- **Email:** Offers a way of interacting with participants individually and collectively. Those individuals, who hesitate to ask questions in class, may feel confident communicating by email. Assignments, examination dates, and special announcements appear on website bulletin boards.
- **PowerPoint Presentations:** Commercial PowerPoint presentations are generally effective and save time. Successful presentations are vibrant, animated, and have interactive hypothetical or real case studies. Instructor-created PowerPoint presentations take considerable time to create but save time in the future.

Empowering participants to become successful learners enhances the possibility that they reach their academic goals and make effective decisions. Independent computer learning generally leads to further exploration and active learning outside the classroom experience. Independent computer learning experiences assist in creating an element of curiosity.

Participants have opportunities to develop and improve course content decision-making skills. Why is on-line testing an excellent reinforcement for learners? Frequent practice sessions allow participants to use multiple senses, build test-taking skills, and decrease anxiety. Encouraging participants to become successful learners enhances their ability to incorporate technology into the learning experience.

In summary, computer technology can individualize learning and provide interactive experiences. Websites diversify the active learning process, extend the influence of the lecturer into another dimension, and build technology skills in the classroom (Smith & Benscoter, 2000). Diverse instructional methods create opportunities for learners to explore and incorporate individual learning styles. The computer revolution created opportunities to develop innovative and dynamic instructional strategies.

Conclusion

This book is about developing your own training success system. The most important qualities are your leadership, training management, and instructional skills. How to invest time and energy remains a basic formula for success. Define your own training success indicators and find your inspiration. Chapter 1: Role Modeling: Dynamic Lecture Strategies is the first pathway to that destination.

CHAPTER 1

Role Modeling: Dynamic Lecture Strategies

"Education is not preparation for life, education is life itself.
— John Dewey

Focus

The purpose of this chapter is to explore the lecture and questioning approach to law enforcement training. Training instructors serve as role models for learners, not purely conveyors of information. Their objective is to communicate a dynamic learning philosophy that applies the principles discussed in this chapter.

A positive mental attitude and diligence fosters success. Moreover, role model professional behaviors, on the podium, and in your personal life. Superior instructors demonstrate positive self-projection, positive self-direction, positive self-motivation, and many of the attributes cited in this chapter to earn the prized accolade – *respected instructor*.

Overview

Instructors present lecture content that enables learners to perform basic progressions requiring critical thinking, problem-solving, and practical applications. The lecture questioning method is a means for transmitting basic law enforcement fundamentals, learning content, and concepts. The purpose of dialogue is to explain and illustrate principles and procedures. The lecture provides opportunities for communicating substantial information in the least amount of time. Learner questions provide feedback on the lecture method.

Instructor Leadership Philosophy

The instructor's leadership philosophy focuses on instructional questioning that encourages learners to maximize their learning potential. The emphasis is not only on content, but also on decision-making skills and problem solving. Refer to Figure 1-1: Instructor Attributes and Philosophy for an illustration.

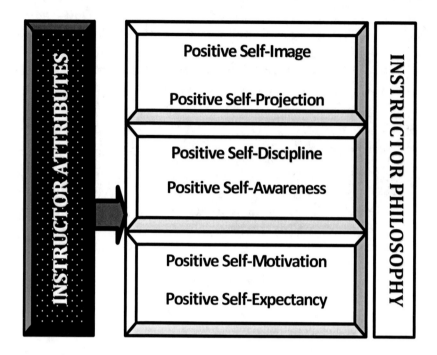

Figure 1-1: Instructor Attributes and Philosophy

Instructor Attributes

One fundamental instructor requirement remains constant—**a positive self-image.** This important quality concerns how the instructor perceives their self-concept. **Self-image** helps establish positive training methods and instructor success. Trainees identify with instructors who have a **positive self-image.** **Self-concept** is a life-controlling mechanism that regulates **self-discipline, persistence,** and **dedication.**

Successful instructors are capable of **positive self-projection,** an asset that creates an aura of confidence and a willingness to try another approach. They present a motivating influence; their charisma instills confidence and develops environments where learner efforts thrive.

Instructors who practice **positive self-direction** envision success. They stay on the cutting edge and position themselves to enter the instructional arena, charting the course for arriving at their destination. **Positive self-discipline** and aspirations are powerful motivating forces. Imagination and inventive thinking help define gifted instructors who respond to fluid situations in creative ways.

Another important instructor quality is *positive self-awareness*. This requires the ability to step back and appraise one's personal impact on the instructional process. The skill demands examining strengths, weaknesses, and potential limitations. *Self-refection* requires personal insight and honesty.

Effective instructors engage in *positive self-motivation* and concentrate on what they desire to achieve. There are limitations; however, fear of failure is not one of them.

Self-motivation to accomplish a series of goals and objectives includes two types of motivation: (1) *external* or *extrinsic motivation* and (2) *internal or intrinsic motivation*. Extrinsic motivation involves external rewards—status, money, and praise. *Intrinsic motivation* flourishes when instructors engage in behaviors for inherent learning reasons, regardless of any rewards.

Superior instructors own *positive self-expectancy*. They have insight into overcoming instructional barriers and insulators. This self-fulfilling prophesy offers powerful learner enticements. Anticipate successful instructional solutions and prompt them to unfold.

Instructors with *positive self-control* take responsibility for their actions and do not rationalize mistakes. They (1) make positive choices, (2) shape and define the learning destiny, (3) lesson plan effectively, and (4) follow the correct course of curriculum action.

Confidence stems from previous successful lectures and classroom experiences. Effective instructors understand that past failures do not matter. However, one important question requires an answer: Did I learn from the experience and will I avoid similar mistakes in the future? Success serves as positive reinforcement for future instructor and participant learning opportunities. Refer to Table 1-1: Instructor Attributes for a Self-Rating Inventory Scale for an analysis of your personal skills. The Rating Inventory Scale Table includes an assessment rating of one to ten (with ten being the *high* and one the *low*).

Table 1-1: Instructor Attributes

Positive Attributes	1	2	3	4	5	6	7	8	9	10
Self-image										
Self-discipline, persistence & dedication										
Self-projection										
Self-direction										
Self-discipline										
Self-awareness										
Self-motivation										
Self-expectancy										
Self-control										
Intrinsic motivation										

Lecture Fundamentals

The lecture is a formal presentation where instructors discuss a series of law enforcement issues, concepts, or events. Lectures also include facts, principles, problem exploration, and inter-personal relationships. Furthermore, instructors solicit learner responses. Instructors emphasize central ideas, related lecture points, and practice lecture continuity. Lectures require smooth transitions and unfold from one lecture point to the other.

Instructors demonstrate relationships among various training lecture points. Therefore, the lecture should be focused on essential information and related concepts. Explanations summarize difficult content, and learners may ask questions. If questions do not arise, instructors initiate discussions to assess lecture content understanding.

Content mastery and subject-matter sequencing offer superior strategies. Plans that present ideas and concepts facilitate audience rapport. They suggest a precise choice of words and training content. Most important, instructors reflect enthusiasm and interest in the subject matter. Refer to Figure 1-1-A: Lecture Fundamentals for an illustration.

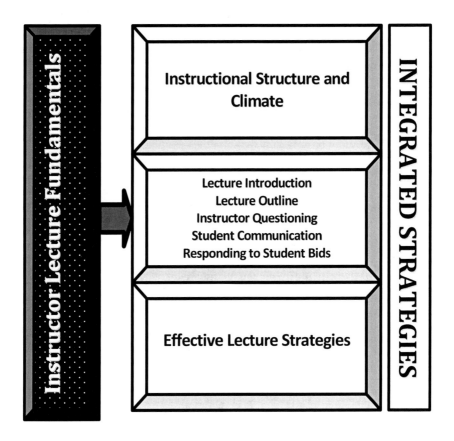

Figure 1-1A: Lecture Fundamentals

Planning defines direction and guides content-related discussion questions. Questions based on goals and performance objectives serve as the main source for audience discussions. Course outlines provide thoughtful foundations for addressing basic questions and provide learner compasses. Questions based on goals and learning objectives serve as guideposts for learner discussions.

Lecture Speaking Points

Excellent communication is in the power of the instructor's words, gestures, and, from beginning to end, their strengths and convictions. Instructor podium demeanors present a relaxed approach, without word-by-word narrations from notes. Focus on learners; move about learning environments while diversifying voice inflection.

Powerful speech is a combination of appropriate volume and effective modulation. The first principle of the lecture: learners should not have to strain to hear in diverse classroom settings. Instructors must project their voice, but not to the point that learners feel verbal sound assault.

Speakers control their rate of speech. Paint emotional pictures by emphasizing voice inflection appropriate to content, emotion, and the words early spoken. In contrast, slower speech patterns may convey concern, sadness, or introspection.

Inflection is a calculated change in the normal pitch pattern and offers increased emphasis on key lecture points. Dramatic delivery encourages audience attention and highlights important points.

Pausing and inflection is a way of punctuating speech content. This technique serves four purposes: (1) gives learners opportunities to evaluate and absorb ideas; (2) provides emphasis and assists in conveying the meaning of ideas; (3) helps speakers to relax and breathe; and (4) offers learners opportunities to anticipate content direction.

Rationale for Questioning

Lesson plans drive questioning and form the basis for guided discussions. Lecture questions form the foundation for understanding and participation. In any case, regardless of the teaching method, the ultimate purpose is to provoke critical thinking and enlightening dialogue.

Excellent instructors become skilled at questioning strategies. The purpose is to communicate accurate information. Why should instructors care about the questioning process? Effective uses of questions offer significant opportunities to learn.

What signals excellent questions? Questions should reveal an expressed purpose, be specific, and relate directly to an understanding of the intended content. Prepared instructors support performance objectives and test questions related to presentations.

The primary reasons for questioning in the lecture process are learner comprehension and retention. The secondary purpose:

emphasize specific content and connect related concepts, thereby shifting responsibility for learning to the audience. Learners pay added attention if they realize questions follow key lecture points, which encourages audience participation.

Open the lecture with a stimulating question that: (1) motivates thinking; (2) clarifies so learners easily grasp the main point; (3) initiates the first discussion component; and (4) prompt follow-up questions that drive lectures and guide discussions. Refer to Corner 1-1: Robinson vs. Ewell for an illustration of stimulating the jury's thinking in a trial situation.

Corner 1-1: Robinson vs. Ewell

The following case dialogue demonstrates the power of the appropriate use of the lecture method. A defense attorney effectively challenges a jury during the course of a moving mini-lecture. The following lecture passage is from *To Kill a Mockingbird*. Atticus Finch delivers the final summation argument in the case of *Robinson vs. Ewell:*

> *"... Nevertheless, there is one way in this country in which all men are created equal—there is one human institution that makes the pauper the equal of Rockefeller, the stupid man the equal of an Einstein, and the ignorant man the equal of any college president. That institution, gentlemen, is a court. It can be the Supreme Court of the United States or the humblest J.P. court in the land, or this honorable court, which you serve. Our courts have faults, as does any human institution, but in this country our courts are the greatest levelers, and in our courts all men are created equal."*

Corner 1-1: Critical Thinking

The instructor pauses until the audience has the opportunity to internalize and ponder the content, and then makes eye contact across the classroom ... "Harper Lee challenges the reader on two basic levels. What do you think she is trying to say in the lecture?"

Lecture Questioning Techniques

Instructors control lecture content and timing. They scan their audience for attention and provide opportunities to ask questions at appropriate intervals. Positive learning climates allow audience interaction with teaching points, an essential component when presenting complex material.

Learner-centered instruction requires acknowledging the audience and encouraging responses. Learners generally prefer to contribute to the learning process. Instructional climates improve when learners ask questions, and rewards follow participation in a positive discussion process. Enthusiasm for the learning process increases when instructors address questions that attend to learner needs or understanding. Frequently, audience members stimulate other participants, rather than simply listening to continuous instructor dialogue.

Ask concise and simple questions and avoid lengthy narrative questions, including unrelated content. Every question should reflect applicable content. Ask questions that require critical thinking, but not necessarily concise answers. The active questioning approach requires instructor creativity, preparation, and feedback. Refer to Training Figure 1-1-B: Lecture Questioning and Feedback for an illustration.

The instructor might add complementary content or develop further examples. Rhetorical questions work efficiently in combination with other instructional methods and are useful in transition points that introduce new content. Pose and answer questions. Redundant rhetorical questioning reduces effectiveness. Responses are components of the lesson outline planning process.

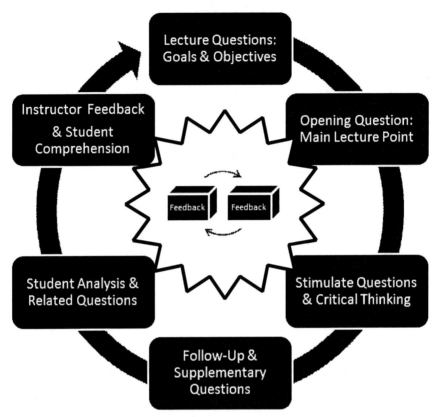

Figure 1-1-B: Lecture Questioning and Feedback

Assessment of Misunderstanding

One superior method to determine comprehension: ask well-formulated questions. Instructor questions assist in revealing misunderstanding and indicate the need for remedies. Instructors adapt presentations to the learning tempo by expanding and refocusing on previous explanations and essential material.

Probing learners for understanding increases instructional method effectiveness. Learner responses reveal weaknesses, strengths, and the need for follow-up and remedial action. Spontaneous questions may discourage active participation. Poor questions leave learners in the shadows of confusion. Excellent questions shed light on the subject matter.

Instructors can learn effective responding skills, for example, by simply rephrasing questions without dismissing the learner's concern. Recognize the learner's question and attempt to offer clarification. Occasionally, learners have difficulty expressing an emotional point of view. The appropriate response is "I'm sorry ... I didn't quite understand your question." Interpreting learner facial expressions and six basic emotions may help clarify misunderstandings.

Reading Six Basic Emotions

"Six Basic Emotions" is a term that refers to the theory of American psychologists Paul Ekman and Wallace V. Friesen. They identified emotions based on studying the isolated culture of people from the Fori tribe in Papua, New Guinea. Tribe members were able to identify these six basic emotions: (1) Anger, (2) Disgust, (3) Fear, (4) Happiness, (5) Sadness, and (6) Surprise. Refer to Figure 1-2: Six Basic Emotions, the Grimace Project for an illustration of facial changes.

Figure 1-2: Six Basic Emotions

"Ekman and Friesen took pictures of facial expressions of people from the Fori tribe with the same emotions and they presented these pictures to people of other races and cultures all over the world. They also interpreted the emotions on the pictures correctly. Gradually, many researchers have confirmed that these emotions are universal for all human beings." Examine Corner 1-2: Learner Communication Bids for illustrations of audience questions, expressive comments, and emotional responses.

Corner 1-2: Learner Communication Bids

Instructors constantly encounter bids for attention. Attempts to communicate can vary from disruptive to supportive. Disruptive learner behaviors take considerable effort and require demanding responses. Bids for attention deserve worthy responses.

Gottman and Declare (2001) in **The Relationship Cure** describe excellent solutions for resolving instructor communication conflict. The authors divulge the need to respond to social bidding effectively. Their insights into the process of bidding for emotional connection are the results of considerable research. Bids may include questions, statements, or comments. Bids typically involve thoughts, questions, feelings, observations, opinions, and invitations. Their research methods involved real-life scenarios and social relationships. These researchers identified three basic bid communication responses: (1) *turning toward*, (2) *turning away* and an extreme form of turning away is the (3) *unrequited response.* Refer to Training Figure 1-3: Learner Communication Bids for an illustration.

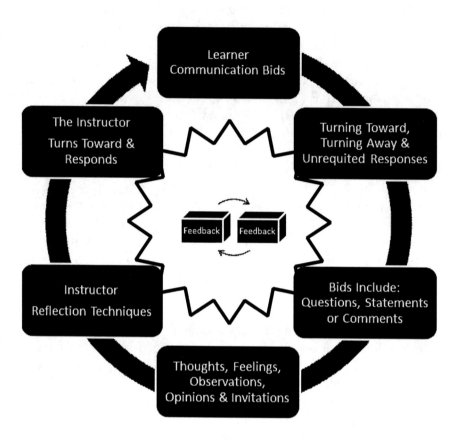

Training Figure 1-3: Learner Communication Bids

Case Study 1: Turning Toward

The *turning toward* communication response is a positive reaction to a bid for emotional connection and requires focus and attention. Instructors look directly at the person and actively listen to bids to establish positive feedback responses.

Sergeant Maryann O'Malley believes you must give fully to others to earn respect. Therefore, she is caring, helpful, supportive, and relationship-oriented, but can be prideful, overly intrusive, and demanding. She functions best when bonding with class members.

Sergeant O'Malley appreciates activities that nurture development and connection. Maryann seeks relationships that offer comfort and support. She cares about the trainees and offers a friendly learning climate. Maryann is concerned about learning and addresses the need for information.

Sergeant O'Malley emphasizes the trainees' role in the learning process. She prepares for presentations—including lecture plans, notes, PowerPoint, and performance activities. Group dynamics play a significant role in fostering learning from others; her lectures are brief and unfold around a central idea.

Sergeant O'Malley's goal is to discuss concepts in an open dialogue. She wants to achieve common understanding and an emotional connection concerning learner bids for attention. This instructor listens carefully to questions, answers, and strives for positive communication. Her objective is to discuss relevant issues and achieve feedback. Bid responses are respectful and enlightening.

The focus of the learning process is on audience participation. Sergeant O'Malley constantly scans her listeners to assess learner response and attention. This technique demands preparation rather than reading from notes.

This instructor demonstrates self-assurance and command of the subject matter. More important, learner attention is on her presentation. Sergeant O'Malley considers posture, classroom movement, gestures, and eye contact. Excellent preparation reduces the nervousness that many experience when in front of an audience.

Case Study 2: Turning Away

The *turning away* pattern of communication involves ignoring another's bid for attention, appearing preoccupied or offering unrelated responses. Consistently turning away from bids for attention is destructive to the instructor/learner relationship.

Corporal Larry Batters believes you must keep a humorous perspective and remain open to assure a high quality life. Accordingly, he seeks pleasure, new possibilities, and is upbeat and adventurous. Sometimes, Corporal Batters avoids pain by appearing uncommitted and self-serving.

He enjoys telling jokes and "fooling around." The downside of Larry's sense of humor results in embarrassment and negative outcomes. His audience often appears disenchanted when his behaviors soar. Larry may feel inhibited, lethargic, or emotionally down when in an under-activated state.

This instructor has great potential; however, his classroom preparation is minimal. The format resembles a "vanity lecture" about self. His pontifications are random and not well correlated. He fails to summarize main points and coordinate learning progressions. Participant questions emerge; however, Corporal Larry Batters minimizes their impact or value.

He may suddenly become energetic, tell a joke, but is off-task when his audience begins to focus their attention. Sergeant Batters ignores the majority of bid requests, wants to be happy, and keeps things upbeat. He enjoys life and appreciates simple things.

He responds to specific questions about himself; however, he ignores bids for personal attention and questions. Sometimes, the Sergeant offers unrelated attempts to appear humorous. His main strategy is to distract participants from the poor presentation, question responses, or omissions. He adjourns the class session, lost in thoughts about his own need to be the center of attention. Unfortunately, Sergeant Batters soon acquires a nickname— "The Joker."

Case Study 3: Unrequited Response

The worst learner bid response is an ***unrequited response***. This unfortunate response occurs when the instructor contin-uously turns away from learners engaging in a series of bids for connection. Negative communication cycles broaden when in-structors habitually ignore bids for attention.

Sergeant Ted Swisher believes you must protect yourself from a world that demands too much and gives too little to assure personal safety. Therefore, Ted seeks self-sufficiency and dwells in his own thoughts. He can be withholding, detached, and overly private, the ideal researcher for finding alternative instructional content.

He is self-aware, introspective, and personalizes issues, be-coming self-absorbed and hypersensitive. Additionally, other temperamental personality traits include self-consciousness, moodiness, and withdrawal. Sergeant Swisher is most effective when seeking information, or involved in sorting, planning, learning, and performance objectives. Ted continues his search, even if it results in fatigue and exhaustion.

Sergeant Ted Swisher does not address learner bids or needs. Trainees find his eccentric tendencies to lecture to the corner of the room a source of rejection. His lectures unfold without eye contact. Ted remains stationary, usually behind the large wooden podium. His deadpan expression reflects a total lack of the emotional involvement.

Ted attempts to break his somber mood with an occasional forced smile. His poker face turns learners off to the presentation. Learners feel they are listening to a tape-recording.

Corner 1-2: Critical Thinking

Analyze the case studies. Compare and contrast instructor methods. What would you change concerning learner bids for attention? Why are instructor responses hurting morale and learner rapport? How would you improve instructor performance and avoid learner conflict? Refer to Corner 1-3 Learner Conflict for an illustration.

Corner 1-3: Learner Conflict Management

Sergeant Larry Armstrong believes you must be strong to achieve resources that satisfy needs and wants. He is decisive, authoritative, and commanding. Sergeant Armstrong dominates his world.

His swagger and boastful attitude create latent morale problems. Fear serves as his best tool for oppression. Only self-assured trainees comment. Attempts to reconcile boundaries induce ruthless and dictatorial retorts. The sergeant becomes combative, intimidating, confrontational, and belligerent, thereby creating adversarial relationships. When challenged, conflict becomes a test of wills.

The sergeant applies threats and reprisals to guarantee obedience from the trainees. The purpose is to keep them off-balance and insecure. However, some seek confrontation. Conflict can be contributory or negative to the instructional process. Learners can test the instructor's human attributes and pose questions that can create disagreement. Audience conflict can lead to additional training management issues.

Larry's demeaning attitude does not offer a positive learning experience. In addition, he announces that on-line practice tests are not available. Instructor apathy creates additional learner anxiety and morale problems. Several class members express anger over this situation; however, he fails to respond.

One participant, an informal leader, expresses audience feedback. Edward Collins, a military police veteran with ten years experience, demonstrates an uncompromising approach. He believes you must be good and right to be worthy. Accordingly, Collins is conscientious, responsible, improvement-oriented, and calm, but he also can be critical, resentful, and self-judging. The following dialogue borders on insubordination and disrespect. Edward likes to influence classmates and voices valid observations.

Collins sits in the front row and states his concerns regarding instructor presentations.

"Your lectures are flat and based on reading from disorganized lecture notes. You never acknowledge us or our questions."

The instructor begins to pull on his collar, his right hand shaking.

"Let me finish the lecture."

Collins appears unyielding.

"I want answers to my questions. We deserve better than this."

Suddenly, Armstrong yells—

"STAND DOWN!"

Collins stands his ground and persists in analyzing the instructor's instructional methods ...

"You're not posting on-line practice tests and grading them? How do we know if we've performed correctly without feedback?"

The instructor glares at Collins as drops of sweat form on his brow. He takes the offensive and attacks.

"You're the only person that has a problem with my instruction! You're a smart ass!"

Collins beams with confidence and responds with unruffled assertion.

"That's where you're wrong. The whole class is ready to sign a petition. Incidentally, other instructors operate on the principle that it's alright to disagree, but not be disagreeable."

Corner 1-3: Critical Thinking

Refer to Don Richard Rizo's book citations in Chapter 2: Group Dynamics for examples of Enneagram personality types. It identifies possible Enneagrams that apply to the case study personalities. Then, compare and contrast frequently appearing Emotional Command Systems. Refer to Chapter 10: Pulling It All Together for additional clarification. How might this content help identify instructor and group member emotions?

Conflict Management

Daniel Wile, in *After the Fight: Using Your Disagreements to Build a Stronger Relationship,* describes some conflict responses. He summarizes his primary philosophy in the following paragraph:

"The quality of life in a relationship depends on our ability to recover from the inevitable periods of fighting or withdrawing; that is, from turning each other into adversaries or strangers. At a minimum, we want to keep such fighting and withdrawing from destroying the relationship. But it is possible to turn these hazards into a means for deepening the relationship by conducting a recovery conversation."

Analyze the case studies according to Wile (1993). Determine if the following three conflict response categories apply:

1. **Attack and Defend:** This happens when you decide the other person's faults or inadequacies are to blame, so you lash out, driving him or her away. If you are the recipient of such an attack, you get defensive, which also leads to alienation.
2. **Avoid or Deny:** You try to ignore or minimize your negative feelings about the problem. You tell yourself, "It's silly to feel this way," or "I just won't think about it and maybe it will go away." As the problem persists, however, it gets harder and harder to hold this position.
3. **Self-Disclose and Correct.** You can discuss how you feel about the problem and work on common understanding.

Even if you do not find the perfect compromise or solution, you have at least established an emotional connection.

Instructors should avoid confrontation with training participants and acknowledge that a learner complaint or concern may be valid and worth addressing. Timely training method assessments allow sessions to move forward in directions that are more positive.

Focus Points

Instructor-led questioning is an important strategy that encourages participant interaction. Learning requires designing questions that motivate learners to exceed expectations. Encourage questions that promote clarification and understanding. The ultimate purpose is to provoke problem-solving, critical thinking, and discussion.

State unambiguous questions, promote retention, analysis, and reflect specific performance objectives. Excellent questions serve a variety of purposes. They encourage active listening and audience attention. Learners increase their attention when uncertain about instructor question timing or direction. Passive learning and complacency are often consequences of too little classroom interaction.

Formal lecture methods represent one technique of disseminating pertinent information; little or no learner participation is problematic. The lecture works best in combination with other methods of instruction.

Pause briefly after asking questions and create opportunities to stimulate critical thinking. If necessary, ask learners to repeat responses. Evaluate answers and praise positive solutions.

The right conversational tone is important. There is a difference between saying words and communicating ideas. Proper voice modulation and pauses enhance attention span.

Dynamic instructors apply skillful strategies and recognize the need to manage the classroom climate. Innovative instructors frequently change the learning pace. Alternating methods enhance and maintain interest for expanded periods.

Lecture strategies are best limited to approximately fifteen minutes. Diverse teaching methods and active learning strategies limit distractions and improve learner attention spans.

Occasionally, instructors misinterpret questions as challenges to their expertise. Instructors should listen to questions and give learners the benefit of their uncertainty. Well-prepared instructors may find that learners ask questions that require further research.

Instructors must resist temptations to demean knowledge-seeking behaviors from learners. Learner disenchantment erupts when instructors do not clarify content or audience expectations.

Competent instructors pay close attention to Learner Guide.

Conclusion

Stop for a minute! Are you reading the case study illustrations and missing underlying messages? If so, you overlook opportunities to apply training content and enhance retention. Case studies offer important "memory hook" principles and supporting content. With a little more concentration, the benefits will outweigh the effort tenfold. Chapter 2: Group Leadership Dynamics provides a pathway to diversify the lecture method, and improve learner participation and morale.

CHAPTER 2

Group Leadership Dynamics

"In such an educational community, students could find an excitement in intellectual and emotional discovery which would lead them to become lifelong learners."
— Carl R. Rogers

Focus

Instructors who encourage active learning strategies foster critical thinking skills and maximize group dynamics. Achieving goals requires group planning and assessments. Understanding group dynamics and the instructor's role is essential to excellent group performance. The purpose of this chapter is to define the role of an instructor who organizes small group learning strategies.

Overview

The application of group dynamics and case study methods generates considerable feedback. Group activities allow interaction between learners from diverse backgrounds and encourage accommodating dissimilar points of view. The chapter emphasis is on learner assessment skills and group development. The small group learning process differs from traditional lecture methods; however, instructors remain content experts.

Group Dynamics: Active Leadership

A basic understanding of group leadership and cohesion is essential. Group cohesion is important because it determines the level of cooperation and communication among members, ultimately affecting the achievement of learning performance objectives. Small groups appear effective in achieving active learning outcomes.

Initially, a quantity of conflict is normal, leadership unfolds, and eventually group norms emerge. Ultimately, the group moves toward higher levels of performance and problem solving.

Instantaneous feedback augments lecture and passive learning strategies. Membership is valued as new friendships develop.

Instructors serve as mentors, leaders, and role models—group members with professional expertise and observer skills suitable for appropriate interventions. The ability to conduct assessments facilitates moving groups through predictable developmental stages.

In the early stages, groups elect temporary leaders who encourage positive performance. Members select two scribes who document findings. They also endorse presenters. The remaining participants serve as group researchers and all assignments rotate. Rotation encourages public speaking and action-briefing skill development.

Small learning groups are superior for peer bonding. Ideal groups comprise four to six members and avoid odd numbers. The instructor leadership style is directive in the initial dependant stage of development—then becomes supportive during subsequent phase completions.

Group Stages

Individual behaviors are unpredictable; however, group behaviors have predictable stages of development. The predictable stages are: (1) *disorganized stage*, (2) *adjustment stage*, and (3) *cooperation or performance stage*. The instructor's objective is to encourage group development to at least the *adjustment stage*, or preferably the *cooperation stage*. The *cooperation or problem-solving stage* is team-oriented. Instructors monitor the progress of groups that move too quickly to the *performing stage*, creating frustration and poor group cohesiveness. Patience, active listening, open communication, and understanding enhance successful transition through stages. Refer to Training Figure 2-1: Group Stages of Development for examples of group evolutionary stages.

Occasionally, learning groups do not arrive at the cooperation stage of development. Several influences may prevent transition. Typically, the group does not coordinate efficiently outside or inside the classroom on performance-oriented tasks. Instructors are not responsible for regression. Responsibility for successfully moving through the three-group development stages belongs to the group.

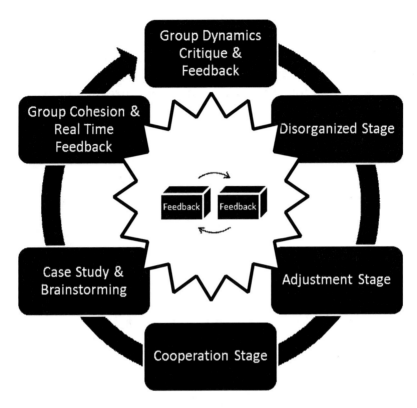

Figure 2-1 Group Stages of Development

Groups must transform to achieve maximum potential for independence and cooperation. Groups experience some conflict as leadership emerges in the *disorganized stage*. There is little feedback in the "go-along to get-along" phase. Members seek approval and direction from instructors. Disorganized groups need praise and direct guidance from their leadership.

As groups move toward the adjustment stage, members bond and form insider relationships. Limited feedback evolves at this stage of development and communication guidelines include: (1) timely information, (2) specific information, (3) nonjudgmental comments, and (4) maintaining training content focus. Instructors serve as limited facilitators until groups arrive at the *cooperation* or *performing* stage. Members are willing to give and receive effective feedback in the *cooperation* stage. Feedback assesses basic task performance and content understanding; instructors permit additional delegation of responsibility.

Group learning settings encourage two simultaneous dimensions: (1) academic content, and (2) group development. The development dimension represents how groups discuss the training content or current topic. Mastering the group development dimension assists in retention.

The keys to facilitating the critical thinking process are *schedule rotation* and *early dismissal* for individual groups. Flexibility allows instructors to focus on individual small group organization and planning. Participants use release time for planning sessions or learning assignment review. Learners interact with each other in small groups and rehearse group presentations—opportunities to review course materials at their own pace.

Group Development Dimension

The development dimension unfolds as groups define operating norms. There are many ways for leadership to emerge. Group members with experience and demonstrated proficiencies generally prevail. Individuals may earn respect because of their status; mature learners often fall into this category.

One member may attempt to seize control and influence discussions by inserting negativity. Instructors quickly interject themselves into the discussion by commenting that it is acceptable to disagree, but not be disagreeable. Negativity can quickly become contagious; consensus is the preferred method.

Group Content Dimension

Generally, the content dimension requires considerable group time. However, lapses in the development dimension may impede or stop group momentum—hampering efficient forward movement.

Keeping groups focused on the training content dimension is no easy task. Training content issues arise when groups lack necessary information from reliable resources. Provide positive guidance in the early stages of group development, including clarification, training summary sheets, and adequate classroom instruction.

Instructor group interventions stimulate learners toward positive outcomes. Short comments may serve to encourage discussion, critical thinking, and problem solving. Excessive lectures stagnate and facilitate group dependency.

Instructor Leadership Interventions

Instructors use *observations* to interpret group progress, including the ability to read nonverbal communication and interpret group dynamics. Accurate observations assist in moving groups forward toward successful task accomplishment.

Instructor feedback addresses group progress and may involve observations from members. Group performance signals efficiency. Instructors identify who has influence, how the individual achieved influence, and, more important, their motivation.

One significant factor is to determine how individuals influence the decision-making process. Once instructors achieve that information, then it is possible to identify the group's stage of development. Instructor behaviors influence the rise to cooperative group thinking.

Instructors assess group dynamics to determine accurate academic content and related growth dimensions. Instructors have three basic courses of action when problems emerge: (1) influence the academic content dimension, (2) influence the development dimension, or (3) choose not to act or influence the group. Instructors determine the appropriate response following stage development assessment.

Conduct a brief group leadership evaluation, including member performance. Acknowledge leaders and star presenters; then maximize their potential and create opportunities for others to develop. Enneagrams assist in making nonscientific group member assessments. *Ennea* is the Greek word for *nine,* and *gram* stands for *model*; therefore, the term *Enneagram* means *nine models.*

The origin of the Enneagram—ancient mathematical discoveries and their history—reveals Greek and Arabic learning during the fourteenth or fifteenth centuries. Enneagrams serve as crude indexes of human personality and behavior. Refer to Corner 2-1: Nine Enneagram Types for an illustration of group assessment applications.

Corner 2-1: Nine Enneagram Types

Don Richard Riso and Russ Hudson (1996, 2000), in *Understanding Enneagrams: The Practical Guide to Personality Types,* identify nine basic Enneagram personality types that can be applied to assessing group dynamics. Enneagrams represent personality systems that describe distinctive personality styles.

"In the Enneagram, as in life, there are no pure types. Everyone is a unique mixture of his or her basic type(s) and one of the two types adjacent to it, is called a 'wing.' Second to the basic type, the auxiliary type, or wing, provides the basic connection type with other psychological functions, sometimes complementing the other basic type, sometimes working in opposition to it."

Enneagrams represent basic propositions or beliefs that individuals require to meet personality needs and personal satisfaction. Enneagrams identify three levels of human performance: (1) **healthy best**, (2) **average**, and (3) **unhealthy worst**. The following nine Enneagrams may require additional research. However, Enneagram personality synopsis statements prove helpful when instructors conduct group member assessments.

Enneagram Type One:

The *Reformer* is principled, purposeful, self-controlled, and a perfectionist.

Healthy Best Reformers: are conscientious with strong personal convictions. They have an intense sense of right and wrong as well as a personal code of moral values. This personality type believes you must be good and right to be worthy. Accordingly, they are responsible, improvement-oriented, and self-controlled.

Reformers are rational, reasonable, self-disciplined, and moderate in all things. They are ethical, truthful, and concerned with justice. Their sense of integrity makes them outstanding moral teachers, personal examples, and witnesses to the truth and other values.

Average Reformers: become dissatisfied with reality and personally feel it is up to them to improve everything. They become crusaders, advocates, critics, educators, and high-minded idealists that promote causes. Related to this role is the need to explain, remedy, debate, and point out errors while striving to maintain standards.

Unhealthy Reformers: can be extremely rigid, close-minded, self-righteous, intolerant, and appear inflexible. They project the idea that they alone know the truth and relentlessly make pronouncements from narrow forbidding absolutes. Their severe judgments require them to prove themselves *right* and others *wrong*.

Enneagram Type Two:

The *Helper* is generous, demonstrative, people-pleasing, and possessive.

Healthy Best Helpers: are empathetic, compassionate, and care for others. This personality type believes you must give fully to achieve love. At their best, they are deeply unselfish, humble, humane, and give unconditional love to themselves and others.

Average Helpers: engage in "people-pleasing" behaviors to gain closer relationships, including: friendliness, emotionally demonstrative, and full of good intentions. Their motivations are: achieve love, express feelings for others, and feel needed and appreciated. Moreover, their goal is to motivate others to respond and vindicate their inner feelings about themselves.

Unhealthy Worst Helpers: can be manipulative, self-serving, and encourage guilt by making others feel indebted. Accordingly, *Helpers* can be prideful, overly intrusive, and demanding. They can undermine people by making belittling or disparaging remarks. This personality can resort to being domineering or feeling entitled to get anything they want from others. In addition, they might feel bitter, resentful, and angry when not receiving positive feedback.

Enneagram Type Three:

The *Motivator* is adaptable, ambitious, image-conscious, and driven.

Healthy Best Motivators: appear self-assured and energetic, with high self-esteem. They believe in themselves and their own value. They are inner directed, authentic, and industrious people, everything they seem to be. They want to feel worthwhile, affirmed, distinguished, admired, and impress others. This personality type believes you must accomplish and succeed to be valued.

Average Motivators: are industrious, fast-paced, goal-focused, and efficiency-oriented. They compare themselves to others in their search for status and success. The *Motivator* becomes image-conscious and concerned about outward perceptions. Moreover, this personality type reflects others' expectations.

Unhealthy Worst Motivators: engage in fear of failure and humiliation. Furthermore, they misrepresent themselves or distort the truth regarding their accomplishments. They can be extremely unprincipled, dishonest, opportunistic, and jealous over the success of others. They may be willing to do "whatever it takes" to preserve superiority. The downside is becoming career driven social climbers invested exclusively in achievement and winning at all costs. They can also be inattentive to others' feelings, impatient, and image-driven.

Enneagram Type Four:

The *Individualist* is expressive, romantic, and can be withholding and temperamental.

Healthy Best Individualists: are self-aware, introspective, engage in a "search for self," and aware of feelings and inner impulses. In addition, they are self-revealing, emotionally honest, and humane. At their best, they are profoundly creative and may express artistic endeavors. Accordingly, they are idealistic, deeply feeling, empathetic, and authentic to self.

Average Individualists: are interested in artistic, romantic environments that cultivate and prolong their personal feelings. This includes a heightened sense of reality through fantasy, passionate feelings, and imagination. To stay in touch with feelings, they interiorize and personalize things and imaginations. They want to be themselves, to express something beautiful, and may withdraw to protect their feelings and take care of emotional needs before attending to anything else.

Unhealthy Worst Individualists: are dramatic, moody, and sometimes self-absorbed. When dreams fail, they become self-inhibiting and angry with themselves and others. In addition, they can become blocked and emotionally paralyzed, ashamed, and unable to function.

Enneagram Type Five:

The *Investigator* is innovative, cerebral, detached, and provocative.

Healthy Best Investigators: observe everything with extraordinary perceptiveness and insight. Furthermore, they concentrate and become engrossed on what has caught their attention. Ultimately, they become skillful and master whatever interests them. In addition, they can become visionaries, broadly comprehending their world. *Investigators* often find innovative ways of perceiving and doing things.

Average Investigators: conceptualize everything before acting. They work things out in their minds first; then, engage in model building, preparing, practicing, and gathering resources. Furthermore, they are mentally alert, curious, and have a searching kind of intelligence. Nothing escapes their attention.

Unhealthy Worst Investigators: become reclusive and isolated from reality. In addition, they display aggression, reject, and repulse others and all social attachments.

Enneagram Type Six:

The *Loyalist* is reliable, committed, and can be defensive and suspicious.

Healthy Best Loyalists: are able to engage others and identify with them. They are steadfast, earnest, and affectionate. They are self-affirming, trusting of self and others. In addition, they are independent as well as interdependent. *Loyalists* cooperate as equals. Their belief in self leads to true courage, positive thinking, leadership, and self-expression.

Average Loyalists: invest their time and energy in whatever they believe will be safe and stable. Organizing and structuring, they seek alliances with authorities for security and continuity. They make commitments to others, hoping for returned acts of kindness. They are constantly vigilant, anticipate problems, seek clear guidelines, and feel secure when system procedures are well defined. Moreover, they want security, and to feel support and approval from others.

Unhealthy Worst Loyalists: are clingingly dependant and self-disapproving, with acute feelings of inferiority. They see themselves as helpless and incompetent, seeking a stronger authority or belief to resolve all problems.

Enneagram Type Seven:

The *Enthusiast* is spontaneous, versatile, distractible, and excessive.

Healthy Best Enthusiasts: are responsive, excitable, and enthusiastic about sensations and experiences. They are extraverted and find everything invigorating. In addition, they are lively, vivacious, eager, spontaneous, resilient, and cheerful.

This multitalented personality type becomes easily accomplished achievers, generalists who do many different things well. Moreover, they assimilate experiences, making them grateful and appreciative for what they have. They want to be happy and satisfied, have a wide variety of experiences, keep their options open, enjoy life, and amuse themselves to escape anxiety.

Average Enthusiasts: appear uninhibited, and do and say whatever comes to mind. They engage in storytelling, flamboyant exaggerations, wisecracking, and mimic "on stage performer behaviors." This personality type fears being bored, so they keep in perpetual motion, but attempt too many things. Some may not fare well.

Unhealthy Worst Enthusiasts: become superficial, self-centered, and greedy, feeling unsatisfied. Additionally, they can become offensive and abusive while going after what they want. In flight from self, they act out impulsively rather than deal with anxiety or frustration.

Enneagram Type Eight:

The *Leader* is self-confident, decisive, dominating, and confrontational.

Healthy Best Leaders: have a "can do" attitude and fervent inner drive. In addition, they are decisive, authoritative, commanding, and take the initiative to make things happen. Therefore, they seek justice and are direct, strong, and action oriented.

They are self-assertive and stand up for what they need and want. Typically, they champion people, are protective and honorable. They carry others with their strength. At their best, they become self-restrained, merciful, and forbearing. *Leaders* are courageous and demonstrate a willingness to sustain serious jeopardy to achieve their vision.

Average Leaders: achieve self-sufficiency, financial independence, and have enough resources for important concerns. They become enterprising, pragmatic, and hardworking risk-takers. In addition, they begin to dominate their environment and become the "boss." Their word is law and they tend to engage in boastful, forceful, and expansive behaviors.

Unhealthy Worst Leaders: may also engage shocking behaviors. They will defy any attempt to control them, and are capable of becoming completely ruthless with an attitude of "might is right." If endangered, they may destroy everything that does not conform to their way or wants, rather than surrender to anyone.

Enneagram Type Nine:

The *Peacemaker* is reassuring, agreeable, and can be disengaged and stubborn.

Healthy Best Peacemakers: are deeply receptive, accepting, emotionally stable, and serene. They are trusting of self and life, and tend to be innocent, patient, unpretentious, and good-natured. In addition, they are imaginative, creative, and attuned to nonverbal communication. Other personality traits include optimism, and bringing people together. Furthermore, they are good mediators, communicators, and have a calming influence on others.

Average Peacemakers: believe that to be loved and valued, you must intermingle. Therefore, they seek harmony, comfort, and stable environments. They become agreeable, "go along to get along" to avoid conflict, and may engage in passive behaviors. Their motivation is to have serenity, peace of mind, and to preserve things as they are.

Unhealthy Worst Peacemakers: have a tendency to avoid conflict and escape problems that require unpredictable demands.

They can be neglectful and irresponsible, unaware of anything that could affect them. In addition, they might not be able to function under stressful circumstances.

Corner 2-1: Critical Thinking Exercise

Enneagrams offer approximate insights into self-appraisals and behaviors. The crude index provides personality and motivation indicators. The Oracle at Delphi wisdom reverberates across the centuries—"Know Thyself." If you were to describe yourself in one word, which Enneagram concept would apply? Select one or two of the following categories: (1) *Reformer*, (2) *Helper*, (3) *Motivator*, (4) *Individualist*, (5) *Investigator*, (6) *Loyalist*, (7) *Enthusiast*, (8) *Leader*, or (9) *Peacemaker*. Refer to Table 2-1: Enneagram Self-Assessment Survey Rating Inventory Scale. Ten is *high* and one is the *low*.

Table 2-1. Enneagram Self-Assessment Survey

ENNEAGRAM SELF-ASSESSMENT SURVEY	1	2	3	4	5	6	7	8	9	10
Type One: The Reformer is principled, purposeful, self-controlled and perfectionist.										
Type Two: The Helper is generous, demonstrative, people-pleasing and possessive.										
Type Three: The Motivator is adaptable, ambitious, image-conscious and arrogant.										
Type Four: The Individualist is expressive, romantic, withholding and temperamental.										
Type Five: The Investigator is innovative, cerebral, detached and provocative.										

ENNEAGRAM SELF-ASSESSMENT SURVEY	1	2	3	4	5	6	7	8	9	10
Type Six: The Loyalist is reliable, committed, defensive and suspicious.										
Type Seven: The Enthusiast is spontaneous, versatile, distractible and excessive.										
Type Eight: The Leader is self-confident, decisive, dominating and confrontational.										
Type Nine: The Peacemaker is reassuring, agreeable, disengaged and stubborn.										
Note: Healthy, Average, & Unhealthy Categories										

Appraise the following case study. It addresses personality and behavioral foundations that unfold in the nine Enneagrams. Apply Enneagrams to case studies to practice assessments and as a general index for reading learner bids. Refer to the following Corner 2-2: Enneagram Case Study for an example of group dynamics applications.

Corner 2-2: Enneagram Case Study

Trainee John Samson believes you must be powerful and commanding to assure protection and regard in a hard-hitting world. He is direct, tough, and action-oriented, but he can also be overly excessive and sometimes impulsive. His motivation is the need to be self-reliant, strong, and avoid feeling weak or dependent. John is overprotective and battles for justice. The following conversation took place in an empty classroom with Ed Collins.

John shakes his head ... puzzled.

What is wrong with this instructor ... does he have dementia?

Then he throws an empty training folder in the trash.

The guy is "out of it" and nobody cares around here!

He glances in the direction of another trainee, Ed Collins, who sits reading a newspaper.

"So what are we going to do about it? We are in the business of saving lives and this instructor is totally lost and confused. He's wasting our time."

Ed looks up.

"Maybe we need to be a little more patient and understanding. He's going to retire in a year anyway and has been around a long time ... even before I was born."

John, untouched by Ed's attempts, continues his brash dialogue.

"He keeps repeating the same old war stories every class session and I'm sick of it."

Ed attempts to introduce humor.

"I think you may be on to something there ... maybe we should take the guy out and shoot him."

The comment amplifies John's annoyance.

"This is no joking matter. We're talking millions of dollars in lawsuits for failure to train. We need information on the use of force and other related issues. Lives are at stake. Do you have any serious ideas?"

"Just one ... we maintain calm and let the old man retire with dignity."

"Forget it ... my patience is gone."

"Why don't we help him get through this year and take an active role in teaching units on the use of force?"

"Do you mean divide the material up between us?"

"Right ... it's a win/win solution. Everyone does his or her share. The old man saves face and retires with dignity—problem solved."

"Maybe you're right. I could live with that as long as we do something ... let's have a meeting and share our thoughts with the others."

Corner 2-2: Critical Thinking Exercise

Which Enneagram Personality description(s) best describe John and Ed? How do John and Ed differ according to the Enneagrams? The case study also reflects frequently appearing Emotional Command Systems. Refer to Chapter 10: Pulling it All Together for additional information. Compare and contrast both personality systems.

Lessons Learned: Minimizing Conflict

A certain amount of conflict exists within groups. Participants assess group boundaries, personal power, and that of others. Group member behaviors vary according to gender, culture, personality, and training.

Some groups demonstrate leadership vacuums and may require outside instructor interventions. The reverse can also be a problem; groups with too many leaders struggle to share influence and power. The transfer and reorganization of group members requires a plan of action and forms the basis for instructor intervention. Enneagrams may assist in the assessment of group members.

Instructors attempt to remedy group interaction problems sooner rather than later. In some marginal situations, wait to see if group members step forward to fill leadership gaps. Consider appointing a leader from another group if appropriate leadership does not evolve.

Group assignments include performance-oriented tasks. Final projects encourage cooperation regarding content and performance. Announce graded group projects during initial sessions and assign topics to encourage competitive team spirit.

The best way to counter off-task behaviors is to require action briefings after group discussions. Present training solutions on the blackboard in appropriate topic sequence. This assignment motivates class session participation.

Content defines group strategies; however, one group member may attempt to dominate discussions by inserting personal agendas. The group discourages off-task behaviors in support of training content presentations.

Problems with off-task behaviors abound and examples include cell phone texting and off-topic personal conversations. Persistent and consistent behavior problems require instructor intervention. Disruptive behaviors damage group-learning outcomes. A few off-task isolates may emerge in the early group development stage. However, ultimately the group will persuade them in the interactive phase.

Case Study Method

The case study method is learner focused and positions learners in a group performance mode. Instructors are not center stage;

learners move into the spotlight. Learners shift into the problem-solving position and generate new questions. This method of instruction represents interactive group questioning.

The emphasis is on group cooperation, case study examination, and accurate information. Group members struggle for harmony and consensus regarding solutions. Members grow and develop during powerful exchanges throughout the group dynamics flow.

Problem-solving case scenarios develop trainees and improve personal performance. Participants learn concept applications and reason cause and effect relationships. Trainees learn judgment skills and apply flexible thinking. Most important, they learn how to analyze the case study problem, discuss divergent points of view, and work with others in a creative planning format.

Instructor-focused questions can be motivating. Instructors maintain low profiles and pose questions. Someone generally steps forward with an answer, generating further discussion and questioning. Instructor responses encourage participants to reexamine assumptions and active learning solution applications.

The case study method provides opportunities for personal expression and content development. However, discussions must emphasize key instructional points that contribute to learning and positive testing results.

A short lecture precedes the case study introduction; participants are encouraged to resolve the case as a group. The case study is generally short, offers specific content applications, mirrors real or hypothetical crimes, and describes facts from the case.

Instructors serve as mentor guides and provide leadership skills. Participants embrace opportunities for verbal expression and group interaction. Instructors conclude the process with a formalized follow-up activity called a *critique.*

Critiques inform learners regarding their academic progress. Critiques assess solutions and provide constructive feedback, without criticizing a particular point of view or solution. Ultimately, critiques clarify, emphasize, or reinforce basic concepts and critical thinking skills.

Case study opportunities offer multiple opportunities for learning and concept applications. Instructors assign hypothetical case study questions that learners can respond to during future class sessions.

Case Study Example: The Cult Leader

The following case study example emphasizes a cooperative classroom climate where participants learn from each other. The instructor presents training content that enables learners to apply basic performance objectives and problem-solving strategies. Instructors circulate Advance Sheets during prior class sessions that describe training performance objectives and relevant references.

Case Study Facts

Prophet Jack Lewis Clayton is a homely, middle-aged white male and born into the Sons and Daughters of the Sanctified Saints. He is charismatic, a pious scoundrel. Jack's leadership style is "carrot and stick" and his violent behaviors ultimately garner power and control. He relentlessly exercises supremacy, convinced that fate has given him privileges beyond others.

The congregation reveres Prophet Clayton; few members challenge his word. He claims to be an instrument of God! Followers who dare to confront him face excommunication from the cult and banishment. His recent rise to cult leadership motivates harsh doctrine and grandiose behaviors. Followers must refer to him as their Prophet; he claims to be clairvoyant and a disciple of universal truth.

Prophet Clayton molests young females after religious ceremonies. He professes they are child brides, and also awards underage children as spiritual brides for the Board of Elders, further examples of his absolute power and control. Clayton may punish innocents as a warning to others.

The Prophet has mood swings that range from depression to mania; his behavior becomes erratic when excited. He preaches Armageddon and the destruction of civilization. Only those sanctified by his presence will live through the annihilation. However, he does not believe in anything except his personal survival.

The prophet is a moral crusader and his divisive sermons proclaim the need for racial segregation. He is adamantly against interracial marriage and social contact. Any interaction with outsiders constitutes religious contamination. Nevertheless, Clayton defies the law, morality, and common decency; he feels invincible.

He plots with the Elders on the possibility of starting a race war. His plan is to initiate Armageddon and armed conflict that will end civilization. The Prophet encourages followers to arm themselves and build underground concrete shelters. Clayton is obsessed with making himself impenetrable to attack.

Clayton consolidates his control and terrorizes followers, jeopardizing children. He vows that law enforcement authorities will never take him alive. Fear tactics suggest that agents plan to raid their community, actions that will initiate Armageddon. He convinces followers that the day of reckoning is fast approaching. Cyanide poison stored in large quantities will serve their exit from the planet.

Excommunicated and fugitive cult members complain to law enforcement officials. The intelligence flow of criminal information offers probable cause. Law enforcement agencies formulate a Special Task Force to decide on a plan of action. Refer to Appendix B: Criminal Cult for an expanded version and support documentation.

Conference Group Method

The **conference group method** represents a participatory approach. This group strategy involves group training, guided thinking, and includes specific goals and objectives. Collectively, participants gather ideas to solve problems. Conference planning requires an instructor maximum ratio of 20 participants, preferably 12 participants. The ultimate form of group work is the conference method.

This conference method represents member-centered discussions with an emphasis on practical problems. The purpose: to explore increased understanding of issues or problem(s). Participants develop insight into decision-making, techniques, procedures, and applications—increased commitments to solve problems because of participant interest and commitment.

The core of this approach is knowledgeable and experienced instructor/conference leaders. However, ideas, strategies, and solutions emerge from group participants, not instructors. Instructors serve as silent mentors for the group; however, they may offer questioning techniques. Instructors guide groups through controlled discussions and toward constructive solutions. Typically, the **conference group method** is ideally suited to in-service programs for training leadership. Members should be similar in educational level, rank, and job description. Group members demonstrate knowledge, experience, and offer applicable information concerning the topic or problem(s). Therefore, relevant background and expertise offer considerable contributions. Instructor/conference leaders occupy supportive roles; they do not provide answers or information.

Focus Points

Unlike passive learning, active group learning requires that participants learn not only from the instructor, but also from each other, while participating in the problem-solving process. Therefore, there is communication learner-to-learner as well as between the instructor and participants. One way to accomplish this is through directed small groups.

Group participation enhances the active learning process and increases the possibility that participants reach their full potential.

Group dynamics, problem solving, and diverse instructional strategies address differing learning styles. Instructors pose hypothetical situations. Groups work independently to solve problems, whereas instructors serve as mentors.

Instructors encourage cooperation, not isolation. A collaborative group process teaches learners that they can master content by relying on themselves and other learners as opposed to exclusive instructor dependence. Instructors encourage the free exchange of ideas and possible solutions.

Some questions require several responses; therefore, allocate difficult questions to several groups. That approach offers the possibility of highlighting multiple complex lecture points. Task groups compare and contrast group solutions. For example, group one reviews one component of the question, whereas groups two, three, four, and five emphasize related training points. Generally, multi-group reporting is superior to singular group assessment.

Group analysis and the application of effective assessments are complex activities. The reader must exceed expectations to reach maximum performance. Critical thinking group exercises support the planning of instruction and appraisal process.

The next progression requires more cooperation and respect for others as the group builds on their former experience and firmly identifies its leadership. To put this in perspective, critical thinking case studies encourage learners to participate in cooperative exploration and constructive disagreement while moving toward problem solutions.

Learners discover respect for differing opinions, therefore, increasing their potential to discuss dissimilar points of view from a wide spectrum of positions. The group case study method encourages learners to think and communicate persuasively and gain experience in working with other people.

Group presentations emphasize collaboration and speaking skills. This level of analysis requires the development of computer research skills to access information on selected topics. Instructors present training concepts in PowerPoint presentations.

Case study exercises support training and require participants to read and comply with advanced study and reading assignments. Hence, without appropriate learner preparation, this approach will be less successful and impede the learning process.

The case study exercise method permits theory applications to real or hypothetical case scenarios and allows maximum use of the senses. Superior presentations insert interactive case studies that require trainee participation and active learning. Learners read the case, present solutions on the blackboard, and then compare and contrast their decisions.

Most educators/trainers agree that active learning applications motivate content retention; participation enhances critical thinking skills. Small group activities encourage autonomous activity and cooperative interaction.

Conclusion

Training awareness acknowledges instructional content, group dynamics, and applications that work toward positive learning outcomes. Instructor influence requires diverse strategies that address learner needs and fluid classroom environments. Spontaneous teachable moments evolve in an atmosphere rich with creative opportunities, feedback, and reflective assessment. Refer to Chapter 3: Dynamic Curriculum Management to support learning strategies.

PART II: THE CURRICULUM SEARCH BEGINS

"We should all be concerned about the future because we will have to spend the rest of our lives there."
— Charles F. Kettering

Figure Part II-A

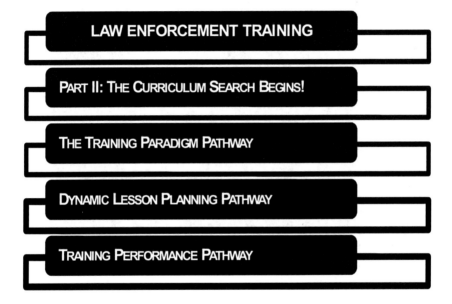

LAW ENFORCEMENT TRAINING

PART II: THE CURRICULUM SEARCH BEGINS!

THE TRAINING PARADIGM PATHWAY

DYNAMIC LESSON PLANNING PATHWAY

TRAINING PERFORMANCE PATHWAY

Figure Part II-B: the Curriculum Search Begins

Connecting Curriculum Dots	Guidepost Pathways
The Training Paradigm: • Curriculum Design • Organizing Centers & Goals • Performance Objectives • Active Learning Case Studies • Program Evaluation • Student Evaluation	• Define Problem • Define Destination • How Will You Get There? • Define Arrival • Select Appropriate Solution
Dynamic Lesson Planning: • Lesson Plan Purpose • Lesson Plan Elements • Lesson Planning Foundations • Lesson Planning Strategies	• Describe "Big Picture" • Define Instructional Units • Instructor Preparation • Blue Print for Instructional Content and Assessment
Training Performance: • Student Learning Styles • Learner Feedback • Define Performance Objectives • Practical Exercise Model	• Assess Student Learning • Conduct Task(s) Analysis • Establish Task Criterion • Prepare and Apply Model

CHAPTER 3

Dynamic Curriculum Management

"An investment in knowledge pays the best interest."
— Benjamin Franklin

Focus

Curriculum management provides the **strategic big picture** and pathway to practical training solutions. A **training paradigm** is a collection of organizing principles, belief systems, or creative models that shape understanding. The purpose of this chapter is to explore training paradigms, curriculum management, and planning. **Find the leadership road map!**

Overview

Curriculum paradigms improve training effectiveness and practical applications. New sets of solutions emerge as training curriculum paradigms develop and knowledge increases. In addition, the examination of curriculum philosophy, critical thinking, and active learning training content enhances positive outcomes. The need to analyze, construct curriculum, and improve the quality of instruction involves a planned effort.

Curriculum Foundations

Bloom's system includes a threefold division of training applications concerning performance objectives: (1) cognitive domain (recall or recognition of knowledge); (2) affective domain (feelings or emotions; changes in interest, attitudes, and values; appreciations); and (3) psychomotor domain (reflexes, basic fundamental, perceptual, and complex motor patterns). The social domain reflects personal and social development. This domain also includes the development of socially acceptable behavior as well as conduct, emotional stability, interpersonal relations, and self-fulfillment.

The following illustrates the principles of curriculum and Systematic Design of Instruction (SDI):

- Identify an instructional goal.
- Conduct instructional analysis.
- Identify entry behaviors and characteristics.
- Write performance objectives.
- Develop criterion-referenced test items.
- Develop an instructional strategy.
- Develop and select instruction.
- Design and conduct formative learner evaluations.
- Revise instruction.
- Conduct summative program evaluation (Dick and Carey, 1985).

Defining the Curriculum Philosophy

A training philosophy must be action-oriented and dynamic. Philosophy is the search for reality, truth, and professional conduct. A training philosophy should include a system of principles of decision-making for performing law enforcement operations. Specifically, philosophy is an on-going assessment of basic beliefs, attitudes, and values that consistently function for deciding worthy law enforcement actions and why the tasks are important. If *where are you are going?* is a valid question; then, the inquiry on what basis (philosophy) establishes *how* and *why* is crucial to the law enforcement mission. In addition, philosophy serves as the foundation for values, ethics, and direction for law enforcement training.

The application of philosophical foundations includes attitudes and values that serve as a basis for determining training curriculum. The philosophical approach serves as a navigational system for learners. The philosophy is dynamic, action-oriented, and involves critical thinking and problem solving. Moreover, the philosophy, goals, and objectives remain a compass for offering training direction and quality instruction. Curriculum philosophies build training climates. Refer to Training Appendix C: (Chapter 3), Building the Training Climate for an illustration of the Universal Design for Instruction philosophy.

Critical Thinking Foundations

Critical thinking integrates well with the training philosophy, organizing center articulation, performance task(s) and training performance framework. One of the earliest tests applied to learner behaviors is the Dressel & Mayhew Test of Critical Thinking (1954).

"Researchers identified five salient skills for critical thinking: The ability to:

- Define a problem.
- Select pertinent information for the solution of a problem.
- Recognize stated and unstated assumptions.
- Formulate and select relevant and promising hypotheses.
- Draw conclusions validly and to judge the validity of references."

Problem Solving

Problem-solving strategies represent essential training requirements. The problem-solving training approach applies problem selection and reasoning strategies. After gathering essential information and carefully analyzing the problem and causative factors, training personnel can implement appropriate responses. This requires field training planning, implementation, responses, evaluating effectiveness, and modifying training approaches.

Training programs should include problem-solving strategies and tactics for law enforcement personnel. Field officers must understand the actions and interactions between offenders, victims, and the law, before developing appropriate responses. Problem-solving training serves as the foundation for effective decision-making.

Decision-Making

Law enforcement personnel make more decisions on a daily basis than corporate executives. When confronted with an important training decision, analyze each alternative and select the best choice. Arrange training schedules around practical exercises that require active learning and decision-making.

Decision-making in the field continues to involve high-risk behaviors that are life threatening. The most important survival strategy is making the right choices. Time considerations may require immediate action; this form of critical decision-making is open to error. Every field situation is dependent on effective decision-making. Therefore, law enforcement training requires field encounters that involve high-risk reasoning and decision-making. High tech *virtual reality* training provides a safe haven for practicing high-risk practical exercises.

Dynamic *virtual reality* training methods involve real world multidimensional situations. There must be a balance in understanding the facets of training content. Training is simply not about being *ready to shoot* but also about *when not to shoot*.

Many decisions are flexible; instructors may defer their preference until the necessary time frame. Longer-range training decisions are more likely to unfold appropriately, along with the application of correct instructional methods.

Active Learning Foundations

Instructor reliance on a single method of training neglects opportunities to relate to trainees through varied learning styles. Instructors interested in meeting individual learning needs encourage the critical thinking process and stimulate learning through a variety of training techniques. The combination of effective training strategies motivates learners, enhances retention, and maintains imaginative learning environments.

Active learning requires participants to learn not only from the instructor, but also from each other, while participating in the problem-solving process. Therefore, communication unfolds learner-to-learner as well as between the instructor and learners. The active learning process thrives on group participation and the diversification of teaching methods.

Diverse methods of instruction encourage refocusing learner attention spans throughout class sessions. Learners integrate the knowledge base rather than memorizing isolated facts for examinations.

Learner applications of knowledge and concepts to practical scenarios offer opportunities to develop significant perceptive and insight skills. Additional support and reinforcement proves helpful when meeting the needs of learners with diverse learning styles

(Nance and Nance, 1990). Researchers report that learners respond best to a variety of teaching methods (Greek, 1995). Teaching methods that involve participants in active learning, that is, role-play (Wilkins, 1996), and the application of factual and conceptual material prove most engaging (Wells, 1997).

The application of knowledge is essential to critical thinking and learning. Four progressions of increasing complexity unfold that stimulate active learning while utilizing a diversity of instructional strategies:

- Small group presentations
- Case study methods
- Moot court proceedings
- Learner performance projects

Training Goals

Training goals acknowledge program objectives and contribute to the development of a harmonious instructional process. They may evolve from agency goals and mission statements. Goals and learning objectives support field applications.

Curriculum design and positive learning benefit from a systematic approach. When a global intent is apparent, then instructional strategies emerge to facilitate specific goal and learning outcomes. The *goals approach* motivates instructors because it offers direction, enhances evaluation in response to specific performance, and meets task-linkage requirements.

Goals do not provide feedback regarding successful accomplishment. Therefore, it is necessary to state required changes in operational performance and measureable evidence for outcomes. This evidence unfolds in measurable, connected goals, organizing centers, and related training objectives. The goals approach is the best foundation for formulating organizing centers and training objectives. Refer to Training Figure 3-1: Organizing Centers and Goals for an illustration.

Figure 3-1: Organizing Centers and Goals

Organizing Centers

Law enforcement trainers pose the first basic question: *"Where are we going?"* The answer determines training goals, organizing centers, and defines appropriate learning objectives. The organizing center is a frame of reference; the emphasis is on focal points of instruction.

The relationship of *required learning* from one stage level to another determines the vertical organization of law enforcement curriculum. Organizing centers provide a linkage basis for vertical and horizontal content articulation and sequencing. Articulation refers to the continuous application of an organizing theme, content, or concepts. Sequencing represents the progressive development of law enforcement skills, professional attitudes, or values.

Organizing centers determine essential facts or concepts and define content emphasis. For example, the intersection of the horizontal and vertical axes defines the organizing center. The following behaviors are included on the horizontal axis: concepts, values, attitudes, ethics, critical thinking, and decision-making. The vertical axis represents content and identified learning objectives. It includes: (1) the use of force, (2) self-defense, and (3) deadly force learning objectives. Identifying core curriculum for deadly force offers a means to organize content, concepts, and active learning methodologies. Refer to Figure 3-2: Organizing Center for an illustration of an organizing center.

In summary, organizing centers represent broad training goals and specific learning objectives. Training or behavioral objectives define and document outcomes or directions. Objectives describe how learners perform after successfully completing the training experience.

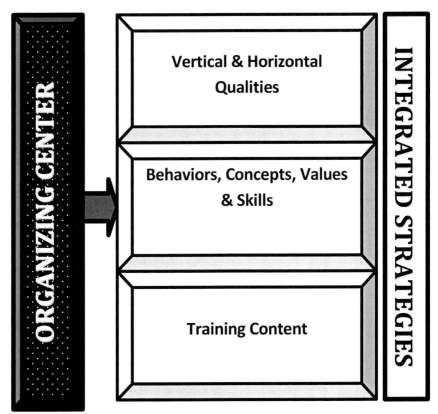

Figure 3-2. Organizing Centers

Training Objectives

Training learning objectives evolve after formulating broad
goals and organizing center training curriculum. This technique
is acceptable; however, it is difficult to formulate training performance objectives without field knowledge or direct experience.

Specific participant **performance objectives** function on the
operational field level. For example, outline field content before
performance objectives become obvious. In most cases, formulate
and refine training objectives following field practitioner advice
and review. Refer to Training Figure 3-3: Identifying Entry Level
Behaviors for an illustration.

Develop goals and training objectives after answering the
second question: *"How will you get there?"* Organizing centers
enhance learning design through the articulation and sequencing
of training objectives. Objectives originate from specific goals and
inform learners of standards and performance progressions.
Training performance objectives occasionally referred to as
behavioral or *learning objectives*, serve as learner-centered
guidance. In addition, they measure specific criteria or learning
competencies. Refer to Chapter 4 for an in-depth explanation of
performance objectives.

The most essential factor in training design is the determination of training elements, which serve as the foundation for curriculum planning. Training curriculum requires consistency, an
essential component of learning. Organizing centers sort out vast
amounts of content. Refer to Corner 3-1: Training Case Study for
an illustration of the training organization and curriculum content.

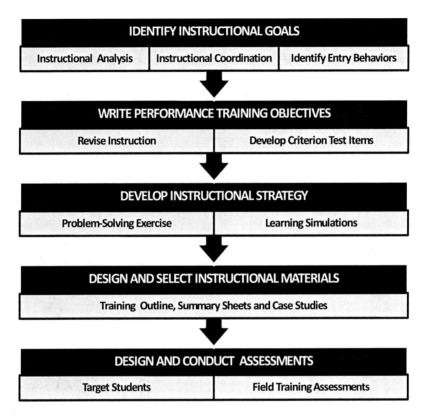

Figure 3-3. Identifying Entry Level Behaviors

Corner 3-1: Training Case Study

Lieutenant John Dunn's recent assignment to Central Training Academy requires designing a new Terrorist First Responder Curriculum. His most recent assignment was the Traffic Division, which may assist in this endeavor. He feels this assignment is going to require an effort beyond his limited training experience. Lieutenant Dunn walks down the hall and approaches Captain Daily waiting in his office.

Lieutenant Dunn sits down and pauses before speaking.

"I have some concerns about the Terrorist Training First-Responder Program."

Captain Daily appears sincere and supportive.

"Lieutenant, I realize this assignment is not going to be easy, but I recommend the Training Systems Model as the basis for any training program. This approach incorporates in-service procedures and deals with entry-level performance. Look to your right; the model is already posted on my wall."

Refer to Training Figure 3-4 for an illustration of the Training Systems Model.

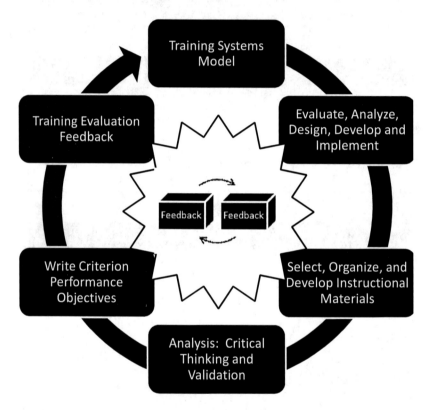

Figure 3-4. Training Systems Model

The Captain opens his training notes and suggests the following preliminary procedures:

- **Step 1:** Review related training literature.
- **Step 2:** Identify references and obtain relevant training content to formulate the philosophy, goals, performance objectives, and assessment procedures.

- **Step 3:** Establish a curriculum topical outline.

- **Step 4:** Develop relevant performance objectives related to the topical outline.
- **Step 5:** Develop active learning activities or practical exercises.

"Thank you for the advice Captain."

Lieutenant Dunn leaves and prepares the following draft training program. Refer to Terrorist First-Responder Curriculum for an illustration of the Training Systems Model.

Terrorist First Responder Curriculum

Training Systems Model programming is dynamic and consists of the following analytical methods:

- **Analyze**
- **Develop**
- **Design**
- **Implement**
- **Evaluate**

Lieutenant Dunn begins the training analysis process by considering a needs assessment and possible problem solutions. The analysis process includes an extensive examination of training problems and collective performance tasks. Examination of collective tasks in many situations, leads to the identification of individual performance task(s). Results from this comprehensive analysis serve as the foundation for developing training activities. In addition, it provides an operational definition of what constitutes a successful training mission.

Training programs address personnel requirements and field environments. The systems approach to gathering information or data provides the basis for the implementation of a training program. Lieutenant Dunn writes the following paragraphs on Curriculum Philosophy and applies the procedural guidelines of curriculum training foundations.

Curriculum Philosophy

The first responder curriculum philosophy encourages critical thinking, problem-solving, and active learning strategies. This course of training instruction emphasizes the protection of life and property. Furthermore, the planning process serves as protection for citizens and responding public safety personnel. Instructors implement and support the curriculum philosophy, goals, training objectives, and evaluation procedures.

The primary *training goals* of this curriculum and related instructional units involve: (1) building homeland security awareness, (2) disaster scene control, (3) coordination, and (4) first responder considerations. The integration of passive lecture learning, critical thinking, and problem-solving strategies provide the foundation for dynamic problem-solving scenarios.

Learning Objectives

Learning objectives evolve from training goals and organizing centers. For example, the organizing center vertical axis content deals with: (1) first responder, (2) crisis management, (3) consequence management, and (4) incident management system. The horizontal axis includes: (1) homeland security values, protection of life and property, protection of citizens, critical thinking concepts, and decision-making skills.

Learning objective contributions advance from training analysis and the entire instructional process. The basic source of the training objective is performance task analysis. The achievability of objectives depends on three basic factors:

- **Learning the task(s)**
- **Capacity of the learner**
- **Knowledge of the instructional task(s) sequence**

In any case, update and review performance objectives as basic components unfold. Listed below are beginning training objective examples.

Unit A: Training Objectives

The learner will apply the following training objectives:

- Define crisis management.
- Define consequence management.
- Identify the importance of a lead agency.
- Appraise the need for unified management command.
- Distinguish the various applications of the incident management system.

Unit B: Training Objectives

The learner will apply the following training objectives:

- List the elements of the front-end planning concept.
- Define an emergency operations center.
- Outline the emergency operation plan.
- Cite the elements of logistics and emergency operations planning.
- Identify the role of liaison relationships with other agencies.

Unit C: Training Objectives

The learner will apply the following training objectives:

- Define convergent responders.
- Appraise the critical importance of scene awareness in a terrorist event.
- List the responsibilities of the first arriving unit during a violent event.
- List the principles of "2 in 2 out."
- Distinguish the elements of:
  - **LACES**
  - **Lookout, Awareness, Communications, Escape, Safety Instructional Design**

A plan is necessary to insure that training programs and support materials move forward in a systematic manner. Tailor the evidence-based design to training setting and trainee needs. This design feedback envisions a strategy to validate the tests and measurement criteria as indicators of trainee competencies.

The intent of *design* is to guarantee the successful systematic development of training programs. The identification of training support and materials will also enhance the overall effectiveness of the entire training system. Design outcomes influence the process. Training analysis serves as a blueprint for the program's design and development.

The terrorist response scenario is a time-phased, problem-solving exercise. Learners receive additional Fact Sheet Summaries as the planning unfolds and responses develop. Instructors distribute well-timed and executed Fact Summary Sheets to formulate practical case study issues. Supplemental scenario information requires coordination, command post requirements, and liaison with related public safety components. The following first preliminary example narrative (Summary Sheet: Terrorist Case Study) demonstrates the application of Emergency Operations Plan (EOP) and informal Incident Action Plan (IAP).

Summary Sheet: Terrorist Case Study

An explosion originates from a parked gasoline truck in New York's Times Square. Scattered bomb fragments result in 10 casualties and 50 injured citizens. Initial law enforcement units arrive at 9:32 a.m. Fire and emergency medical services units arrive at 9:45 a.m. Soon thereafter, there is a massive explosion in the subway system immediately adjacent to the truck explosion site.

Several first responders are injured. One building collapses (estimated occupancy 500 people). The Medical Emergency Center admits numerous injury patients from the bomb incidents. Multiple explosions threaten secondary disruptions such as power grid failures and downtown communication interruptions. In addition, many survivors sustain chemical burns from the combination explosive/chemical attack. (Summary Sheets and case scenario intelligence reports continue in systematic release procedures.)

Summary Sheet: Intelligence Information

Preliminary intelligence analysis warns that this terrorist attack is the work of a covert Neo-Nazi group. The terrorists call themselves by the code name: "Underground Socialist Movement." Their primary goal is to seize power and establish a new order.

Their leader, Thomas Bullock, is profoundly ruthless, and rejects the government and its laws. He is delusional and convinced he possesses omnipotent powers. He takes credit for the recent explosions and chemical attacks.

According to a psychological assessment, Bullock's mind is capable of sudden chaos, precipitating more irrational and potentially devastating behavior. As his terroristic-directed acts increase, so does the isolation that feeds the terror, a vicious circle. Underneath the façade, he is terrified of harsh punishment for his many crimes, so heinous as to warrant death. He may break with reality and become suicidal.

First Responder Emergency Response Requirements

Feedback represents a basic requirement of the Training Systems Model. Training thrives on the feedback process; without it, the system will not achieve satisfactory success. Systematic training increases the probability of positive outcomes; it emphasizes evaluation and needs assessment. This form of organized training establishes accountability and focuses on training safeguards, which enable modification and improvement. Systems training methods result in improved effectiveness and efficiency.

Generally, the first learning assignment involves lecture and media presentations that prepare learners for the problem-solving phases. In addition, the first assignment is a lead-up, small group activity that allows trainees to engage in preliminary steps toward active learning and critical thinking feedback. The instructor poses hypothetical case study situations, and learners apply basic public safety concepts as members of prearranged groups.

Most important, the instructor acts as a group facilitator, guide, and mentor. Participants provide feedback on the application of basic learning objectives and demonstrate competencies on the blackboard. The first assignment is a warm-up exercise where learners focus on the mastery of specific first responder learning objectives. Direct participation generally motivates learners involved with their own instruction and small group activity. Training feedback is a basic step toward higher progressions and practical exercise performance objectives.

Case Study Problem-Solving

The terrorist project elaborates on the above-mentioned case study. Learners analyze the scenario and apply the principles of planning, critical thinking, and problem solving. This is an active learning project; groups present solutions based on group consensus. Trainee groups present individual solutions, then compare and contrast remedial reactions.

The purpose is to conduct a briefing on the implementation of an emergency response plan. Learners assume various roles in public safety organizations, such as police, fire, and emergency service commanders. The remaining group members serve as the planning section. Five trainee groups compare and contrast a composite solution, which provides feedback and integration of a holistic response picture.

Development and Implementation

At this point, the develop process supplements design outcomes or training products. This results in training program readiness for implementation and related support materials. There is an overlap between design and development. Agencies assume development activities during the design phase or may reverse the process. However, there is a need to validate training support materials. In addition, instructors and training needs should be identified and included in the training management plan.

Training implementation concerns instructional unit presentations to law enforcement personnel. This requires the coordination of training management records such as training schedules and time factors, progress performance, performance testing, training completion, and related subjects. Reporting systems support the validation, evaluation, modification, and improvement of programming.

Evaluation: Curriculum Planning First Responders

Finally, Lieutenant Dunn applies the dynamic systems approach to training, which emphasizes analysis and evaluation. This process creates an opportunity to alert future planning changes in job performance. In addition, revision or development training for job description changes is more likely to demand management attention. Program assessment surveys offer this information.

Systems training programs are particularly responsive to modernization concerning departmental or individual job performance requirements. The first responder and terrorist exercise evaluation process includes:

- Peer evaluation
- Instructor evaluation of the practical exercise
- Exercise notebook grade
- Written examination

Specific training objectives and performance testing make training assessment meaningful and easier to accomplish.

Corner 3-1: Problem-Solving Exercise

Several weeks pass and after considerable research, Lieutenant Dunn submits a draft proposal for the First Responder Program. Captain Daily approves the draft proposal, commends the professional training accomplishment, and recommends a staff planning review. What would you do to improve the proposal in terms of content? Refer to Chapter 4 Lesson Planning and the Practical Exercise for some additional format and content applications.

Curriculum Evaluation

Summative evaluation focuses on the global nature of instruction. The feedback provides information to continue, eliminate, modify, or adjust the goals and performance objectives. Summative evaluation provides opportunities to improve the quality of instruction and modification of future strategies. Survey questionnaires serve as one method of obtaining summative feedback.

Summative evaluation involves a general judgment of the instructional delivery process. This process requires the continuous monitoring of the academic course or training program. Specifically, this involves program verification and validation. In addition, evaluation consists of monitoring the training program during the initial preparation and completion phases.

Evaluation is not just a process following the implementation of the training program. The term *summative evaluation* refers to a broad spectrum of uninterrupted monitoring of the training program as an entire function that involves both verification and validation. The process consists of internally evaluating training during each phase of preparation, while concurrently externally evaluating the total training function. Therefore, following implementation, feedback:

- Assists in evaluating the program
- Assesses the quality of trainee performance
- Confirms agency responsiveness to training needs

The process demands implementation feedback to assess the quality of the programming. In summary, evaluation includes:

- Analysis of needs assessment
- Curriculum design
- Program Development
- Implementation
- Evaluation

Programming design considers performance-oriented learning content. Reenter the development cycle when training program evaluations indicate the need for change. Make necessary changes to enhance the delivery of quality instruction. Identify programming characteristics that meet the needs of quality instruction, and enhance and repeat what works well. Refer to Figure 3-5: Curriculum Evaluation for an overview and illustration.

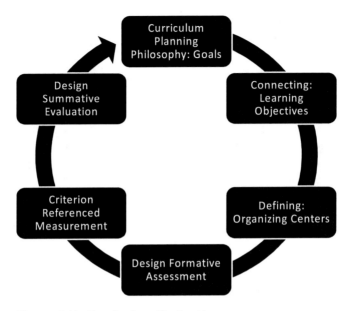

Figure 3-5: Curriculum Evaluation

Evaluation concerns the effectiveness of informational delivery systems. The questionnaire survey strategy focuses on whether course programming produces intended learning outcomes. Measuring instructional methods assists in achieving instructor goals, performance objectives, and avoids unintended consequences.

Learner Assessment Procedures

Learner assessment is necessary to determine the effectiveness of instruction and overall program design. The emphasis is on fairness and equity by meeting the needs of diverse learning styles. The formative evaluation process is essential to determining the final question: How will the instructor know when learners have arrived? This may be the most important question. Final judgments reflect an encompassing assessment of learning over the course of the training exercise.

The process of assessment is necessary to determine instructional effectiveness. The process offers opportunities to measure learning outcomes and future course revisions. Critical thinking essay questions offer opportunities for insightful solutions. In addition, test bank questions and critical thinking learning opportunities reinforce the learning the process. Critical thinking case studies offer additional outlets for learner participation and instructor assessment.

Criteria standards are essential for assessment based on goals, organizing centers, and supporting training objectives. The assessment process determines learner knowledge, skill level, and progress throughout instructional units. In addition, assessment allows learner feedback at the end of an instructional phase. Generally, assessment involves a grading process concerning learner objectives and related standards.

Focus Points

Active learning strategies allow the application of training objectives and assessment to unfold in the training environment rather than exclusively on classroom examinations. Active learning objectives concerning critical thinking, problem solving, and decision-making may serve as a superior method of trainee assessment.

Critical thinking remains a core necessity for law enforcement training. The various indicators of critical thinking include:

- **Persistence**
- **Restraining impulsiveness**
- **Listening**
- **Flexibility**
- **Precision**
- **Questioning**
- **Creativity**

Critical thinking, active leaning, and group dynamics are mutually reinforcing instructional strategies. Diverse teaching methods address a wide range of preferred learning styles (Costa and O'Leary, 1992):

- **Visual Learners:** prefer pictures, images, and so on.
- **Auditory Learners:** prefer sound and music
- **Verbal Learners:** prefer words used in speech and writing

- **Physical Learners:** prefer using their bodies—hands and sense of touch
- **Logical Learners:** prefer using logic, reasoning
- **Social Learners:** prefer learning in social groups
- **Solitary Learners:** prefer to work alone in self-study

Research indicates that *doing* achieves learning retention best. Moreover, it is superior to listening, visual teaching methods, or the combination of the two.

The Training Systems Model includes learning content in support of trainee professional development. In summary, instructional applications include:

- **Educational philosophy**
- **Organizing centers**
- **Instructor goals**
- **Performance objectives**
- **Assessment and evaluation of training programs**

Organizing centers represent central points for curriculum design and learning. Training managers define organizational training goals. Instructors specify training objectives, tasks, conditions, and standards. Define objectives by means of measurable criteria and a timetable for completion is established.

The evaluation process begins with establishing organizing centers, educational goals and training objectives. Evaluation is a continuous process, based on progressions, which involve training verification, validation, and assessment of information feedback. Assessment is pointless unless leaders initiate appropriate remedial actions to correct deficiencies and discrepancies.

Excellent instructors engage in informal assessment procedures to provide feedback. Measurements of learner behaviors, or feedback, provide information on learning accomplishment. Assessment is the most important component of instruction because it involves justice and equity. Trainees need to feel that their instructor is fair and impartial. The best way to achieve equity is equal application of standards.

Then, instructors encourage learners to embrace commitment, ownership, and responsibility for completing assignments that promote positive accomplishments. Assessment involves a guide or benchmark effort to determine the level of knowledge learners achieve.

Unlike passive learning, dynamic learning requires participants to learn while engaging in the problem-solving process. The process is enhanced though group participation and diversity of instructional techniques. This planned curriculum itinerary increases the possibility that participants aspire to higher accomplishments. Dynamic methods of instruction emphasize decision-making strategies by emphasizing a cooperative training climate.

Conclusion

Why should trainers experiment and attempt to apply diverse methods of instruction? *Stagnation* results without field experimentation and evaluation. Instructors and learners miss opportunities to learn and reach their potential. Experimentation, analysis, and evaluation, on the other hand, foster new and improved futuristic ways to learn. Find the dynamic curriculum map! Refer to Chapter 4: Dynamic Lesson Planning for an illustration of the final draft requirements of a lesson plan.

CHAPTER 4

Dynamic Lesson Planning

"Dynamic instruction requires imagination, creativity, and thoughtful lesson planning."

— Thomas E. Baker

Focus

This chapter explores advantages of active learning and practical exercise applications. Curriculum instructional progressions include: (1) lesson planning and (2) hostage negotiations practical exercises. The purpose of this chapter is to illustrate the ***central focus*** of law enforcement training: ***the lesson planning process***. **Chart the destination!**

Overview

The planning process is essential to critical thinking and active learning. It serves as a bridge between instructors and learner destinations, and identifies successful methods to achieve training goals and performance objectives.

Instructors initiate lesson plan modifications. Their objective is to expedite and facilitate superior instructional practices and requires attention to details. Lesson plans reflect performance objectives.

Lesson Planning Foundations

Lesson planning defines the *what, when,* and *how* performance task(s) standards timeline. In addition, planning content forms the foundation for trainee learning destinations. Lesson plans are standard courses of action relevant to real-time learning circumstances. Teaching units serve as foundations for lesson planning.

Lesson Planning Check Points

1. Serve as a blueprint for planning instructional content
2. Ensure lessons are complete

3. Suggest instructional methods
4. Suggest allotted time to devote to each lecture point
5. Facilitate instructor ability to anticipate learner questions
6. Check on instructor preparation
7. Define administrative instructional support
8. Define instructor and learner related activities
9. Serve as an outline for theories, concepts, main points, and illustrative support material
10. Serve as the foundation for personal notes and comments
11. Are not substitutes for lecture notes
12. Offer future opportunities to reform and improve the quality of instruction

Instructors draw on related content from recent historical and descriptive research. Research and brief notes serve as the primary source of training content. However, instructors peruse planning notes to structure instructional details. Instructor notes and PowerPoint serve as classroom content guides.

Lesson Planning Phase

Few instructors have total recall memories; therefore, lesson plans are necessary. Lesson plans are subject to constant revision, improving lecture topics, training points, and activities. Instructional content reflects appropriately sequenced lesson plans and performance objectives.

Knowledgeable trainers apply the **back-step planning** sequence. This process begins by defining desired outcomes and then works backward to establish related accomplishments. The planning process provides an overview of training plans, such as long-range, short-range, and near-term plans.

Conduct content analysis after incorporating the philosophy, organizing centers, and performance objectives. Instructors support performance objectives with classroom lecture points and related objectives. Instructional points cover theories, concepts, and facts related to the subject matter. The most important goal is to achieve overall program coordination.

Instruction consists of a series of instructional units. Occasionally, *unit* describes a lesson or topic block. A **clustering of units** refers to a phase, level, or section. Each unit includes designated **performance objectives** and related tasks. Essential content elements serve the achievement of specified performance objectives.

Generally, begin by presenting the *big strategic picture*, then restate it again. Start with basic definitions and continue to build the groundwork for difficult requirements. Plan to apply additional formats of instructional support. Innovative techniques might include examples, illustrations, and comparisons to other training units. Then determine how to organize the instructional materials and training content.

Outline a distinct hierarchy of learning progressions. Consider how to organize the subject matter and sequence concepts that lead to central lesson points. Learning that involves *chronological steps* requires arranging them in the sequence in which they logically occur. Refer to Training Figure 4-1: Develop a Curriculum Course for an illustration.

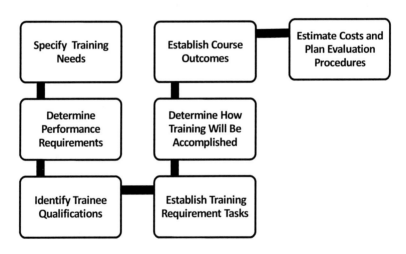

Figure 4-1: Develop a Curriculum Course

Instructors provide *training outline/schedules* on the first day of class. Outlines draw attention to procedures that incorporate additional requirements. Instructors insert or modify original content to meet learner needs. Training schedules assist in charting successful outcomes. This strategy requires focusing learners on future lectures.

Lectures compliment and support lesson plans, lecture notes, and instructor outlines. The outline facilitates presentation attention. An excellent lecture technique is to provide lecture notes at the beginning of the class or post them on the training website. The goal is to expedite and facilitate superior instructional practices. This professional effort requires instructor attention to details. Refer to Corner 4-1: Terrorist Lesson Plan Example for an illustration of case study research related to hostage negotiation scenario.

Corner 4-1:
I. Introduction: Terrorist Lesson Plan

The basic essentials of a lesson plan include:

- Introduction and learning hook
- Main body
- Review
- Conclusion
- Logistical/technology support

The Introduction has six basic sections:

- The attention hook
- Training objectives
- Related lesson connections
- Motivation
- Body of supporting knowledge
- Reviewing lesson planning content

Effective training programs remain the foundation for proactive crisis intervention strategies. Corner 4-1: Hostage Negotiation Practical Exercise describes the lesson planning process.

Learning Hook: *The learning hook is the primary method of gaining trainee attention. An emotional component and the recognition of learner attention spans is the primary objective. The ability to capture learner attention reflects instructor status, prestige, and expertise. Trainees listen best when they respect their instructor. Learner audience is the most important aspect of designing attention hooks. The topic is also relevant to formulating the right hook to lead the lesson content.*

For example, the instructor pauses for a moment and waits for the audience to detect the silence. Glancing around the room and making eye contact sets the stage for the *instructor hook*. The emotional tone is grave; as the instructor describes life and death issues when dealing with the terrorist scenario. The final introductory statement:

"You may be required to respond to a variety of emergency responses—pay particular attention to this lesson. The appropriate response requires exceptional knowledge, training, and preparation. The right response can make a career; the wrong response can end a career. Good luck in meeting today's hostage negotiation exercise requirements."

A. Introductory Learner Orientation

- Welcome
- Trainee group assignments
- Lesson purpose and objectives
- Practical exercise requirements
- Learning objectives requirements

Divide the class into small groups of four or five persons. Assign identifying group numbers and names, and apply the Task Force concept:

- **Group One:** Command Operations Center
- **Group Two:** FBI
- **Group Three:** Emergency Response Team
- **Group Four:** Special Reaction Team
- **Group Five:** State Police
- **Group Six:** Montgomery County Police

In addition, explain various provisions and lesson requirements. Describe the active learning, critical thinking, and problem-oriented approach purpose of the Practical Exercise (PE).

B. Lesson Training Objectives: *Lesson training objectives communicate performance objectives and basic requirements—the importance cannot be understated. Training performance objectives describe accomplishments to achieve arrival at proper learner destinations. Perform-*

*ance learning objectives are directly connected lesson plan
components.*

C. Related Lesson Connections: *A training unit consists
of a series of related instructional units. Each training
unit represents one subject or topic and requires a lesson
plan that relates to another lesson plan or series of lesson
plans. Therefore, a lesson plan does not stand-alone; the
lesson content impacts other lesson units. For example,
review the following related lesson units:*

- First responder staff planning operations
- First responder procedures
- Terrorist response scenarios
- Cult case study scenarios

II. Lead-Up Activities

A. The first learning assignment involves lecture, PowerPoint,
and media presentations that prepare trainees for active learning
phases. The first assignment is a small group activity that allows
learners to engage preliminary steps toward active learning and
critical thinking. Instructors pose a hypothetical case study;
learners apply basic concepts as members of prearranged groups.

B. The instructor acts as a group facilitator, guide, and mentor. Participants provide feedback on the application of basic
learning performance objectives and demonstrate competencies
on the blackboard. The first assignment is a warm-up exercise
where learners focus on performance objectives and the mastery
of specific first responder training objectives. For example,
trainees define the following terms:

- First responder
- Crisis management
- Consequence management
- Incident management system

C. Direct participation generally motivates trainees involved
with their own instruction, and small group activity. The ability
to apply performance objectives is a basic step toward higher
progressions and practical exercise completion. The integration

of passive learning, critical thinking, and problem-solving strategies provides the foundation for a practical exercise.

D. The active learning progression encourages learner transitions to higher level planning for progression three—the hostage negotiation scenario. The instructor presents information that guides leadership in a decision-making process. The process reduces uncertainty and assists participants in developing emergency responses. Lessons learned are part of the after–action briefing, and forms the basis for revising the planning process and changing goals, objectives, and procedures.

Motivation: *One of the most important qualities of the hostage negotiation case study is positive self-awareness. This requires the ability to step-back and appraise one's personal impact on the on the emergency task(s). This skill demands examining strengths, weaknesses, and potential limitations. The self-refection process requires personal insight and honesty.*

Instructor Summary Sheets:

- Provide clear instructions that help learners complete performance objectives and achieve success

Lecture Tips:

- Initiate the PowerPoint presentation
- Move the lecture into a sight and sound visual presentation
- Lecture no more than twenty minutes.
- Keep learners in groups and apply the remote viewer from different group locations.
- Respond to individual learner questions at group locations
- Apply an active learning approach and promote group dynamics

III. Body of Supporting Knowledge

This section is the most important part of the lesson plan. Therefore, the body of knowledge dominates the time factor for learner interaction. Supporting knowledge drives the learning process and learner abilities. This section provides substance for learners to master training perform-

ance objectives. Training points are in the proper learning sequence and prioritized for positive learning outcomes.

Circulate training references several sessions in advance in the form of Advanced Sheet Pre-Training Handouts. The ideal time—during First Responder Planning Staff Operations and First Responder Procedures class sessions. Trainees are responsible for reading support documents prior to Hostage Negotiation Practical Exercise requirements.

IV. Body of Supporting Knowledge:

Refer to Appendix D for an Illustration

V. Case Study: Hostage Negotiation

The terrorist hostage negotiating learning simulation requires trainees to respond to a hostage scenario. The time-span case study allows trainees to manage the incident and apply hostage negotiation and tactical skills.

A. Dynamics of Hostage-Taking and Negotiation

1. Introduction:

- Early history of hostage-taking
- Typologies of hostage-takers
- Times, trust, and the Stockholm Syndrome
- Guidelines for hostage event
- Kidnapping and terrorism
- Surviving hostage situations
- Analysis and conclusion

The core of the lesson plan is the case study exercise. Some instructors describe this learning experience as the most important factor of any lesson plan. All instructional steps set the foundation for vital application of performance training objectives. This training strategy requires participants to apply their knowledge and skills in a practical field setting.

Case Study: Terrorist Hostage Negotiation

The terrorist hostage negotiation case study requires participants to respond to a hostage scenario. The time-span case study allows learners to manage the incident and apply hostage negotiations and tactical skills. The following scenario serves as an example of a practical training exercise.

A police desk sergeant receives a telephone call concerning a hostage situation at approximately 4:00 p.m. on a Thursday. The caller makes the following demands: "I have the governor and his wife held hostage—follow my instructions exactly. I want five million dollars and a helicopter that will fly the hostages and me to the International Airport. I want my demands met within six hours or I will kill them."

Law enforcement agencies surround the Governor's Mansion, isolating and controlling three basic circles of perimeter security. They attempt to establish hostage negotiations and persuade a positive outcome. The goal of the hostage takers is to engage in terrorist attacks and finance their operation through hostage taking and bank robberies.

Intelligence Summary Sheet

Hostage negotiation scenario Intelligence Summary Sheets continue throughout the practical problem exercise. The psychological assessment indicates the terrorist leader, Ted Canfield, is unstable. Canfield does not have insight into his mental state and fails to understand his self-hatred. If conditions do not change for the better, his despair will take a violent turn.

Canfield will destroy others when feeling hopeless and helpless. He focuses on terrorist rhetoric, believing that everything depends on his successful revolution. Canfield may view suicide as an escape option from possible capture and as the ultimate act to avoid his suffering and failure.

The Instructor Role

The instructor monitors discussion groups and avoids intervention or interruptions. Participants apply the planning process and coordinate possible negotiation and tactical options. The group's goal is to organize hostage negotiations and special reaction teams. The first stage of the scenario involves threat analysis and preliminary assessment.

Strategies involve a dialogue, which requires the application of hostage negotiation strategies. Special reaction teams stand ready, while initial contact and communication continues. Learners present group solutions as the terrorist scenario progresses.

Problem-Solving Exercise

Instructors task participants to explore positive hostage negotiator traits. The solution will require oral reports during class discussions. Assign relevant chapter readings and specific chapter graphics or concepts to specific groups for classroom presentations. The approximate time span is one week.

- **Group One:** Hostage Negotiations: Basic Techniques
- **Group Two:** Three Styles of Negotiation
- **Group Three:** Negotiating with the Hostage Takers
- **Group Four:** Stockholm Syndrome and Hostage Safety
- **Group Five:** Time-Phase Model
- **Group Six:** Surrender Phase

Groups brief solutions on the blackboard—then compare, contrast, and contribute to the solutions. Solutions require group PowerPoint presentations during class discussions. In addition, they offer a brief description of their group's Task Force law enforcement agency. This exercise serves as warm-up to further group endeavors.

Maintain learners in groups and apply the remote viewer from different group locations. Respond to individual questions at the group's location. Compliment learners concerning their participation at the end of class and pose the question for the next class. Remind participants to prepare to brief the class during future presentations. Provide time at the beginning of class to organize the presentation. Make reading assignments for the next class session.

VI. Lesson Conclusion

Group Practical Exercise Solutions:

Encourage positive competition among group solutions. Friendly competition can promote creative responses, superior learning, and improve learning concentration. Competition should focus on the lesson plan and performance training objectives. Group members vote on the best presentation. In case of a deadlock vote, the instructor decides the best group solution.

Special Note: **Each group presents their solution to the case study.**

Review: Lesson Plan Content

The summary and closing statement offers the last opportunity to capture learner attention and imagination. The purpose is to summarize essential instructional points and emphasize performance objectives and practical exercise points. The focus is to recapture the learning process and apply one last learning hook. One ideal supporting strategy and final technique is to pass out a Summary Sheet that reviews major unit lesson points.

Learners present, compare, and contrast solutions. The *critique* examines a possible integration of group solutions. Generally, the diverse application of group solutions is better than one presentation. The *instructor critique* is positive and team building. However, inconsistencies and controversial issues may require diplomatic comments.

Learners participate in critique discussions; however, they do not necessarily address essential instructional points. The critique is participant centered. Instructors reserve time for additional comments at the critique's close—the perfect opportunity to address valid concerns.

The *closing statement* offers an opportunity to praise learner performance and training skill applications. For example, "This training process serves positive career outcomes that save lives and property. An emergency hostage negotiation scenario like you practiced for today may arise at any time during your career ..." Finally, participants may ask questions.

VII. Logistics and Technology Support

The ideal situation is a high-tech classroom. Instructors have the flexibility to browse websites and PowerPoint presentations. Wireless accessories allow instructors to advance PowerPoint from any location in the classroom. Related instructor PowerPoint presentations support lesson plans and practical exercises.

VIII. Evaluation

The evaluation process includes:

- Peer evaluation
- Instructor evaluation
- Exercise notebook grade
- Written examination

Refer to Chapter 4: *Dynamic Lesson Planning (Annex E)* for related citations for the Terrorist Lesson Plan.

Corner 4-1: Problem-Solving Exercise

Curriculum lesson planning is always a work in progress. Perfection is never possible, only new learning and revision opportunities. The classroom experience prompts additional changes. Immediately after the training session is over, revise the training lesson plan. New insights emerge from the training experience, trainee interaction, and reaction. Experience serves as the best source of inspiration! What format changes would improve the quality of this instruction?

Planning Instructional Methods

Lesson planning requires selecting appropriate *instructional methods*. Performance objectives match teaching method(s). Proper selection encourages maximum learning opportunities. The content of the lesson determines *instructional method* selection. The correct match may include the following examples:

- Lecture
- Demonstration

- Role play
- Case study
- Practical exercise
- Small group exercise
- Media/computer
- Other methods or combinations

Refer to Training Figure 4-2: Lesson Planning and Selecting Instructional Methods for an illustration.

In summary, lesson planning is necessary to direct the learning process and helps orient the instructor. It answers two crucial questions:

- **Where are the learners going?**
- **How will learners arrive at their instructional destination?**

Lesson planning provides the map for developing goals and performance objectives; furthermore, it provides a plan for assignments and related tasks. The ultimate form of lesson planning is *programmed instruction*. This method of instruction requires maximum learner participation and provides instant feedback. **Programmed instruction** creates opportunities for independent learning and is suited to in-service training.

Programmed Instruction

Programmed instruction is a highly structured form of self-study. Instructors present training content in a series of carefully planned instructional steps and units. Learners progress from fundamental performance objectives to an orderly transition to the complex. Feedback is immediate and connected to positive learning progressions. Learners prove their understanding before progressing to the next level.

Programmed instruction provides a systematic understanding of information. Moreover, it allows self-paced advancement. This format provides immediate feedback, reinforcement, and learner involvement.

Name of course of instruction:

Select items: 1-5 as appropriate:

Students must develop Skills: 1

Introducing new materials or content: 2

Students must develop interpersonal skills: 3

Students need to see skills performed: 4

Students have never performed task(s): 5

Students need to share ideas concerning the subject content: 3

Students need to be involved in be decision-making: 3

Students must develop skills in problem-solving, leadership or team building: 3

The instructor wants to establish student rapport: 3

Instructor must evaluate student performance: 1 & 3

There is a need to build student confidence and skills: 1 & 3

LEGEND: 1. Practical Exercise 2. Lecture/Demo 3. Small Group (Role Play)

4. Media/Computer 5. Demonstrations

Figure 4-2: Lesson Planning and Selecting Instructional Methods

Programmed instruction offers several advantages:

- Instruction is autonomous
- Instructor explanations are not necessary
- Instructions are explicitly planned and systematically presented
- Anticipated questions are pre-programmed
- Remedial programmed content explains why a learner driven response is incorrect
- Immediate feedback is accessible

Programmed instructional opportunities include: (1) learning detailed content material at the learner's own pace; (2) supporting practical exercises; (3) preparing for complex lesson or advanced seminars; and (4) providing training when instructors are not available.

Focus Points

The most important tool the instructor can have in the steady pursuit of training success is *lesson planning*. Correctly recorded, this effort will mirror every training activity of daily learning. With amazing energy, it will enable the instructor to direct successful training outcomes.

Lesson plans center on instruction unit content. The plan connects to previous and future units of instruction; it ensures that the instruction is correctly organized. The lesson plan consists of an introduction, body of knowledge, and review.

The lesson plan targets topic sequence and instructional methods are identified and organized. Learning progressions offer opportunities for learning success. The introduction garners learner attention and encourages motivation. Lesson plans define performance objectives and determine learner destination.

The body of knowledge subsection represents an essential component of the lesson plan, followed by the practical exercise that focuses on practicing performance task(s) related to the body of knowledge. Prearrange content in the proper sequence and hierarchy of skills.

The *final review* is a mini-lesson that incorporates performance objectives. The instructor passes out a Summary Sheet before summarizing basic lesson plan points. Finally, the instructor offers positive comments about learner performance and concludes the lesson with a dramatic training observation.

Conclusion

The law enforcement lesson-planning phase is important and serves as the foundation for dynamic training. Training faces numerous challenges concerning quality instruction. The new frontier encourages revising curriculum and necessitates additional lesson planning, experimentation, and practical applications. Innovative instructional and practical exercises may help facilitate the transition to better-prepared law enforcement personnel. Chapter 5: Leadership Feedback provides a pathway to lesson planning outcomes.

CHAPTER 5

Leadership Feedback

"Truth is tough. It will not break, like a bubble, at a touch; you may kick it about all day, like a football, and it will be round and full at evening."
— Oliver Wendell Holmes

Focus

The word **feedback** defines learner knowledge and results. Effective instructors recognize the role of **feedback** in the learning process. The justification for feedback is to improve performance. Feedback provides constructive advice, direction, and guidance to advance the learning process. Learner performance objectives correspond to feedback and training assessment. The purpose of this chapter is to explore learner performance objectives, communication, and leadership feedback.

Overview

Feedback is an individual training necessity that acknowledges learning styles. Effective feedback requires focusing on task(s) development. Instructor feedback enhances task understanding and recognizes learner perspectives. Assess performance before giving feedback. Feedback is a four-step leadership communication process that assesses:

- **Learning style**
- **Task readiness**
- **Performance appraisal**
- **Instructor response**

Learning Styles

Some learn best from listening or reading, whereas others thrive while actively involved. Therefore, using diverse teaching methods and the active learning approach attempts to reach the needs of learners. Active learners achieve a deeper understanding of the material than passive learners do. They incorporate their senses as they advance forward in the learning process.

Considerable research demonstrates that the use of multiple senses like reading, hearing, seeing, and application increases learner retention (Emerson & Mosteller, 1998; Olliphant, 1990). The application of multiple senses fosters aspects of problem-solving (Flavel, 1976). "Most learners acquire 83 percent of their information from seeing and only 11 percent from hearing, and generally remember only 20 percent of what they hear compared to 30 percent of what they see and 50 percent when they hear and see something" (Holkeboer, 1993:4).

How does learning style influence learning and retention? Some individuals learn best by listening (auditory learners). They rely on hearing information from others. Other learners depend on visual presentations, such as educational videos and Power-Point. A third learner depends on psychomotor awareness (tactile) and learns best by physical activity. For example, Ferrett (1994: 143) comments: "A visual learner may say, 'I see the big picture;' an auditory learner may say, 'I hear you;' and a kines-thetic person may say, 'I think I have a grip on this problem.'"

In summary, research suggests that learners retain more information when all senses are involved. The combination of listening, visual, and hands-on experiences reinforces the learning process even when there is a preference for one learning style. When learners have opportunities to respond to varied instructional methods, they assess and select their preferred style. Learners should explore theories and concepts before integrating them into their individual learning styles (Young & McCormick, 1991; Wilkens, 1996).

Instructors assess preferred learning styles during the feedback process. Determine the best approach for providing feedback. For example, a mini-lecture benefits auditory (listening) learners, whereas hands-on (tactile) learners might profit from website links and additional direct practice. Learning strategies have primary or secondary applications, or possible combinations. Effective feedback takes many forms depending on learning styles and teaching methods.

Performance Objectives

Training performance objectives have three parts: (1) *action verb*, (2) *content area,* and (3) *measurable criteria.* The learning hierarchy distinguishes the relationship between lower-level training objectives and higher-level training objectives. Address lower-level performance objectives first, setting the foundation for higher-level objectives. Some performance objectives are terminal and do not require sequencing hierarchies.

The action verb provides direction, defines learner performance and activity completion. Training objectives may include specific learning criteria and describe the conditions under which the learner performs the task(s). Standards describe measurable criteria for assessment and a system for achieving accountability.

Performance objectives represent present tense declarative statements, including an action verb. The action verb defines necessary task accomplishments. Avoid passive or weak verbs. For example, verbs like "understand" are difficult to measure. Performance objectives are brief, clear, and involve one subject. Refer to Figure 5-1: Performance Objective(s) for an illustration.

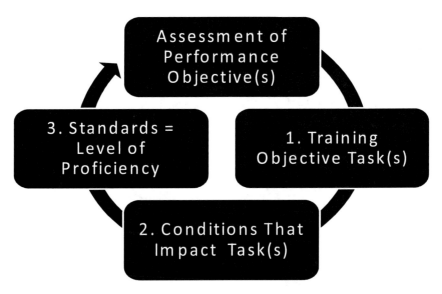

Figure 5-1. Performance Objectives

Instructors determine performance objective(s) rationale and define learning outcomes.

For example:

- What new knowledge should learners be able to apply because of the instruction?

Classic purpose examples:

- Issue a traffic citation
- Administer constitutional rights waiver requirements
- Interrogation procedures

The most important criterion of a training objective is that it identifies the purpose of performance and acceptable evidence of the achievement of the task(s). Learners must identify instructor expectations. Traditional assessment formats include oral or written testing. However, field performance is the best measurement.

Training objective(s) must be attainable and measurable throughout learning progressions. Performance objectives define what the learner must accomplish to achieve success. Instructors assess outcomes by observing learner performance during problem-solving exercises.

Appropriate actions or reactions are the core of learner performance objective(s). Most important, responses reflect the enforcement operation and have a direct relationship to job performance and successful mission accomplishment. Simulated task training conditions may reflect authentic field applications. Conditions represent valid scenarios in which the performance task(s) are required.

Feedback Assessment

The feedback principle is complex. The spectrum of human behavior offers dissimilar meanings and results. Learners receive feedback from five basic sources:

- **Personal insight**
- **Instructors**
- **Learning task(s)**

- **Peers**
- **Training staff**

Each learner is unique and situations vary considerably. However, as feedback responses emerge, instructors may find opportunities to understand learner behaviors.

The most common feedback response is correcting learner performance errors. Positive feedback motivates or encourages learners to improve performance and establish rapport. Positive instructor comments can motivate learners to increase efforts and improve learning behaviors. Positive feedback is generally acceptable when offered with a genuine, honest, and friendly manner.

Effective feedback focuses on learner performance, not instructor partiality. Instructors provide feedback on the merits of the situation, not agreement, or disagreement with learner values or personal preferences. Objective feedback requires avoiding personal opinions and maintaining impartial relationships. Refer to Training Table 5-1: Training Performance Assessment/ Feedback for an illustration.

The foremost dilemma stems from instructor *favorites*. Over-identification with a learner can serve as a barrier to objectivity and alienate other participants. An evaluation based on performance achieves objectivity. Conversely, some learners are conflict-oriented and may influence instructor judgment. Feedback must be candid; however, it must not ridicule or make light of learner opinions in front of peers. Learners require recognition, self-confidence, and approval. Constructive feedback takes place in private settings, environments where learners profit, not suffer, from relevant feedback.

Insightful instructors assess the learner's response to feedback. Stonewalling or non-compliance is not a positive indicator. The learner is not listening or receptive to the feedback.

Feedback does not have to be negative or disapproving to succeed. Learners typically have a tolerance level for criticism; however, some perceive critical comments as personal attacks. Defensive behaviors may include instructor rejection. Perceived threats may encourage anger outbursts and poor improvement.

Positive communication may well enhance rapport and future feedback acceptance. Criticism is uncomfortable; unwarranted praise may not prove helpful. Instructors encourage the positive aspects of learner performance, while communicating weaknesses. In addition, instructors identify improvement requirements.

Table 5-1:   Training Performance Assessment/Feedback

☆	TRAINING PERFORMANCE	☆

Date & Time   **Assessment/Feedback**
STUDENT NAME:
_____

Training Task(s) & Location:
_____

EVALUATOR (Name/Number) _____
LACK OF MOTIVATION
- ❑ Boring response
- ❑ Unpleasant response
- ❑ Personal Knowledge
- ❑ Finds the task(s) or subject difficult
- ❑ Concerned about personal risk or danger
- ❑ Personal distractions, family, etc.
- ❑ Other:

LACK OF SKILL OR KNOWLEDGE:
- ❑ Does not understand materials
- ❑ Cannot perform skill
- ❑ Emotional response questionable
- ❑ Not Evaluated

Student Responses

Incorrect performance response because:
- (1) The easy way out
- (2) More enjoyable not to do the training task(s)
- (3) No consequences for not performing
- (4) Other reasons

Information Assessment   **Obstacles to Performance**

❑ Recommend follow-up	❑ Not enough time
❑ Unverified	❑ Lack of Information
❑ Verified	❑ Inadequate equipment or supplies

The best advice is to accent the positive. Discuss positive feedback first, offering the possibility of skill improvement. Rapport, timing, and receptiveness offer genuine opportunities for learner growth and development.

Feedback is flexible and specific to trainee needs, reducing stress and offering helpful remedies. Tactful feedback requires timely assessment of the situation and the tools for improvement. Active listening enhances rapport and encourages learner motivation to achieve task success.

Task Analysis

Experienced law enforcement personnel identify training standards. Consensus offers the best solution for defining measurable standards. When agreement on a training standard is not possible, select the lower standard. Do not expect trainees to perform at the expert level.

Task analysis inventories evolve from individuals who demonstrate performance expertise and field experience. Also, analyze related standing operating procedures and former job descriptions. Policies, procedures, memorandums, and related training documents serve as valuable sources of information. Refer to Training Figure 5-2: Elements of Task Analysis for an illustration.

Practical exercises may involve a scaled-down version in safe, controlled conditions. For example, the warrantless search of an automobile, the Carroll, Preston, Cooper Doctrine, can unfold in a parking lot. Stash bogus drugs and weapons in the interior and trunk of a staged vehicle. Learners establish probable cause, conduct a traffic stop, and apply the Plain View Doctrine.

Performance standards state the degree of correctness the learners must demonstrate during the task(s). There are two basic standards:

- **Accuracy**
- **Speed of response**

For example, firearms' training represents the ideal training environment for measuring those standards. However, other training tasks are more difficult to apply precise standards. This form of performance training requires analysis and planning.

Action Verb + Object Acted Upon + Qualifier

ELEMENTS OF TASK ANALYSIS

TASK ANALYSIS: Coordination of efforts from every level is essential. Central requirement is to know the definition of a task:

* ✶ Related activities directed toward a goal
* ✶ Generally has a beginning and ending point
* ✶ Involves a student interacting with other people or equipment

* ✶ Results in a meaningful outcome, action or decision(s)
* ✶ Includes a combination of perceptions or physical activities
* ✶ May involve a degree of complexity, has a specific purpose
* ✶ Performance is independent of other tasks
* ✶ May be related to one or more tasks
* ✶ Instructor observation permits measurable assessment

TASK ANALYSIS AS LISTED:

* ✶ Development of an inventory of tasks comprising the job
* ✶ Rate the Task or Tasks
* ✶ Analyze the Rating
* ✶ Select the tasks relevant for training
* ✶ Assign performance criteria to the task(s)

+DEVELOP A TASK INVENTORY

Figure 5-2: Elements of Task Analysis

Practical Exercise Model

Five basic issues are addressed in a practical exercise: (1) the ***goal component*** of the training objective identifies the intent of the task(s); (2) **performance or behavioral task** activity describes the action verb, specific learner behavior or activity; (3) **content reference** describes the subject in which the behavior is applied; (4) **criterion standard** indicates the minimum acceptable level of performance success in measureable terms and determines success in achieving the goal of the learner performance objective(s); and (5) **conditions** feature physical factors or other criteria under which participant learning occurs. On the other hand, the training standard is similar to the entry job level.

Prepare training performance objective(s) during the curriculum development phase. Curriculum instruction includes detailed descriptions of field behaviors and related task(s). Performance-oriented training includes lead-up and rehearsal learning activities. Learning objectives differ on emphasis and may not describe the conditions, which affect the task, or the level of proficiency required.

The practical exercise has specific training objectives and criteria for performance. The practical exercise is a training activity, which applies specific practice task(s), and creates multiple feedback opportunities. Practical exercises permit the

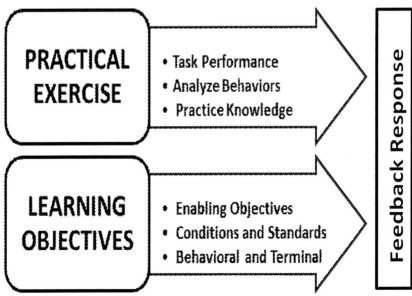

Figure 5-3: Practical Exercise Model

application of training knowledge. In addition, the practice is limited in purpose and scope to the training task(s). Refer to Training Figure 5-3: Practical Exercise Model for an illustration.

Practice and lead-up activities approximate field tasks and assignments. The feedback process may include unsupervised programmed instruction or mock scenes. The FBI *Hogan's Alley Shoot/Don't Shoot* practical exercise is a classic example. Some practical exercises demand immediate task feedback. Refer to Corner 5-1: Suspect Stop Practical Exercise for an illustration.

Corner 5-1: Suspect Stop Practical Exercise

Lesson Content: *Terry v. Ohio*, **Citation:** 392 U.S. 1, 88 S. Ct. 1868, (1968)

Brief Facts Summary: John W. Terry (the "Petitioner"), was stopped and searched by an officer after the officer observed the Petitioner seemingly casing a store for a potential robbery. The officer approached the Petitioner for questioning and decided to search him first.

Synopsis of Rule of Law: An officer may perform a search for weapons without a warrant, even without probable cause, when the officer reasonably believes that the person may be armed and dangerous.

Supreme Court Facts of the Case: The officer notices the Petitioner talking with another individual on a street corner while repeatedly walking up and down the same street. The men periodically peer into a store window, and then continue their conversation. They also speak to a third man whom they eventually follow up the street. The officer believes that the Petitioner and others are "casing" a store for robbery potential. The officer decides to approach the men for questioning, and given the nature of the behavior, decides to quick search the men before questioning. A quick frisking of the Petitioner produces a concealed weapon. The officer charges the Petitioner with carrying a concealed weapon.

Legal Issue: Is a search for weapons without probable cause for arrest an unreasonable search under the Fourth Amendment to the United States Constitution?

Decision Held: The Supreme Court of the United States held that it is a reasonable search when an officer performs a quick seizure and a limited search for weapons on a person he reasonably believes is armed. A typical beat officer would be unduly burdened by being prohibited from searching individuals that the officer suspects to be armed.

Discussion: The facts of the case are important to understand the Supreme Court's willingness to allow the search. The suspicious activity was a violent crime, armed robbery, and if the officer's suspicions were correct then he would be in a dangerous position to approach the men for questioning without searching them. The officer also did not detain the men for a long period to constitute an arrest without probable cause.

Special Note: The law can change and the legal quantum of proof of "reasonable suspicion" and "Stop-and-Frisk Doctrine" modified. Superior instructors research the law and stay current. For example, recent law enforcement controversy and court decisions regarding "stop-and-frisk" procedures in New York City can create confusion and debate.

Goal Component Is: To provide safety and protection of officers and innocent bystanders.

Behavioral Activity: Learners participate in a "Stop-and-Frisk" Practical Exercise.

Content Reference: *Terry v. Ohio* (1968)
Synopsis: The standards for a Stop-and-Frisk originate from the 1968 Supreme Court case *Terry v. Ohio. Stop-and-Frisks* do not violate the Constitution under certain circumstances. Observing *Terry* and others acting suspiciously in front of a store, a police officer concluded that they might engage in an armed robbery. The officer stopped and frisked the men. A weapon was found on Terry and the suspect was convicted of carrying a concealed weapon. The Supreme Court ruled that this search was reason-

able. Stop-and-Frisk depends on the definition of "reasonable-ness." The Justices were very careful not to define the terms "stop" or "frisk" with specificity. Instead, they decided that whe-ther an officer behaved "reasonably" must be determined by "the totality of the circumstances."

Condition: For example, a "Stop and Frisk" intervention unfolds in a darkened warehouse. The suspect is dressed in black clothing and acts evasively.

Criterion Standard: The standards for criteria might specify: (1) stop and interview, (2) scan for possible weapons and listen, (3) request identification, (4) establish reasonable suspicion standard of proof, (5) conduct a legal search: pat down outer garments, (6) secure weapon, and (7) search for secondary back-up weapons.

A brief list of circumstances that law enforcement officers have lawfully utilized to justify a Terry stop would include:

- The suspect is in a known high-crime neighborhood
- The experience and training of the officer
- Suspect makes a sudden movement that is consistent with criminality or guilt, otherwise referred to as "furtive move-ments"
- The reliability and accuracy of information provided by a third party, commonly known as "criminal information"
- Criminal information provided by another law enforce-ment person or agency
- The suspect's appearance and modus operandi behaviors are consistent with a predefined "criminal profile," that is, a drug courier or gang member
- Suspect flees from the police or intentionally avoids law enforcement when he notices their presence
- Suspect says something incriminating or suspicious dur-ing a voluntary interaction with law enforcement

Instructor Demonstration: Exchange a few words with a learner who demonstrates good judgment. However, an even better solution is to recruit another instructor to play the suspect role. **The Practical Exercise Rules: total cooperation and**

no physical resistance during the *stop and frisk* scenario. The "suspect" conceals two or more simulated weapons, one in an obvious place, the others well hidden. In addition, the suspect conceals a plastic baggie full of white baking flour to simulate a dealer concealing cocaine. Two additional learners play the role of police officers. The remaining audience serves as supporters and coaches.

Critique: Typically, learners are reluctant to conduct a search beyond the "pat down," miss evidence, and the second weapon. Conduct surprise endings; the suspect produces the second back-up weapon and placebo package of drugs. The life-saving lesson requires finding all weapons! This practical exercise drives an etched tombstone memory and unforgettable lesson.

In Summary: Producing the drugs sends another memorable moment and secondary evidence message. The dramatic ending communicates the difference between survival and violent death. Learners now recognize the constitutional "reasonable suspicion stop" and "probable cause" quantum of proof for arrest on multiple charges. The charge of attempted robbery, possession of weapons, and drug contraband are in place.

Practical Exercise Feedback

Practical exercise opportunities prevent learners from repeating similar mistakes in real world scenarios. Learning outcomes offer opportunities to make mistakes in a safe classroom, rather than in field encounters. Learners obtain information and apply knowledge in intense, highly volatile situations.

Practical exercises solicit correct responses; instructors establish the acceptable quality of the response (task criteria). The learner is confronted with task(s), receives the signal to perform, and demonstrates the proper behaviors. Timed signals to perform are an option. Task(s) often require immediate instructor feedback:

- **Pass**
- **Fail**

Generally, training tasks are narrow in scope, for example, performing the field traffic stop. Sufficient practice scenarios offer learner opportunities to demonstrate proficiencies. Successful task completion serves as an encouraging accomplishment. Ineffective participants repeat the training experience. Offer feedback as soon as possible after the practical exercise.

The training process requires announcing learner training performance objectives, including learning activity descriptions, and required equipment. One classic example: shooting range requirements.

- Weapon mechanics
- Safety requirements
- Sight picture and alignment
- Detailed lessons follow

Excessive information, in the early stages, can be counter-productive. Insufficient learner readiness may lay the foundation for confusion. Complex concept comprehension improves subsequent to mastering foundation skills. Direct feedback mirrors performance objectives.

Appropriate learning progressions encourage a greater level of competence and the ability to embark upon complex tasks. For example, learners master basic accident measurement skills before introducing the *coefficient of friction formula*.

Field Training Feedback

On-the-job training, under the supervision of a field training officer (FTO), follows the basic pre-service academy program. The FTO serves as a mentor and role model for performance-oriented task(s). The position requires specialized training and is not randomly assigned.

Field training programs offer feedback advantages. The probationary field experience offers realistic training under the supervision of an eminently qualified trainer. Field training programs focus on practice skills and real world applications.

Field instructors evaluate task performance requirements and provide feedback to the field training supervisors. Field trainee supervisor programs target the needs of federal, state, or local agencies. General comments that may apply to state and local law enforcement agencies include the following goals and objectives.

According to Jack B. Molden's article, "The FTO Trouble Shooter," published in the *TRAINER*, there are:

Four Field Training Program Goals and Objectives:

- To provide a structured and standardized learning experience for recruit officers in preparation for solo patrol.
- To transfer and apply classroom training to real problems and situations encountered in the course of an officer's daily activities.
- To provide a mentor, guide, advisor, and role model in the form of an FTO.
- To provide documented evaluation of recruit performance in order to:

  o **Validate selection procedures**
  o **Assist in retention/termination decisions**
  o **Determine readiness of officers for solo patrol**

Advantages of a Formalized FTO Program:

- Training under standardized conditions will promote an improved self-image, better performance; contribute to the safety and welfare of citizens.
- Incompetent, ill-fitted candidates will be discovered and terminated, thereby reducing liability and increasing quality and productivity.
- Performance outcomes can be predicted based on standardized training and evaluation.
- Discrimination and liability charges can successfully be defended with records generated during the training cycle.

Qualified law enforcement field instructors are responsible for performance training objectives. Competency assessment commences with performance objectives, the basic measurement tools for determining an acceptable level of trainee proficiency. Officers tackle training progressions at a moderate pace, until they achieve proficiency.

Corner 5-2: The Field Training Officer's Evaluation

You serve as a Field Training Officer (FTO) in a large metro-politan police department. Officer Doyle is a probationary officer under your supervision. At the end of the field training program, trainees perform duties and responsibilities independently. However, Officer Doyle constantly seeks advice from classmates and senior officers.

Officer Doyle's goal is to graduate last in his class—a joker and class clown who enjoys the laughs. Everyone in his academy class likes him. Doyle completes field training after several extensions. You rate him *below average* on his performance objectives.

Doyle's positive attributes include on-time arrival, inter-personal skills, community relations, and citizen praise, including letters of commendation concerning performance. He wears the uniform well and makes an impressive short-term impression.

Corner 5-2: Decision-Making Exercise

The Training Commander requests a Final Field Probationary report concerning Doyle's strengths and weaknesses on the per-formance-oriented task(s). Your report determines Officer Doyle's current career outlook: *retain* or *dismiss*. List his weaknesses and strengths. Would you recommend retaining this probationary officer? Refer to the Enneagrams in Chapter 2 for motivational considerations.

Focus Points

Instructors provide clarification in the feedback process. The training situation may require additional accurate information or possible alternative responses. Highlighting positive or negative consequences prove useful.

Learners accept feedback from instructors who earn their re-spect. Confidence in the instructor's qualifications and compe-tence is foremost in criticism acceptance. Moreover, trainees generally accept feedback when instructors demonstrate assur-ance and sincerity.

Instructors establish rapport and mutual respect with trainees before the feedback process. If not, the instructor's positive attitude and expertise serves as a substitute.

Knowledge that relates to the learners' experiences has further meaning and relevance. Personal feedback that addresses goals and improved performance has significant value, including intrinsic meaning that enhances retention. Instructor willingness to adopt flexible methods of instruction serves learners best. This approach includes understanding learner behaviors, participant involvement, and training feedback.

Some learners fail to apply feedback recommendations or ignore a suggestion. Confident learners, who exceed performance, often pay little attention to unwarranted feedback and may find the process demeaning. Avoid over-supervision and performance feedback. Address participants who require remedial support.

Instructor roles differ during feedback, practical exercises, and presentations. The focus shifts to learners during practical exercises; the learner is the essential source of information. The instructor serves as the main source of information during direct participant feedback.

Specific feedback produces rapid improvement, achievement, and superior performance. Feedback related to performance improves the response and increases the ability to correct errors. Skill development in the early stages is simple and direct. However, timing is essential; learning progressions must be in the proper sequence.

Training objectives serve as learner-centered guidance. Moreover, performance objectives differ; they measure task criteria, performance conditions, and include competency measurements. Specific performance objectives pave the road to successful training task completion.

Instructors establish the criteria for successful task performance. Another related factor concerns a method for measuring and scoring criteria. Instructors focus on conditions, logistical considerations, and essential factors that support performance objective(s). Refer to Appendix A for an illustration of the performance objectives.

The ideal situation: connect performance objectives to practical exercises and assessment procedures. Although this connection is important, in most cases, *how* to merge learning techniques is unstated. The practical exercise describes how to blend logical combinations of related tasks.

Why should instructors apply the practical exercise strategy and active learning approach? Simultaneously, diverse instructional strategies reinforce the learning process. Instructors provide structure for addressing individual learning styles.

The practical exercise and case study method have overlapping qualities; on the other hand, they both emphasize feedback. The case study is target specific; however, the practical exercise demands instant feedback.

The *practical exercise* offers venues for problem-solving applications. Excellent question techniques encourage learner analysis and problem-solving strategies. The practical exercise proposes that participants increase their potential to perform similar field problems in the future.

Conclusion

Practical exercises offer superior strategies for dynamic training and reflect an instructor's experience, imagination, and creativity. Instructor field experience, innovativeness, and the ability to take calculated risks enhance resourcefulness for appropriate practical exercise scenario development. Allow learners to attack the problem! Practice develops skills and enhances opportunities for successful task(s) achievement. Chapter 6: Organizing the Practical Exercise provides a pathway to station training points and learner performance applications.

Part III: Find the Leadership Road Map

"For all of your days, prepare, and meet them ever alike: when you are the anvil, bear—when you are the hammer, strike."

— Edwin Markham

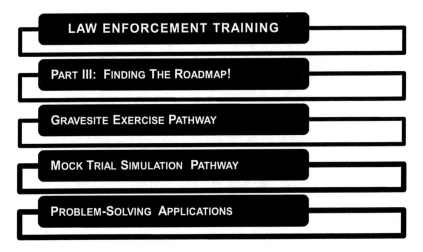

LAW ENFORCEMENT TRAINING

PART III: FINDING THE ROADMAP!

GRAVESITE EXERCISE PATHWAY

MOCK TRIAL SIMULATION PATHWAY

PROBLEM-SOLVING APPLICATIONS

Figure Part III-A: Find the Leadership Roadmap!

Dynamic Training Dots	Guidepost Pathways
Gravesite Practical Exercise: • Practical Exercise Summary • Instructional Support • Victim Identification • Case Study Applications • Practical Exercise • Instructor Supervision and Coordination	• Case Study Example • Facts of the Case • Prepare Model • Coordination Procedures • Gravesite Support • Check - Points • Monitoring & Feedback
Mock Trial Simulation: • Simulation Training • Simulation Role Playing • Mock Trial Foundations • Learning Progressions • Developing Witness Skills • Exercise Evaluation • Instructor Supervision and Coordination	• Case Study Method • Case Study Example • Role Assignments • Simulated Investigation • Crime Scene Processing • Witness Skill Development • Suppression Hearing • Trial Simulation • Exercise Evaluation
	• **Special Note:** Learning simulations require intensive planning time and energy. In addition, instructor training, experience, and expertise are vital to positive outcomes.

Figure Part III-B: Find the Leadership Roadmap!

CHAPTER 6

Organizing the Practical Exercise

"Develop a passion for learning. If you do, you will never cease to grow."

— Anthony J. D'Angelo

Focus

The purpose of the gravesite excavation practical exercise is to assist in developing investigative skills, procedures, and appropriate protocols for protecting the crime scene. Learners address preliminary investigative and follow-up reports and coordinate with appropriate scientific laboratories and forensic experts. Training stations correspond to related practical exercises.

Overview

The field of forensic science has an increasingly significant impact on law enforcement training. The gravesite excavation exercise appeals to multiple learning styles. Five practical exercise stations evaluate learner performance. **Source:** the *Forensic Examiner* originally published Sections of this chapter with permission: Baker, T. E. (2009). "Police criminalistics: Learning modalities and evaluation." *Forensic Examiner*, 18 (3), 50–55.

Practical Exercise Summary

Participants play forensic roles and related websites support the Gravesite Practical Exercise. A scenario description of potential suspects and trace evidence clues offer investigative leads. Case Summary Sheets provide additional criminal information for solving the case. Moreover, trainers post investigative leads that provide additional information for solving the unidentified human remains mystery.

Three essential components promote a successful practical exercise:

- Active rather than passive learner participation
- Approximation of investigator field experiences
- Performance-oriented related-task behaviors

Excellent field performance requires competent investigators equipped with multitasking, critical thinking, and problem-solving skills. Classroom instruction related to performance objectives helps participants succeed and offers opportunities to apply knowledge. Refer to Training Figure 6-1: Gravesite Practical Exercise Organizing Center for an illustration and overview of the practical exercise.

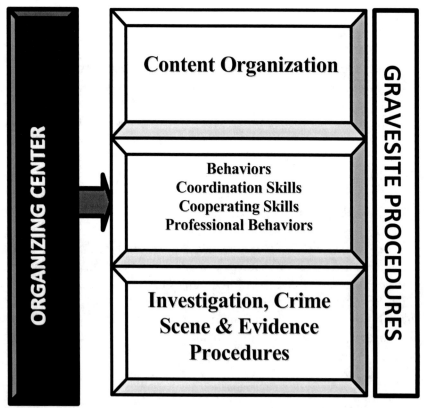

Figure 6-1: Gravesite Practical Exercise Organizing Center

Realistic scenarios provide opportunities to participate in advanced field applications. Instructors emphasize team interaction and coordination with appropriate forensic specialists. The gravesite excavation problem requires the application of investigative concepts and relevant practice exercises.

Instructors evaluate training stations 1 to 5 for successful completion of all requirements, and devote special attention to appropriate evidence collection and chain of custody procedures. Primary assessment tools include preliminary, supplemental, and related laboratory reports. Refer to Training Figure 6-2: Gravesite Organizing Center & Goals.

Figure 6-2: Gravesite Organizing Center & Goals

Designated participant leaders assume command, supervise peers, and coordinate learning stations. In addition, they arrive early and rotate through the learning stations before the problem solving begins. Everyone serves as evidence technician when collecting evidence samples and taking crime scene photographs. The practical exercise requires extensive planning. Refer to Corner 6-1: PREPARE Model for an illustration.

Corner 6-1: PREPARE Model

PREPARE is an acronym that describes:

- **Plan**
- **Rehearse**
- **Early Intervention**
- **Proceed**
- **Active Learning**
- **Review**
- **Evaluation**

This planning process provides instructors with basic steps for developing successful practical exercise outcomes. Those basic steps include timely preparation, successful progressions, practice sessions, one-on-one training assistance, active learning, and assessment.

Preparing to Train Synopsis

P = PLAN: Planning is the first essential step that leads to the successful implementation of the practical exercise in the training environment. Instructors need time to design case scenarios, role scripts, and logistical support items. For example, items might include evidence tags, chain of custody forms, evidence log, preliminary and follow-up report forms, and items needed to process the crime scene. Instructors provide support items and anticipate logistical requirements.

R = REHEARSE: The old maxim that "practice makes perfect" is appropriate. Websites offer relevant investigative links and postings, which are especially important when task(s) are highly specialized. Moreover, websites create opportunities for time-flexible training and practice. Learners participate in case studies and laboratory exercises as preparation for the mock gravesite excavation. Lectures and PowerPoint presentations support practical exercise requirements.

Instructors review planning stations and positions while directing the exercise. A wise instructional strategy is to preview support/logistical materials before learner participation and encountering questions.

Practical laboratory exercises offer opportunities to target and shape specific role expectations and anticipate problems that may arise during the practical exercise. The pressure of performing before an audience can make simple problems difficult to resolve. Practice sessions lower anxiety, increase morale, and give participants a feeling of increased control during actual case study scenarios. In addition, practice sessions prepare learners with the expectation of optimal performance and success.

E = EARLY INTERVENTION: Some participants resist or struggle with the practical exercise experience. Identify learners who demonstrate difficulties and take proactive steps to relieve anxiety and provide support. Instructors initiate positive interventions by assigning experienced participants to work with those who need additional assistance. The concept of "learners helping learners" accomplishes more in less time than "one-on-one" instructor assistance. The goal is to empower learners toward confidence and a feeling of positive accomplishment.

P = PROCEED: Initiate the field experience once learners arrive at the appropriate level of readiness and subsequent to covering preliminary performance progressions. For example, participants complete classroom case studies, evidence exercises, and related readiness learning progressions. Instructors evaluate learners and provide feedback on performance improvement. Deficient learners re-examine training content and seek remedial support.

A = ACTIVE LEARNING: The application of diverse instructional strategies reinforces the learning process. Learners select their preferred learning style. Classroom environments that integrate multiple senses—hearing, seeing, active learning, and computer applications—increase learner retention.

Problem-solving lead-up activities represent fundamental training strategies. Learners enhance their capacity to access information. Instruction is active learner driven and focuses on field-oriented computer exercises and systematic instruction. Computerized learning individualizes training and emphasizes field performance requirements. Computer applications continue to expand, limited only by software developer imagination.

R = REVIEW: Law enforcement trainers focus on content and facilitate participant learning, offering options that enhance training experiences. Trainers understand the "learning curve" principle. Trainers train-up to the required level of proficiency in the minimum amount of time. Additional review and retraining enhances law enforcement skills.

Every learning curve contains a "forgetting curve," a quantitative curve that leads to decline in the learning process. The forgetting curve follows peak proficiency devoid of updated, reviewed, and sustained training. The *review process* serves training best when applied with a consistent and persistent approach. Conduct an exercise review during the final classroom instruction and at the beginning of the field training practical exercise.

E = EVALUATION: What does program-training evaluation accomplish? Training agendas provide the skills for accomplishing the law enforcement mission. Leaders/managers establish goals and objectives that support the mission; instructors provide direct support for learners. Assessment and program evaluation represent integral components of the training cycle. Sustained performance review is essential to the learning process and a necessary component of any training program. Leadership responsibilities include targeting deficiencies that obstruct training programs.

Learner assessment concerns the successful measurement of learner outcomes. Evaluation answers two fundamental questions:

- **How will the instructor determine arrival at the proper training destination?**
- **Where is the next training journey going?**

Never skip or eliminate the evaluation process. **Source:** Adapted from U.S. Army training **PREPARE** model.

Instructional Support

Instructor support effectiveness is critical and seeks to accommodate diverse abilities. Varied instructional methods support different learning styles. Learners receive advanced notice regarding report submission requirements and deadlines. In addition, sample reports assist learners in the report writing process.

A grading system for report or project submissions states performance expectations and lists requirements for learner assessments. Model formats and reinforcement support successful task completion. Gravesite practical exercise goals and related performance objectives provide additional guidance and reflect final assessment performance standards.

PowerPoint notes support the learning process and help move learners forward in their preparation for the gravesite practical exercise. Creative presentations that include reader-friendly line spacing, illustrative images, and enlarged fonts enhance learning environments. Computer technology provides instructors the option of posting lecture notes, an additional learner support activity. Empowering successful learners influences future field decisions. Independent computer applications generally lead to further exploration and may assist in creating opportunities to expand law enforcement expertise.

Demonstration and Check Points

Advanced planning and preparation is important. The goal is to avoid interruptions or problems that influence the demonstration component of the instructional process. Group leaders arrive early. Instructors identify station operational task(s) that group leaders will be required to duplicate for class members.

Demonstrate performance steps in a straightforward manner and sequence the learning progressions. Explain essential steps, emphasize essential points, and identify written materials and equipment essential to the tasks. Describe *when, where,* and *why* the tasks are important.

Instructors assure that group leaders understand demonstrated steps and tasks. Most important, encourage questions and probe for learner comprehension at every station.

A first priority—identify areas where safety issues may evolve. Group leaders represent the first line of defense and an early warning system. Identify appropriate corrective actions in case of an emergency and prepare participants. Verify learner understanding regarding instructions and rules surrounding the gravesite practical exercise. Instructors inventory necessary learner support items including notebooks, gloves, pens, rulers, clipboards, and so on.

Provide clear and concise instructions at each training station. Emphasize directions on important steps, so that learners know what to do and when to accomplish each task. Walk learners through individual training stations and demonstrate performance objectives. Most important, emphasize critical points and safety considerations. Learners will generally meet the required performance objectives once they recognize instructor criteria.

Encourage a learning climate in which everyone feels comfortable, capable, and competent. Ask questions that assess procedural understanding; then, give the signal to begin. Learners conduct an investigation to determine the unknown victim's identification and locate the offender(s).

Instructors frequently require assistance, opportunities to take advantage of assigned group leader support and intervention. Therefore, instructors address learner concerns by exception. Accomplished learners, who complete the exercise early, may assist by coaching others.

Instructors determine whether group leaders can adequately monitor individual learner progress. Consider the number of learners and time constraints regarding task completion. If necessary, modify the training agenda, stations, or instructions. Unpredictable learner responses may require real-time adjustments.

Case Study Applications

The case study method combined with practical exercises allows learners to apply theories to hypothetical scenarios and entice multiple senses. Learners read case studies; present solutions on the blackboard, then compare and contrast their solution decisions. Lead-up case studies and hands-on lab experiences form the foundation for gravesite practical exercise stations. Learning progressions relate to skills that ensure successful completion of the practical exercise.

Case studies and scenarios encourage learner activities that enhance retention. Group dynamics present opportunities for involvement, personal expression, and investigative applications. The emphasis is on the integration of concepts, analysis, and problem-solving skills related to addressing the case scenario. Examples of learner preparation case studies and labs include:

- **Chain of custody**
- **Laboratory request forms**

- Marking and measuring the gravesite
- Victim identification
- Homicide investigation cases

The primary purpose of this practical exercise field project: follow-through on protecting the crime scene. Performance objective achievement and the completion of training stations serve as primary goals.

The following FBI case example concerns personality reconstruction from unidentified remains. Decomposed bodies are difficult to identify. Relatives, even after a reasonably short time, fail to recognize family members. Refer to Corner 6-2: Victim Identification for an example.

Corner 6-2: Victim Identification

Case Study: The badly decomposed remains of a human were found in an isolated wooded area adjacent to an industrial park. The crime scene investigation disclosed that the skeletal remains had been dragged a few feet from the original location, and it was suspected that this dislocation of the remains resulted from animal activities. An intensive search produced only a few strands of hair, a medium-size sweater, and a few pieces of women's jewelry. The physical remains were taken to the medical examiner's office, where the time of death was estimated to be three to six weeks before the discovery of the body. A subsequent review of missing persons reports for the pertinent time produced no additional clues.

With the question of the victim's identity still unresolved, the remains were forwarded to the curator of physical anthropology at the Smithsonian Institution in Washington, D.C. Based on an examination of the skeletal remains, it was concluded that the skeleton was that of a Caucasian female, approximately 17 to 22 years of age, who was of less-than-average stature. She had broader-than-average shoulders and hips, and was believed to be right-handed. Her head and face were long; the nose was high-bridged. Also noted was the subcartilage damage to the right hip joint, a condition that had probably caused occasional pain and suggested occupational stress. An irregularity of the left clavicle (collarbone) revealed a healed childhood fracture.

Local police officials then began a social and personality profile of the deceased based on an analysis of the physical evidence obtained through the crime scene search and related photographs, medical examiner's reports, and reports from the FBI laboratory. In addition, aided by a physical anthropologist from the Smithsonian Institution, a police artist was able to provide a sketch. The sketch was published in a local newspaper, and police officials immediately received calls from three different readers who all supplied the same name of a female whom they all knew. They confirmed that she resembled the sketch, and they further estimated that she had been missing for approximately four months.

A search of the local police files disclosed that the individual with this name had been previously photographed and fingerprinted. These prints were compared with the badly decomposed prints from one of the victim's fingers, and a positive identification was made.

Further investigation by the police determined the victim was 20 years of age. Associates related that when she worked as a nightclub dancer, she occasionally favored one leg. It was further determined that she suffered a fracture of the left clavicle at age six.

Source: Cherry, D. G. and J. L. Angel. (1977). "Personality reconstruction from unidentified remains," *FBI Law Enforcement Bulletin*, 46, (49) pp. 12 – 15.

Forensic artists may assist in developing clay sculpture models from skeletal remains. Computer facial reconstruction can be useful in identifying unknown victims. The author created the sketch below using Inter Quest FACES Software. Refer to Training Figure 6-3: FACES Computer Software for an illustration of the ability to capture facial descriptions.

Corner 6-3: Gravesite Practical Exercise

Summary Sheet #1

A jogger finds several bones near a remote park area. Numerous investigative questions quickly emerge:

- Are they human bones?
- Can the person's identity be established?
- What was the cause of death?
- What other details will the crime scene reveal?

Figure 6-3: FACES Computer Software

At this point, the learners require basic knowledge concerning crime scene processing and should understand the need to coordinate with scientific experts, that is, forensic archeologists, forensic anthropologists, forensic entomologists, and forensic odontology scientific specialists.

The Trainee Commander releases the investigative evidence teams to the site and assigns learners to one of five investigative teams that rotate through five performance stations:

- Station 1: Primary Skeletal Remains
- Station 2: Additional Skeletal Remains – Hair and DNA Evidence
- Station 3: Additional Skeletal Remains: Entomology Site
- Station 4: Clothing and Related Blood Spatter
- Station 5: Chain Of Custody Performance Objectives

In addition, stations 1 to 5 require evidence collection, note taking, crime scene photography, and sketching.

Initially, teams conduct a walk-through preliminary search. This involves finding all associated evidence, such as missing body segments, clothing, weapons, shell casings, hair, blood, and other related items. The search focuses on the skeletal remains and surrounding gravesite. Visual inspection involves moving outward from the center to related sites until all body parts are recovered. Thus, the search starts at the site, moving away in the cardinal directions and fanning out *away* from the body (Byers, 2002).

The responding officer preserves the scene and notifies headquarters immediately. The shift commander dispatches the investigative and evidence teams to the site. You are a member of one of the teams.

Case Summary Sheet #2: Detective Gordon Piland preserves the scene and notifies police headquarters. He detains a jogger witness for an informal interview. The Detective's goal is to obtain preliminary information.

"Wait a minute ... why the rush to leave?"

"I'm upset ... she is wearing a gold cross—just like the one I gave my girlfriend."

"What do you mean ... *she*? Those skeletal remains could be anyone, male or female. We do not have an autopsy report or physical anthropologist on the case. The skeletal remains are the center of this investigation, even more important than the location."

"I want to know what's going on ... is this the same serial killer I read about in the newspaper?"

"We don't know for sure if this is murder, suicide, or death from natural causes. Who knows if it's the serial killer's work?"

"I feel like blowing my brains out! I need to know if this is my girlfriend! I have been waiting for over two hours. You are the first investigator to give me the time of day!"

The witness bolts toward the car again.

"Wait a minute! I need your name and address."
"Take down my license plate number and check me out."
"We need to identify the gravesite remains."
"Well, that's your job, not mine!"
Beads of sweat appear on Detective Piland's forehead, "We need your cooperation."
"I want to find out who did this. What if it is my girlfriend? She has been missing for months. I want you to solve the case. You cops do not seem to care. She worked only a few blocks down the road."
The witness slams the car door, starts the engine, and burns rubber. Detective Piland records the license plate number ... *My first and only witness, but he behaves more like a person of interest or suspect.*
Puzzled by the witness response, Piland returns to the crime scene where shreds of torn clothing were recovered. The evidence appears ravaged by carnivores and possibly a sharp instrument. Investigators respond to the scene; the medical examiner arrives. Crime scene photographers photograph the entire site, including the skeleton, before it's transported to the city morgue.

Summary Sheet #3: Refer to Appendix A: Gravesite Excavation Exercise for an illustration of the five-station planning process.

Summary Sheet #4: At the morgue, the medical examiner examines the remains for evidence of trauma, such as stab marks or blunt trauma to the skull and mandible. In addition, the medical examiner looks for broken bones. Photographs of the body show that bullet markings are noted. In addition, an examination of the clothing reveals no wallet or personal identification.

Forensic pathologists determine "cause of death." The best determination in this case appears knife and gunshot wounds to the ribs. The pathologist concludes the manner of death as being *homicide*—ruling out other opinions under the classification system such as natural, accidental, suicide, and undetermined.

Additional results by the forensic entomologist estimated "time of death" as approximately two months, according to the forensic examination of insect cycles.

Identification of the skeletal remains is the first consideration. The forensic autopsy leads to positive identification of limited remains. When attempting to make positive identification, the first method is fingerprint identification; this was not possible in this case. Positive identification results from forensic odontologist examination of dental records.

Monitoring Progress and Feedback

Instructors identify problems during the gravesite practical exercise. Issues may evolve from poor preparation, motivation, or social climate responses. Provide assistance; however, encourage learners to perform skills independently as the exercise unfolds.

Offer positive feedback that reflects successful performance at training stations. Instructor encouragement is important. Positive evaluation reinforces performance objectives.

Identify incorrect performance behaviors promptly. Corrective action helps prevent others from interpreting the behaviors as acceptable, therefore repeating mistakes. Encouraging feedback helps learner performance. Harsh comments are destructive to the learning process. Provide reduced feedback as learners advance through the training stations.

Learners are sensitive to task correcting behaviors, especially experienced law enforcement officers. Praise publicly; correct privately. Present universal concerns by offering general observations.

Practical Exercise Evaluation

Evaluation is necessary to redirect the curriculum and help reorient the planning process. It provides the future road map for developing strategic goals and objectives; furthermore, it provides plans for directing learners to future behavioral objectives.

It answers three crucial questions:

- Have the learners arrived?
- Where is curriculum now?
- Where does the instructor go from there?

Twenty-six respondents participate in a course evaluation survey. Questions address twelve general items concerning field-learning experiences. The Likert Scale choices are collapsed because of the small population. Survey participants respond to items by indicating one of the following: (1) agree, (2) undecided, or (3) disagree. Survey results indicate that 100% of the respondents agree that they improved their knowledge of forensic evidence coordination. In addition, 88% agree they improved their understanding of the investigative process, team investigative process, and coordination with scientific laboratories. Moreover, 85% agree they improved their crime scene reconstruction skills and 96% agree that their ability to coordinate the investigative process improved.

Seventy-three percent agree that preliminary and supplemental investigative report assignments improved understanding. Classroom lectures, hard copy models, and website links support writing assignments. Instructors often encounter resistance to writing assignments. Moreover, considerable instructor support motivates completion of investigative and laboratory reports.

Survey items on learning styles reveal that approximately:

- 12% of the participants describe themselves as primarily *auditory learners*
- 31% of the participants describe themselves as primarily *visual learners*
- 50% of the participants describe themselves as primarily *tactile learners*

Auditory learners express further undecided or disagreement responses.

Questions measuring gravesite simulation preferences indicated that:

- 85% agree that the experience offered insight into the scientific community
- 92% agree with the tactile (hands-on) component

The gravesite excavation survey provides preliminary data regarding the learning process and practical exercise approach to instruction. Responses measure the opinions of these respondents and results generalized beyond this target audience are inappropriate. The purpose of the survey: to illustrate how instructors might experiment and evaluate learning environments in their quest to meet trainee needs. The intent is *not* to generalize beyond these learners.

Focus Points

This training philosophy reflects the premise that participants learn best when *involved* in active learning. The gravesite excavation practical exercise offers opportunities for realistic role applications that support active learning. Key critical thinking responsibilities include leadership, coaching, and guidance during the case study and gravesite simulation process.

Trainers pose two questions:

"Where are we going?"

The answer determines goals, organizing centers and defines appropriate performance objectives. The organizing center (gravesite practical exercise) is a goal frame of reference. The emphasis is on the focal point of instruction, that is, the gravesite excavation exercise and concepts around targeted instruction and learning.

The second question:

"How will you get there?"

Answer this question by developing goals and derived performance objectives. Organizing centers enhance learning design through the articulation and sequencing of related goals and performance objectives. Objectives originate from specific goals and inform participants regarding standards and learning progressions.

Case studies and laboratory exercises motivate the application of theories to real or hypothetical scenarios, allowing maximum

use of senses. Interactive case studies require learner participation.

Learners read the case; present solutions on the blackboard,
then compare and contrast their decisions. Learning progressions
consider skills necessary for successful completion of the gravesite
practical exercise.

Participants play forensic roles and easily identifiable websites support the excavation exercise. The case study and Summary Sheets that offer descriptions of potential suspects and
related trace evidence clues provide pathways to solving the case.
Furthermore, web-posted investigative leads provide additional
information for solving the mystery of the unidentified human
remains.

Group dynamics offer opportunities for participation, self-expression, and academic development. The emphasis: integration
of concepts, analysis, and problem solving related to addressing
the case scenario.

Instructors provide feedback via electronic communication, an
essential component of team organization and cooperation.
Learners meet independently and as a group in preparation for
the gravesite practical exercise stations.

Instructors serve as resources, planners, and facilitators; tran-
sitioning from lecturer to coach. Instructors coordinate countless
details and address potential staging dilemmas, including
location, equipment, and training aids.

The investigation does not terminate at the simulation
conclusion. Preliminary and follow-up investigations continue
during the course of instruction. Preliminary and follow-up
reports set the foundation for the forensic reports. Participants
control 40% of their grade by addressing details that emerge from
the gravesite practical exercise experience, assuming responsibility from beginning to end.

Conclusion

The purpose of the gravesite practical exercise is to **spark the
investigative process fire** and its relationship to closing cases,
a tiny component of what actually transpires at a gravesite
excavation. Nevertheless, the learning process encourages insight
into scientific community collaboration and team coordination.
Coordination with scientists and securing exceptional forensic

evidence can mean the difference between a closed or open cold case file. Chapter 7: Organizing the Learning Simulation provides a pathway to advanced learning.

CHAPTER 7

Organizing the Simulation

"Education has as its objective the foundation of character."
— Herbert Spencer

Focus

Mock trial instructional strategies offer interactive learning simulation opportunities and suggest dynamic implications for criminal investigation, forensic science, and other training programs. Critical thinking and learning simulation strategies transfer to dynamic training applications. The chapter explores the mock trial learning simulation.

Overview

Learning simulations offer ideal venues for problem solving and the application of newly acquired active learning investigative skills. Learning simulations are realistic applications that parallel field/courtroom environments and encourage opportunities to apply knowledge. This unique learning experience allows participants to practice investigative behaviors in the simulated courtroom scenario.

Mock trial learning strategies encourage the application of multiple senses and diverse learning modalities. The Mock Trial Simulation enables participants to perform five basic learning progressions:

- **Problem solving**
- **Active learning**
- **Preliminary and follow-up investigations**
- **Suppression hearing rehearsal and practice**
- **Moot court simulation**

Source: the *Forensic Examiner* originally published sections of this Chapter with permission: Baker, T. E., Cimini, J. & Cleveland C. (2010). "Mock trial journey: An assessment." *Forensic Examiner*, Winter, 32–43.

Simulation Training

The main argument for advocating simulation techniques revolves around **motivation**. Active participation, rather than passive bystander learning, stimulates interest. Active participants involved in conflict can visualize and internalize the simulation role-play experience. More important, the simulation excites curiosity to pursue knowledge outside the classroom.

When conducted properly, the learning simulation becomes a motivational driving force, which can produce unexpected and peak performance experiences. The use of multiple senses and interactive learning strategies enhances instructor presentations. Participants have opportunities to move outside themselves and bond to the role-playing process.

Role-play refers to problem solving that enables learners to explore training environments that offer spontaneous enactments. Role-play permits not only content internalization, but also emotional responses that mirror characters. For example, the resulting conflict between the prosecuting and defense attorneys when they examine witnesses at a murder trial *produces realism*.

The decision to introduce the learning simulation is a significant event in the training environment. Successful instructors encourage critical thinking and stimulate learning through a variety of instructional techniques. The combination of effective instructional strategies enhances retention and assists in maintaining a creative learning climate. Empower participants to become successful learners that enhance their peak performance and ability to make effective field decisions.

Organize groups into prosecution and defense teams, which are responsible for opening remarks, case details, relevant laws, and summation. Assign other participant roles to include investigators and witnesses. Select possible defendants from outsiders rather than from the participant pool.

Conduct rehearsal during the Suppression Hearing; remaining class members serve as jury members during the moot court. They decide the outcome of the case. Most important, jury members support verdicts and analyze conclusions using critical thinking skills.

Simulation Role Play

The role-play instructional strategy is not novel; enforcement-training applications abound. Simulations create alternative scenarios that are not perfect but approximate learning opportunities. These learning strategies produce a sense of *flow* and the potential for a *peak experience*. Refer to Chapter 8 for additional information.

Role-play demands rules, regulations, authentic settings, and hypothetical situations. Complex role assignments stimulate social interaction and relationships. The main distinction: the extent role-play reflects realistic situations. Role-play and simulation training are parallel and work well together.

Role Assignments

The solutions to moot court simulations require flexibility, imagination, and realistic role scripts. Participants learn by internalizing role requirements. Case studies, related laboratories, and suggested readings prepare participants for professional roles. Refer to Tables: 7-1 and 7-2 for Role Assignments and Learner Responsibilities.

Table 7-1 Mock Trial Roles Sign-up Form

Trial Judge	Magisterial Judge/Court Officer
Chief of Staff	Assistant Chief of Staff
Chief of Police	Captain of Detectives
Lt. Evidence Commander	Lt. Arrest/Search Team Cmdr
Police Officer: At The Crime Scene	Search Warrant Detective
Crime Scene Photographer	Arrest Warrant Detective
Sketcher & Evidence Collection Officer	Detective Interviewer
Sketcher & Evidence Collection Officer	Detective Interviewer
Primary Evidence Custodian	Detective Interviewer

Alternate Evidence Custodian	Detective Interviewer
Chief Prosecutor	Chief Defense Counsel
Assistant Prosecutor	Assistant Defense Counsel
Assistant Prosecutor	Assistant Defense Counsel

Table 7-2 Mock Trial Roles Sign-up Form

Pathologist/Doctor	Witness #1: Defendant
DNA Expert	Witness #2: Neighbor
Foot Impression Expert	Witness #3: Bartender
Firearms Expert	Witness #4: Roommate
Fibers Expert	Witness #5: Potential Defendant
Fingerprint Expert	Witness #6: Alibi Witness Parent

Mock Trial Foundations

Mock trial participants require supportive guidance and excellent curriculum foundations. Instructors concentrate on organizing centers, goals, and performance objectives that address three basic curriculum questions:

- Where are you going?
- How will you get there?
- How will you know when you have arrived?

Assessment and evaluation represent basic requirements for determining destination arrival. Refer to Training Figure 7-1: Mock Trial Organizing Center for an illustration of the primary coordination point for training goals and objectives.

Mock trial foundations require extensive planning and organization; instructors are responsible for guiding this process. Refer to Training Figure 7-2: Mock Trial Organizational Cycle for an illustration.

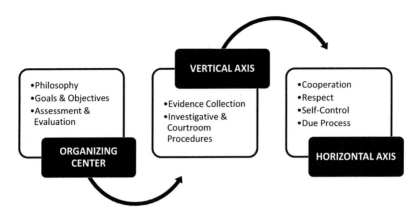

Figure 7-1: Mock Trial Organizing Center

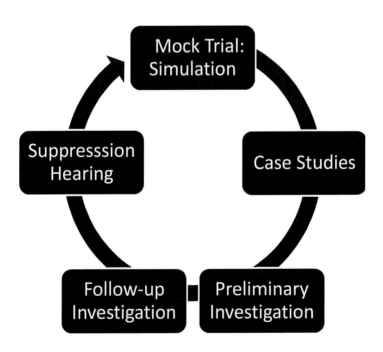

Figure 7-2: Mock Trial Organizational Cycle

Philosophical Foundations

The philosophical approach, a navigational tool, is dynamic, action-oriented, and involves critical thinking and problem solving—a compass for quality instruction. Philosophy addresses decision-making and course requirements.

Organizing Centers

Organizing centers enhance learning design through the articulation and sequencing of performance objectives. They arrange appropriate behaviors, concepts, attitudes, values, and skills in proper progressions on the horizontal axis. The intersection of the horizontal and vertical axes locates the ***organizing center***.

For example, the following behaviors emerge on the ***horizontal axis*** of the mock trial simulation: cooperation, self-control, due process, and respect for the rights of others. The ***vertical axis*** documents content and learning objectives: evidence collection and preservation, chain of custody/scientific laboratory procedures, interview strategy models, courtroom testimony, and so on.

Participants write related reports with an emphasis on format and style. The advantage of using a homicide-simulated case is the abundance of physical evidence and reports. Identifying the core curriculum offers the means to organize subject matter.

Direction: Performance Objectives

Performance objectives originate from specific goals and objectives, and support standards and participant-centered learning progressions. In addition, they measure specific learning competencies. Refer to Training Figure 7-3: Mock Trial Goal.

Once participants have a clear understanding of the road map to success, learner anxiety may diminish. The goal is to focus on the learning process and mock trial requirements. Personal distractions hinder understanding and performance.

The mock trial simulation is conceptually oriented and based on the scientific method, problem-solving and decision-making principles. It represents an intellectually disciplined process of analyzing, synthesizing, and applying newly acquired skills. Excellent critical thinking and active learning methods enhance witness testimony skills. Authentic courtrooms offer multiple learning opportunities and participant outcomes.

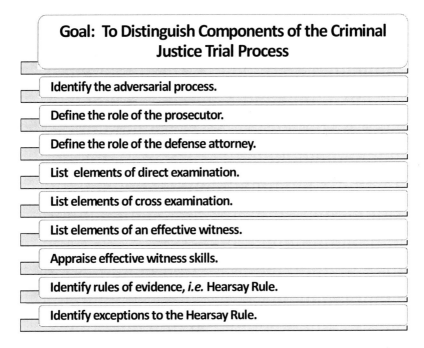

Goal: To Distinguish Components of the Criminal Justice Trial Process

Identify the adversarial process.

Define the role of the prosecutor.

Define the role of the defense attorney.

List elements of direct examination.

List elements of cross examination.

List elements of an effective witness.

Appraise effective witness skills.

Identify rules of evidence, *i.e.* Hearsay Rule.

Identify exceptions to the Hearsay Rule.

Figure 7-3: Mock Trial Goal

Training Progressions

Criminal investigation and forensic courses are ideally suited to learning simulations. The investigative process course applies a role-play approach that creates opportunities for active learning. The goal is to integrate and create a scenario that involves as many learning modalities as possible.

The Case Study Method: Progression One

Approximately 20 case study and laboratory exercises support the Investigative Process course. These practice exercises offer opportunities to develop learning simulation skills and practice problem solving. The case study method requires reviewing and complying with Advanced Study Sheet and reading assignments.

Without proper participant preparation, this approach will be less successful, diminishing the learning process.

Short lectures precede introductions to case studies. Participants ask questions; however, they are encouraged to resolve specific concepts as a group. The cases reflect real or hypothetical crimes, describe complete scenarios, and offer relevant facts.

The Simulated Preliminary Investigation--- Progression Two

Learners prepare for progression two after completing case studies, related laboratories, and readings. Simulated homicide problems involve complex role assignments and programmed scripts. Participants opt for role assignments based on interest. Traditional criminal justice roles include every aspect of an investigation. The primary advantage of homicide simulation scenarios: an abundance of physical evidence and report generation that must be preserved for trial. Case studies serve as foundations for stage two problem-solving and writing requirements.

Role Assignments

Identify roles early to allow time for research and planning. Participants arrive in time-phased stages: The Chief of Staff and safety personnel arrive at 10:00 a.m. to set up the crime scene and evidence. Witnesses arrive at 11:00 a.m. for rehearsal and script preparation. At noon, law enforcement personnel arrive to solve the homicide problem.

Participants complete the preliminary investigation. The instructor and Chief of Staff release records and reports for the investigative staff at appropriate times. The trainer attends staff briefings, providing limited guidance. Sustained emphasis is on crime scene evidence, chain of custody, and interviewing witnesses to move on to progression three.

Crime Scene Processing

The sketch team documents and measures the exact location of physical evidence. Several standard search methods assure the successful collection of vital crime scene evidence. The collection team secures, marks, tags and initiates chain of custody forms with precision and using established protocols. The ultimate purpose of crime scene investigation is to maintain proper care, custody, and control of evidence. Moreover, crime scene procedures allow proper coordination among crime scene investigators, scientific laboratories, expert witnesses, and defense and prosecution teams.

After securing the scene, one officer administers the crime scene log that documents all personnel who have the right of access to the crime scene. A preliminary survey requires written notes, sketches, and the identification of fragile evidence. The first officer who arrives on the scene alerts investigators and crime scene investigation (CSI) technicians regarding the location of fragile evidence.

This officer establishes a clear pathway for investigative and medical personnel; the pathway prevents destruction and further contamination of physical evidence. In addition, the pathway allows follow-up investigators opportunities to establish obvious physical evidence including weapons, blood spatter, footprints, and so on. The initial point-to-point search locates additional evidence for the CSI photographer. The lead follow-up investigator establishes a systematic search plan for the crime scene.

The basic rule of criminal investigation requires that evidence never be touched, altered, or moved before taking multi-angle photographs. Exacting procedures prevent evidence contamination. The CSI team meticulously records the crime scene with well-documented photographs and videotaping procedures. The fingerprint examiner, blood evidence technician, fibers expert, and footprint technician gather fragile trace evidence.

The CSI's primary role is to photograph, sketch, record the crime scene, and finally collect evidence. Investigators estimate boundary determinations, including inner and outer crime scene boundaries that divide the crime scene. The investigator attempts to identify probable offender entrance and exit routes for evidence preservation, reconstruction, and forensic mapping.

Summary Sheet: Case Study

Sergeant Thompson responds to a homicide call and discovers the body of young man in the shower of a bathroom. His name is Bob Jones, white male, approximately 30 years of age. His roommate, who recently returned from spring break at the local university, found the body. The victim is in a state of advanced decomposition and the smell in the bathroom is overwhelming.

The position of the body, blood trail, and physical evidence indicate homicide. There were multiple stab wounds on the victim's back, shoulder, and chest. Defensive wounds and bloody trail indicate flight from the assailant. However, it appears that the attacker dragged the body from the bedroom entrance into the shower. Evidence suggests the purpose—an attempt to conceal or destroy evidence.

The lead investigator notices a high velocity blood mist that formed a bloody halo on the far side of an adjacent bedroom wall. The angle of incidence concerning the bullet wound in the head appears to occur from above with a muzzle distance of approximately two feet. The victim's wounds indicate that the body was in the prone position. The shooter had to be standing above and to the rear of the victim.

His girlfriend, Terry Adams, claims she does not know anything about his death. Her alibi – she was in another state on the way to meet another man. Preliminary interviews suggest her body language and statement of innocence to be contradictory.

One remark gains the attention of investigators. Terry mentions that the victim owned a weapon, a PPK/S Walther, 380 automatic, and it is missing. Terry claims that Bob had another girlfriend named Monica, who he intended to wed. In addition, Monica is the likely killer because she is a prostitute. She probably stole the weapon. However, friends indicate otherwise. They report that Bob talked about terminating both relationships and was pursuing another woman.

Two primary persons of interest emerge in this investigation. Investigators must eliminate one and establish probable cause for arrest. It is hoped that the evidence trail and *theory of transfer* will prove one of them guilty "beyond a reasonable doubt" in the mock trial simulation.

Follow-Up: Progression Three

It is at this stage that critical thinking and the problem-solving process advance forward:

- Identify central issues
- State the investigative problem
- Collect additional information

- Recognize underlying assumptions of motive and opportunity
- Accumulate evidence
- Identify persons of interest
- Identify primary suspects

Laboratory Support

Simulation role players follow-up, complete reports, collect data, and draw conclusions. Investigators seek evidence to support guilt or defendant exoneration prior to arrest and moot court problem. Participants complete preliminary and follow-up simulations in preparation for the suppression hearing. Rehearsals signal readiness for the eventual mock trial simulation.

Homicide investigators distinguish what transpired at the crime scene by reconstructing events; scientific analysis reconstructs an accurate sequence of events. Physical evidence helps investigators focus on a possible suspect(s). The reconstruction of events and sequencing requires accurate measurements. The measurements may involve experimental simulations with bloodstain patterns, incident angle (impact angle), cast-off, high and low velocity blood spatter, and so on. High velocity blood spatter may produce a shadow of the victim on the wall or the approximate angle at which a blood droplet struck a surface.

Bullet trajectory physics assist in determining the path of the projectile. For example, when a bullet penetrates both sides of a wall, the path and angle of incidence is plotted with a probe, string, and protractor. The laser light method for determining bullet trajectories represents a high-technology approach for accomplishing the trajectory of a bullet.

Target residue pattern from the weapon muzzle is absent. There is no indication of a powder contact wound or star pattern wound on the victim's head. The lack of gunshot residue traces on the victim's hands suggests he did not fire the weapon.

Scientific tests and simulations eventually prove the lead investigator's hypothesis as being correct. Proving the case requires reliance on additional scientific evidence, witnesses, computer evidence, cell phone evidence, and photographic evidence from the defendant's personal camera.

Suppression Hearing: Progression Four

The main purpose of *suppression hearing* simulation is to challenge evidence concerning chain of custody. In addition, the suppression hearing serves as a secondary practice session in the witness development phase. Role-playing attorneys, police officers, and witnesses develop understanding concerning the adversarial nature of the criminal justice system.

The prosecution team demonstrates everything that the investigative staff successfully accomplished. Moreover, the defense team demonstrates everything that participants failed to accomplish within specific investigative guideline requirements. Team players eliminate unacceptable courtroom behaviors and shape satisfactory protocols during rehearsals. The learning environment is open and positive; mistakes remain acceptable as a component of the learning process.

The ideal time for *coaching* is during the suppression hearing, before the courthouse mock trial. The defense team challenges evidence admissibility. Suppression hearings present nonthreatening rehearsal opportunities to develop witness skills and instruct learners how to play various investigator and expert witness roles.

Magisterial District Judge

A former federal magistrate judge serves as the Magisterial District Judge. His responsibilities include:

- Probable cause examination
- Fourth Amendment constitutional requirements

Learner investigators receive specific coaching on the arrest and search warrants. The goal is to provide a meaningful simulation that requires critical thinking on the application of factual reliability, particularity, and probable cause. The emphasis is on problem solving and the establishment of guilt-laden facts.

The Role of the Judge

A federal deputy clerk of court serves as the trial judge for the mock trial—an expert in courtroom procedures and the rules of evidence. One significant advantage is his familiarity over many years with the mock trial simulation. The goal is not to turn the simulation into a full-scale trial but to allow opportunities for witnesses to develop basic courtroom skills. His role is that of coach, facilitator, and arbitrator of prosecutor and defense attorney roles. The emphasis is on problem solving, and the establishment of law enforcement and expert witness skills.

The goal is to encourage and teach effective witness skills that emphasize proper demeanor, honesty, integrity, and foremost credibility. Offering testimony before a judge and jury is a natural cause for producing anxiety in any witness appearing before a real courtroom. The mock trial simulation offers a less stressful environment. The classroom setting facilitates the necessary skills to ensure success during the mock trial experience (i.e., problem solving, response to stress, and subject matter knowledge).

Developing Witnesses

Properly prepared witnesses serve as a foundation for the criminal justice system. The mock trial is an adversarial process that requires exceptional performance under demanding and stressful circumstances. Basic law enforcement and expert witness skills flourish during the mock court learning simulation. Courtroom career aspirations often unfold after experiencing the results of successful mock trial preparation.

Proper witness progressions and learning simulations improve lay witness, investigator, and scientific witness potential. Initial witness participation and preparation in less-threatening social settings offer preferable learning experiences. Mock trial learning simulations ensure opportunities for group interaction that foster problem-solving skills.

Mock trial learning simulations require plot driven strategies. The case scenario has two principal characters. Only one character is subject to prosecution. In addition, one character actor serves as a distracter for elimination during the investigative process. The participants arrest one subject after reviewing witness interviews, physical evidence, and probable cause requirements. Mock trial investigators and forensic specialists follow the predetermined pathway to the *prima facie* case and conviction based on guilt beyond a reasonable doubt.

Participants who portray expert witnesses play a crucial role in the mock trial by how well they prepare and expand their role as an expert witness (i.e., medical examiner, fingerprint expert, etc.). Thoughtful selection of the pathologist and DNA expert is essential; prior courses in forensic science facilitate excellent role transition. In addition, the expert witnesses require considerable effort and instructor rehearsal.

The prosecution and defense teams have considerable responsibility in the outcome of the mock trial experience. They must oversee all aspects of the case from arrest to trial, evidence preservation, witness preparation, and organization of the entire pretrial and trial process. In addition, the role of the prosecutor sets the tone of how the entire scenario will evolve. Basic communication skills unfold during opening statements, the examination of witnesses, and final summations.

The defense team plays a crucial role in the adversarial simulation process. The judge mediates the conflict, and assures a positive learning experience for the prosecution and defense. Numerous teachable moments unfold during and after the trial judge's debriefing. The debriefing emphasis is on learning from mistakes, which ultimately prepares participants for professional performance in a real courtroom setting.

The instructor/coordinator role requires patience, timing, leadership, and coaching skills. The successful culmination requires monitoring by the instructor to ensure the role playing scripts are following a pattern toward the goals and objectives of the course destination. This positive outcome requires the instructor's concentration and participant dedication.

Mock trial simulation is a courtroom experience that demands expertise and experience from the instructor/coordinator. This instructional method is not to be taken lightly by the inexperienced. Mock trial requires considerable time and energy. If that commitment is not present, the learning experience can result in less than successful outcomes. The mock trial simulation is where all previous efforts and suppression rehearsals come to fruition. The judge analyzes and clarifies everything the participants accomplish, both positive and negative.

The measure of success is not *conviction*. A win/lose attitude is not encouraged; everyone in the class is a winner. Class members are responsible for their roles, and mistakes are essential components in the learning process. The judge's after-action critique emphasizes a positive learning climate. Learner participants receive helpful commentary regarding proper witness procedures and professional presentation. The coaching process is essential to a positive trial outcome. Evidence competency and chain of custody become central themes. Moreover, laying the foundation for witnesses, especially expert witnesses, remains essential for a successful trial experience.

Methods of Evaluation

Program evaluation focuses on the global nature of instruction. Feedback provides information to continue, eliminate, modify, or adjust the philosophy, goals, and performance objectives. Global program evaluation provides opportunities to improve the quality of instruction and modification of future strategies (Davis, 2001). The quality and effectiveness of instruction improve when global instructional strategies require maximum effort. The modification of future learning strategies requires feedback. Experimentation, analysis, and evaluation foster new and better ways to learn.

Evaluation provides new directions and motivates innovative instructional methods, ultimately enhancing contemporary training programs. Experimentation, analysis, and evaluation advance new and improved methods of instruction. The following survey questionnaire serves as one method of obtaining mock trial simulation feedback. Refer to Training Figure 7-4: Curriculum Assessment & Evaluation for illustration of the process.

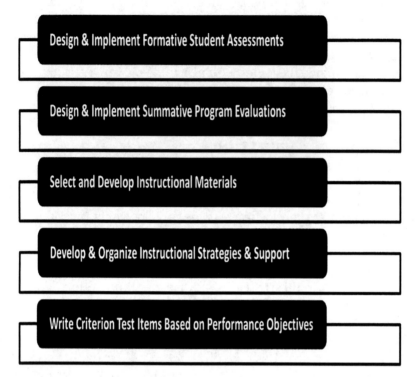

Figure 7-4: Curriculum Assessment & Evaluation

Survey Measurement Method

A Likert-scale survey measured respondent attitudes. The respondent could indicate one of the following choices: (1) agree; (2) disagree; or (3) have no opinion. The format measured critical thinking, problem solving, and the mock trial simulation. The participants also responded to learning outcome questions about the mock trial experience. The survey results are specific to this group of participants; consequently, generalizations beyond this population are not appropriate.

Sample Respondent Population

The overwhelming majority of respondents felt positive about the learning experience. All respondents felt that the mock trial learning simulation was an excellent learning experience and rated it high (94%) for critical thinking applications. In addition, 97% preferred learning experiences that supported critical thinking. Respondents indicated a preference (91%) for critical thinking activities over memorization.

In addition, 100% of the respondents preferred critical thinking learning and case study applications, and 94% preferred learning experiences that required the application of basic concepts. The related issues of meaningful problem solving scored a 97% respondent response, and knowledge applications to scenarios scored 97%. In addition, 100% agreed that case studies helped develop critical thinking skills.

The survey strategy is useful in obtaining participant reaction to critical thinking, problem solving, and mock trial learning strategies. The survey asked participants if their skills improved because of the suppression hearing and mock court learning simulation, signaling opportunities to provide feedback concerning the training experience.

Focus Points

In summary, mock trial active learning strategies encourage:

- **Problem solving**
- **Decision making**
- **Critical thinking skill applications**

Basic active learning concepts emphasize cooperative instructional environments that encourage learner interaction and mutual learning experiences. Participants build the experience necessary for trial procedures after several rehearsals during suppression hearings.

Simulations represent training models that reflect realistic field situations. Scenario roles approximate criminal justice system responsibilities and interactions. The simulation mirrors prescribed laws and procedures. The moot court simulation acknowledges the premise that participants learn best when directly involved with their own active learning.

Simulations offer opportunities for realistic role applications that support critical thinking and decision making. Role-play presents opportunities to practice social interaction skills in realistic, but controlled situations. Instructors take responsibility for classroom leadership, demonstrate enthusiasm for task achievement, coach players, and provide guidance during the simulation process.

Instructors distribute brief scenario descriptions, and brief participants regarding role-play responsibilities. Learners perform within the confines of the simulation and create the scene. The objective is to practice skill applications related to lesson content. Instructors create safe, non-threatening learning climates. They serve as mentors during the development of positive courtroom and expert witness skills.

Simulations require procedures and rules; however, role players create alternate strategies within operating constraints. Clear goals, performance objectives, and immediate feedback represent essential ingredients for success.

Conclusion

Select participants view the Mock Trial Simulation as a professional "calling," sensing fulfillment and meaning from their contribution, including future service to their community and nation. Learner applications offer opportunities to expand significant understanding and develop peak performance. Supreme efforts lay the foundation for future success and personal recognition. Chapter 8: Peak Performance Training provides pathways for triumphing over challenges.

Part IV: Connecting the Leadership Pathways

"Self-confidence is the first requisite to great undertakings."
— Samuel Johnson

LAW ENFORCEMENT TRAINING

PART IV: CONNECTING THE PATHWAYS!

TRAINING FOR PEAK PERFORMANCE PATHWAY

STUDENT GUIDANCE AND REFERRAL PATHWAY

PULLING IT ALL TOGETHER PATHWAY

EPILOUGE: SELF-ASSESSMENT REVIEW

Connecting Training Dots	Guidepost Pathways

Peak Performance Training
• Define Peak Performance
• Types of Peak Performance
• Peak Performance Training
• Flow, Excellence, Creativity
  & Brainstorming
	• Peak Performance Flow
	• Self, Object & Relationship
	• Experience on the Task
	• Strong Indication to
	  Complete Task
	• Expression of Personal Power
	• Application of Case Studies

Dynamic Guidance: • Counseling & Advising • Interview Stages • Instructor Guidance	• Learner Attitude Problems • Case Study Applications • Counseling Approaches • Student Referrals
Pulling it All Together: • Training Management • Emotional Command Systems • Training Leadership • Positive Training Climate	• Evaluate Training • Training Management • Identify Emotional Command Systems • Johari Window Applications • Bid Busters • Legal Mandates • Self-evaluation Inventories

Figure Part IV-B: Connecting the Leadership Pathways!

CHAPTER 8

Peak Performance Training

"The only person who is educated is the one who has learned how to learn and change."
— Carl Rogers

Focus

The purpose of this chapter is to explore training strategies that lead to total involvement of *flow* and *peak performance*. Striving for *peak performance* and *flow* helps learners reach their full potential. These related concepts lead to other related learning strategies: (1) pursuing excellence and (2) creativity. Peak performance is an important goal because it enhances growth and development.

Overview

Instructors and learners benefit from the dedication and determination of having high standards. Striving for **peak performance** facilitates a sense of creative *flow*. Sport psychologists offer insight concerning *peak performance* and *flow* experiences that transfer to law enforcement training.

Defining Peak Performance

Peak performance represents extraordinary moments when we achieve enhanced self-esteem and concern for excellence. The experience is especially valued when instructors help learners achieve their own personal *peak performance*.

Privette defines peak performance as "behavior that transcends or goes beyond predictable functioning to use a person's potential more fully than could be reasonably expected (1981, p. 58). The task that elicits peak performance represents an intrinsic value to the person and culminates in a direct, active engagement with the valued subject" (1981, p. 64). Peak performance is superior behavior at a task(s), not just a personal experience while occupied in the task(s).

"This suggests that peak performance is not a specific type of activity, but rather a high level of functioning. Peak performance is not specific to any particular context, activity, or situation; it represents the 'full use of any human power.'" (Privette, 1983)

Four *peak performance* parameters include:

- Clear focus on self, object, and relationship
- Intense involvement in the experience
- A strong intention to complete the task
- A spontaneous expression of power

There are two basic levels of the *peak experience.* The first level is **novice peak performance.** For example, a citizen stumbles on an airliner crash and saves passenger lives. Therefore, unusual courage and perseverance is demonstrated at a level beyond the citizen's training and experience. This tragic scenario unfolded spontaneously and without prior planning. In some cases, *peak performance* is not deliberate or planned. Individuals describe a sense of calm, purposeful, and calculatedly focused responses.

The second level of peak performance unfolds subsequent to extensive training and conscious efforts to achieve a *peak performance:* Olympic athletes, first responders, police trainers, and others. Refer to Training Figure 8-1: Defining Peak Performance for an illustration of various components.

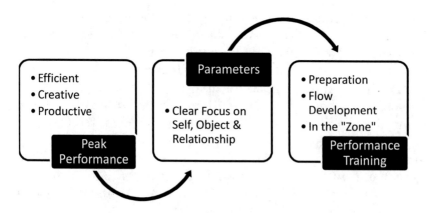

Figure 8-1: Defining Peak Performance

Peak Performance: Level One

Sometimes, inexperienced law enforcement officers achieve greatness. Their peak performance—deliberate "beyond the call duty" actions in a crisis. Some recount slow-moving time, self-confidence, and a sense of optimism in the face of danger. Veteran officers may brush-off a spontaneous response as beginner's luck.

Instructors remember cherished moments when trainees surpass expectations during a Practical Firearms Course, after failing the course ... *twice*. Individuals understand their performance exceeded the norm when awarded the Expert Medal. Everyone recognizes the impressive moment relating to a peak trainee performance.

Peak Performance: Level Two

A law enforcement trainer worked tirelessly for years before experiencing a peak performance while speaking before the Police Academy graduating class. However, some individuals achieve excellence in unpredictable situations. Knowing what triggers a peak performance is difficult to recognize. Refer to Corners: 8-1, 8-2, & 8-3 for opportunities to apply peak performance concepts.

Corner 8-1: Level One – The Mock Trial Prosecutor

The participant is the silent type and never comments or asks questions. He is tall, handsome, and scores at the top of the class on examinations; however, he appears aloof during peer interactions. To the instructor's surprise, he volunteers for the role of mock trial chief prosecutor.

Reluctantly, the instructor approves his request. Concerned the assignment might exceed his grasp, the instructor initiates several inquiries concerning role script progress. The participant assures the instructor that all is well concerning his preparation for the mock trial.

After the preliminary and follow-up investigation, the mock trial prosecutor interviews investigators and witnesses. The stealth-like performance introduces further instructor concerns. The Suppression Hearing date arrives and anxiety soars in anticipation of the mock trial. The prosecutor calls his first witness and performs at an average level; however, he improves with each witness, as a sense of dramatic flow unfolds.

The instructor feels more confident that the prosecutor's presentation is going to be effective, but not necessarily outstanding. *Practice* is extremely important. The prosecutor must be motivated and demonstrate a strong determination to win—focusing on strengths and improving weaknesses. The prosecutor's main weaknesses are low energy and weak voice projection. Several weeks pass and the trial date emerges.

The trial starts with the prosecutor's opening remarks, a near-perfect performance. He clarifies "burden of proof" and outlines how witnesses prove guilt "beyond a reasonable doubt." His words resound sincere and poignant. Everyone is impressed, especially the instructor and judge.

The prosecutor continues to perform with a sense of effortless flow and confidence. He demonstrates clear goals, and plays chess with the defense team during the mock trial challenge. The prosecutor gains positive respect and feedback from peers. He moves outside his comfort zone, finds his calling, an increased sense of well-being, and personal awareness ... *peak performance.*

Direct and redirect examinations unfold with merit. His performance exceeds what you would expect from a learner and approximates an exceptional real-world prosecutor. After closing summation, there is a sense of awe concerning his delivery and timing.

The prosecutor achieves *peak performance*—checkmate after closing rebuttal. Everyone acknowledges team contributions that enhance the enthusiastic performance momentum. The prosecutor motivates participants to reach their personal best. There are no losers on this day—only winners!

Corner 8-1: Critical Thinking Exercise

Examine case study facts and appraise the chapter content. Try to apply peak performance and related concepts.

Corner 8-2: Level Two – The Promising Instructor

Lucid flashbacks haunt a 25-year-old university freshman and future instructor on leave from a local police department. Former military police veterans and trained police officers are not commonplace on a college campus.

He initially evaluates the quality of instruction as *disappointing*. His professor sits behind a desk, reads from the textbook, and seems detached while students doddle and nod off. The snack bar offers learners a refuge from the monotony. However, the officer returns to the abandoned auditorium and glances around elevated layers of tables and chairs ... *I could do this job better than this professor—without even trying!*

The officer returns to law enforcement as a deep undercover investigator after completing two degrees. Soon thereafter, orders require his involvement in a Police Academy presentation on surveillance. He prepares relentlessly; memories of the former professor drive the fear of a similar failure. None the less, he approaches the assignment with self-confidence and optimism.

He arrives early and mingles with trainees who are curious about his undercover role, dress, and demeanor. The goal is to establish rapport before approaching the podium. His deep involvement, commitment, and emotional connection achieve communication links and more.

The detective glances around the room and pauses before speaking.

"Many of you are sitting there thinking that this surveillance lecture does not apply to you. That is what I thought—I was wrong. My replacement is probably in this classroom."

The hook succeeds as a lead-up to the presentation. Attempts to bond with his audience work—*they listen!*

Intense involvement in the surveillance experience serves as a valuable asset. The quality of instruction motivates audience involvement and enthusiasm. The investigator closes the lecture by reviewing basic concepts. Questions emerge and many trainees opt to remain throughout the break. A new learning opportunity serves as an enthusiasm builder.

The new instructor divides trainees into surveillance teams and arranges a field practical exercise. Trainees view photographs and follow two suspects (detectives) through city streets.

Anxious to apply surveillance strategies, they return after following identified suspects successfully. Trainees proudly display the fake cocaine package stashed in the dumpster after the drug transaction exchange.

The instructor's total commitment and dedication fully emerge at summation. He feels a sense of accomplishment when the presentation exceeds expectations. Trainees demonstrate excitement about the learning experience. Applause fills the classroom— hence *peak performance.*

Corner 8-2: Critical Thinking Exercise

Examine the case study facts and appraise chapter content. Apply peak *performance* concepts as applicable.

Corner 8-3: Level Two – Case Study Briefing

Lieutenant Jameson is the ideal investigator when pursuing research and knowledge. She enjoys the chase of investigative facts and applies extraordinary perceptiveness and insight. The lieutenant is mentally alert, curious, and initiates thorough inquiries. Most impressively, she displays foresight, predictive abilities, and little escapes her attention.

She walks to the podium, confident in her investigative abilities. "Good morning gentlemen. For the record, my name is Lieutenant Amanda Jameson. All of you know me as Jamie. I will suspend the formalities and present my analysis in action briefing format."

"Eight homicide cases emerge that indicate Joe Jenson's signature."

Jamie introduces the first crime-mapping slide.

"Our investigation focuses on eight cold cases ... all serial murders and sexual assaults. As you can see, they form a distinct cluster in Central Park and near the affluent part of the city.

The second cluster of hot spots appears near DeKalb Avenue in Brooklyn. Our investigation uncovered that Jenson was born there. Further investigation revealed that he lived in the troubled neighborhood until his early twenties. We used the circle crime mapping method, MO, and signature clues to link the cases."

Captain Thompson leans forward. "Did you find any similarities among the eight cases? For example, did the victims have bite marks ... psychological signature clues?"

"Yes, we also determined other interesting case analysis factors. The escalation of offender violence from strangulation to biting suggests scientific analysis.

"...We have problems with DNA analysis. About 80% of the population falls into the secretors, they have the potential to leave DNA traces in salvia. Traces of saliva appear around bite marks. That's how we located the distinguishable DNA profile."

Jamie pauses for a moment, "None of the seminal fluid retrieved from the crime scenes contained sperm cells. This test result generally occurs in males who have undergone a surgical vasectomy."

Jamie pops up the first actual crime scene slide. "You're now looking at the nude body of the victim who was discovered near a jogging trail. She died of strangulation and multiple stab wounds to the chest.

"...The blow fly eggs collected from the wounds indicate no embryonic development. You can check the timeline out with our forensic entomologist.

"... A police interview canvass of individuals found in and around the park revealed that – the victim was observed talking to a man in his fifties. In addition, the victim was in contact with her parents that afternoon, prior to her discovery, and murdered during the hours of darkness."

One veteran detective questioned. "Do we have a description on the suspect?"

"Yes ... and I would like to say that it's especially nice to see that you're back on the case."

Jamie offers another slide with a smile of satisfaction. "In case two, we located a unique fingerprint clue. Children playing tag in the park find a partially clothed, deceased woman. That traumatic episode triggers a full-scale homicide investigation.

"... Her skin was extremely fair and the bloody fingerprint impression formed a red portrait. CSI set up a superglue tent over the victim and located several prints on her thighs.

"... The fingerprint examiner photographed the print and located ten-ridge characteristics on one thumbprint. Then he conducted a computer search and got a hit on our suspect."

"I'll bet that was Lenny Camp ... he's the best."

"You're right, Captain. He *is* remarkable ... *bulldog tenacity.*"

Jamie presents the third and the most gruesome slide of the series. "Another nude woman, found on a rooftop in the Bed-Sty area, strangled to death with her blouse. She was older than the rest of the victims, but attractive, with multiple post-mortem stab and bite wounds.

"... It is possible that the killer was surprised that he picked an older woman ... she did not fit his usual victim profile. In any case, it was probably too late to change his mind."

The Captain expresses another opinion. "On the other hand, perhaps the killer's victim profile has evolved and her age no longer matters."

"One of our CSI staff flashed her body with ultraviolet light and detected saliva. The close proximity to the bite marks suggested a possible DNA source for laboratory examination.

"... We have test results," Jamie said. "Nevertheless, the lab will have to connect crime scene DNA evidence to the suspect. They cannot compare the results without a saliva sample from our suspect. He may be a secretor."

The Captain leans forward. "No problem. I think we can provide that as soon as we locate Jenson."

"I'm sure we will find a way ... I can run through these other cases, but they don't have the same hard and physical evidence."

"You're right Jamie. We need to get the facts together for an arrest and search warrant. The word on the street is he supports and visits his mother on a regular basis. We hope to arrest him during one of our stakeouts."

Jamie displays her usual "The End" conclusion slide. "Let's break for lunch. I will go over the gory details when we come back. Eat light ... the afternoon presentation gets gruesome."

The Captain approaches the podium. "Jamie, you're in flow and glowing with confidence. *We're impressed.*"

"Thank you Captain ... I appreciate your comments."

The presentation was a peak performance.

Corner 8-3: Critical Thinking Exercise

Examine the case study facts and appraise the chapter content. Apply as many peak performance concepts as possible.

Peak Performance Training

Sports psychologists develop training programs for athletes—efforts to develop potential peak performance. Garfield and Bennett (1984) found eight conditions that accompany exceptional performance (Williams, 1993):

- Mentally relaxed, sense of calm, high concentration, and often the perception that time slows down
- Physical relaxation—loose and fluid movements
- Self-confidence and optimism even in the face of challenges
- Focus and a sense that one's body performs automatically
- High energy level along with positive emotions, such as joy, as well as a sense of being "hot" or "charged"
- Extraordinary awareness of one's own body
  - Often accompanied by an uncanny ability to know what the other athletes are going to do
  - The ability to respond to them instantly
- A sense of total control without undue effort to create or maintain that control
- "In the cocoon"
  - Refers to a sense that one is in an envelopment that allows one to be protected from distractions
  - Allows easy access to one's powers and skills

The following outline serves as a possible source for transferring the conditions to law enforcement instruction. Beginning with flow, or being "in the zone," sports psychologist Jackson and Csikszentmihalyi (1999) offer practical suggestions that support enhanced performance:

- Move beyond one's comfort zone
- Challenge obstacles
- Believe in one's skills
- Stop nagging self-doubt
- Focus on the process or moment-by-moment activity
- Be self-aware, not self-conscious
- "Set the stage" or accomplish necessary preliminary preparations before competition
- Practice a simple meditation exercise to help focus on the present and control unnecessary and distractive thinking

The *flow concept* seems to merge with *peak performance*. However, some subtle differences begin to emerge when sport psychologists differentiate the two concepts. A difference exists between what one experiences as being in the *zone or flow* and what it takes to improve performance. These concepts transfer to the application of law enforcement training. The following paragraphs explore the function of training in developing the *flow* experience.

The Flow Experience

Csikszentmihalyi (1975) defines the *flow* concept after many interviews and subject response analysis. He offers insightful observations regarding psychological well-being. Subjects describe how it felt when doing something enjoyable and the activity was going well. The results paint an astonishing verbal portrait of moments when everything flows in perfect harmony. The following paragraph describes Csikszentmihalyi's definition:

Flow denotes the holistic sensation present when we act with total involvement ... It is the state in which action follows upon action according to an internal logic, which seems to need no conscious intervention on our part. We experience it as a unified flowing from one moment to the next, in which we feel in control of our actions, and in which there is little distinction between self and environment; between stimulus and response; or between past, present, and future (p.43).

In summary, Csikszentmihalyi describes a *flow experience* as maximizing complete concentration, attention, and awareness. In addition, the individual entirely focuses on the activity. This focus allows the individual to feel as if they are in complete control of their actions. Their concentration feels effortless without nervous tension or aggressive effort to control or suppress thinking. There is a loss of self-consciousness during *flow*.

Time appears to pass quickly or it may appear as slowed down. During many occasions, time seems to slow down, as the person tends to feel a state of relaxation. There is a lack of anxiety about making the next decision. Flow is an altered state of consciousness that produces effective decision-making.

Csikszentmihalyi believes building a sense of flow results in a personal challenging situation. The challenging activity pushes one's skill level; then, the required concentration can induce the *flow* experience. If demands are high and skill levels are low, the person will generally feel anxiety. If demands are low and skills high, the person feels bored. Flow is possible when the situation demands a challenge to the person's skills.

Chasing Excellence

Excellence defines extreme personal performance efforts that demand practiced expertise and the application of related skills. Organizations occasionally apply the term *excellence* to the services they provide. The implication is that excellence is learned. Undoubtedly, the expression is relevant to creative training and instructional strategies.

The Resonance Performance Model (RPM) Newberg et al. (2002) is a four-stage model that begins with (1) "The dream or the feelings a person seeks when engaged in an activity. This is not a goal for the future, but a sense of what the person wishes to feel like in the present. (2) The person must be involved intensely and engage in preparation. This stage involves intense practice, but it is engaged practice rather than drudgery.

Inevitably, a person encounters (3) "Obstacles." In the RPM, however, when obstacles are encountered, one does not simply try harder. That is, a person does not necessarily believe that "When the going gets tough, the tough get going." Instead, she or he (4) "Revisits their dream," or reconnects with the feelings that give spark to their dream. This reconnection with original feelings allows a person to embrace the obstacles, to avoid the trap of trying harder and enjoying it less, and to move forward with the development of skills. RPM offers one system to help people achieve excellence in a number of areas.

Instructors who pursue *excellence* incorporate advanced performance behaviors. Professional performance reflects motivation and commitment. Instructors who do extremely well on *excellence* are committed to the learning process and apply resolve to prevail even in the face of adversity. Their commitment is to discover and apply dynamic instructional strategies with consistency.

Chasing Creativity

What do we mean by *creativity*? The quest for a simple definition baffles psychologists. One definition suggests a process that produces novel responses that contribute to the solution of problems (Simonton, 2000).

Creativity requires "dreaming the dream" in pursuance of positive images. Inspired dreams and images generally unfold at night or at unexpected moments and quickly vanish. Record the experience when you awaken or in the moment; hesitation may result in lost insight.

The *confluence model* proposed by Lubart and Sternberg (1995) states that six resources need to work together in creativity:

- Intellectual abilities
- Knowledge
- Personality traits
- Motivational style
- Thinking styles
- An environment that is supportive of the creative process and creative output

Tardif and Sternberg (1988) summarize research and group creativity studies into four general areas:

- Creative person
- Creative process
- Creative products
- Creative environments

Those we label "genius" demonstrate similar qualities associated with people who achieve excellence in their field. They are extremely dedicated and committed to their area of expertise, motivated, and willing to work long and hard – absorbed in the search for knowledge about their craft. They are so intensely involved in their work that they may appear self-absorbed. In contrast to those who are creative (but not geniuses), geniuses tend to exhibit extremely high levels of self-confidence.

Creative instructors are intensely interested in their field and are willing to work hard. Generally, it takes instructors three or more years to develop dynamic approaches to training. Creativity generally takes time; however, insight gleaned from *experiences* can jump-start the dynamic instructor approach.

Brainstorming: Striving for Creativity

Brainstorming applies a creative problem-solving process. The final product is to produce practical recommendations, and represent a group effort that includes four to five participants. The instructor introduces the topic and reviews the brainstorming problem-solving process.

Assigned group members review instructor-generated problem scenarios. The *brainstorming* process works best when problems overlap. Integrate and explore solution connections at the end of the session. The comfortable learning environment accommodates group members; however, dividing the groups into individual locations helps circumvent detractions.

Groups receive problems—members document solutions without prior evaluation and post observations for viewing. Participants discuss group options and settle on the best solution.

Instructors support *brainstorming* sessions by stating performance objectives and rules for participation; encourage participation in a nonjudgmental exchange of ideas; and recognize nonverbal communication cues and stimulate passive participation. Members collect suggestions without prejudice regarding significance or correctness. Everyone encourages diverse opinions and conclusions.

Each group assigns two scribes to record session discussions and suggestions. They record recommendations for future presentation. One participant serves as moderator and presenter; their assignment is to coordinate problem-solving ideas. The instructor keeps time and allows 30 minutes for group discussions.

The instructor introduces the groups and tasks them to present their findings. The final step is group solution presentations. Groups vote on favored solutions during brainstorming sessions, distinguishing between free-floating ideas and those that produce favorable options. Instructors connect the learning solution dots.

Brainstorming requires accomplished instructors who support open and flexible learning environments. Suggestions require non-threatening social settings. Participants understand the process and enhance individual recognition.

Ultimately, the *critique* is a method of clarifying, emphasizing, or reinforcing basic concepts and critical thinking skills. The instructional emphasis is on freethinking and mutually agreed-upon solutions—incorrect responses do not incur negative consequences. Consequently, the critique is an effective procedure for informing participants of their problem-solving progress, assessing solutions, and providing constructive feedback.

In summary, the criteria for **brainstorming** evaluation include:

- **Creative solutions to problems**
- **Participation of all group members**
- **Novel solutions**
- **Valuable ideas**
- **Trust**
- **Non-punitive social environments**

Focus Points

Instructors recognize a *peak performance*; it appears on the faces of their audience. Accurate perceptions lead to constructive feedback and the opportunity to achieve a *peak performance*. Instructors acknowledge the positive result with enthusiasm and pride. Persistent and consistent efforts concerning training issues enhance creativity and opportunities for successful outcomes.

Creative instructors aspire to introduce imaginative approaches. The ability to engage in creative thinking is associated with supportive leadership climates. Training environments can facilitate an agreeable openness that allows creativity to flourish through collaborative efforts. In addition, basic resources and brainstorming cooperate to increase creativity.

The first component of genuine *excellence* is law enforcement knowledge. Excellence is the ability to apply insightful learning strategies. Prepared instructors discover learning solutions earlier. *Practice* serves another important component in the achievement of excellence and superior performance.

Practice sessions are extremely important in the development of expertise. *Peak performances* and *flow* experiences are more likely to occur during practical exercises or simulations. Accomplishments may exceed expectations.

Listen to your intuition and triumph over new frontiers. When you start something new, you can choose to either put yourself down and succumb to the inner critic or enjoy the process of personal growth. Focus on the moment and immerse yourself in the positive creative flow of skill practice.

Personal achievement starts in your mind. Training knowledge assists in anticipating the expectations and creating new training cycles and innovative trends are always possible. Through training preparation, you bring into play training imagination.

Peak performance compels you to seek and achieve an exceptional action—*excellence*. Moreover, you enhance your ability to initiate peak performance at will.

Conclusion

Immerse your senses in your surroundings, seek challenging tasks, learn something new, and nourish your strengths and passions. Like athletes training for peak performance, when you visualize something extraordinary, you can embrace it with more intensity. Gratitude for earned accomplishments opens your mind to the possibility of further positive reinforcement. Believe it is possible, and then you can accomplish it—dare to aim high! Chapter 9: Leadership Counseling provides a pathway for learners to achieve peak performance.

CHAPTER 9

Leadership Counseling

"The attitude of importance in creating a climate for change is acceptance, or caring, or prizing—what I call "unconditional positive regard."
— Carl R. Rogers

Focus

Generally, the literature on *counseling* offers three options:

- Help others make prudent choices and decisions
- Support emotional adjustments
- Promote mental health

This chapter emphasizes counseling or advising on improving or modifying learner choices and decisions concerning training progress. In addition, the counseling/advisement process focuses on:

- Requests for assistance
- Helping connections
- The referral process

Overview

Chapter content describes basic counseling approaches that support learner decision-making. This approach analyzes learner behaviors, assessment, and instructor listening skills. In addition, the content examines some instructor leadership advising, counseling, and guidance proficiencies. Promote diagnostic or mental health adjustments by referral; seek assistance from trained professionals.

Counseling/Advising Foundations

Training, counseling, and the advisement process require helping relationships directed at an improvement or change in learner behavior. This form of instructor/advisee counseling includes preliminary steps:

- Establishing a mentoring relationship
- Learner self-exploration
- Adjustment to the problem

Instructors apply active listening skills, responses, and reflective questioning. This form of communication requires respect and genuine consideration.

Instructors help learners gain self-understanding once relationship foundations are in place—no easy task. Two factors affect the process: (1) defensive behaviors and (2) denial or blockage. Pondering problems is not enough; solutions require acceptance and behavioral changes. Learners may recognize their issues but fail to address them because of emotional barriers.

The final step requires insight into the problem, acceptance, responsibility, and commitment to change. The learner and instructor must agree to a plan of action for resolving the problem. Alternate plans need reviewing, along with consequences for learner choices. Learners select one planning option, highlighting the achievement of attainable goals, objectives, and positive outcomes. Observable behavior changes indicate positive learner outcomes. Refer to Training Figure 9-1: Advisee Guidance Steps for an illustration of the counseling process.

Advisee Guidance Steps

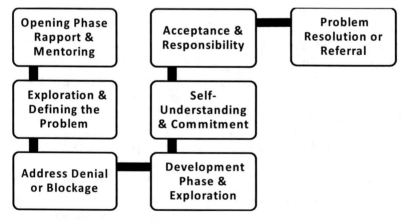

Figure 9-1: Advisee Guidance Steps

Learner Privacy

Confidentiality is the first consideration in the counseling/ advisement process. Learner-seeking impulses will occasionally arise just before or after class, while instructors prepare or collect support items. Restrain impulses to respond to sensitive learner needs publicly. Address privacy concerns, express your willingness to assist, and suggest an immediate appointment.

Learners may reveal intimate, personal information, and occasionally divulge embarrassing predicaments. Sensitive information remains private; learners assume a confidential relationship exists. Instructors are obligated to respect and preserve discretion.

Keep meticulous records of every session. Do not make notes during interviews. Record your observations and conclusions after learner departures. Include problem summaries, action plans, and outcome decisions. Safeguard confidential records under lock and key.

Interview Stages

The counseling interview process has three overlapping phases:

- Opening
- Development (self-exploration, self-understanding, commitment)
- Conclusion

The following paragraphs focus on opening and closing phases.

Opening phase: the emphasis is on rapport. Interviews begin with neutral topics—attempts to encourage understanding with open and friendly dialogue. Provide positive feedback. Be attentive to learner needs and demonstrate genuine interest in their concerns. Refer to Training Figure 9-2: Instructor Professional Attitudes for an illustration of the counseling process.

The best way to achieve rapport and establish positive relationships is *active listening*—avoid ridicule and judgmental comments. Positive leadership and the free expression of ideas enhance learner climates. Supportive environments contribute to

rapport and mutual esteem. Encourage problem-solving exchanges that reduce resistance and encourage future communication. Focus on deciphering learner motives. For example, "I
know you have something important to discuss ... What's on your
mind? How can I help you?"

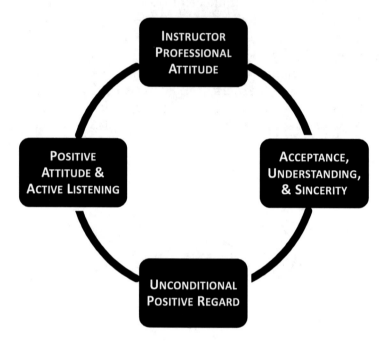

Figure 9-2: Instructor Professional Attitudes

Unsatisfactory performance evaluation discussions are emotionally laden and require instructor understanding, a test of
counseling skills that demands immediate remedial advisement.
Offer support, recommendations, and the hope for corrective
solution success.

Concluding phase: Prepare for closure and avoid encouraging new concerns. However, indicate your willingness to
assist if new issues emerge. Generally, a brief summation ends
the session. Appropriate closures offer opportunities; advisees
leave feeling positive about the counseling experience. Moreover,
a supportive non-threatening environment diminishes any hesitation to seek future assistance.

Instructor Guidance

Performance attitude problems differ from testing issues; the former highlights reasons that influence learner potential. Symptoms include poor attendance, disrespect, poor attention, and attitude issues. Practice test scores decline, followed by failed examinations.

Defining the problem provides a systematic approach for performance assessment. **The two-step process includes:**

- Collecting information
- Determining the cause(s)

Analyze deficits and poor performance motivation. Examples include late arrivals, missed training sessions, and failure to attend the practical exercise. Symptom examinations are priority concerns.

Assessment skills include observing, listening, analyzing, and rapport. Satisfactory interventions require forecasting, reading behaviors, and understanding underlying causes. Instructor forecasting abilities improve when they disregard unconfirmed assumptions and focus on the problem. Accurate assumptions based on fact offer superior solutions. Refer to Training Table 9-1: Advisee Coping Skills—Rating Inventory for an illustration.

Assessing Coping Skills

Assess *coping skills* as soon as possible. Accurate behavioral analysis determines positive outcomes. Positive coping skills become difficult when challenges reach beyond advisee resources. Instructors provide support and guidance. The goal: to motivate practical decision-making and problem-solving behaviors that help advisees cope and adjust to emerging problems.

The process requires a change in performance behaviors: "A response aimed at diminishing the physical, emotional, and psychological burden that is linked to stressful life events and daily hassles" (Snyder & Dinoff, 1999, p. 5). Compas (1987) suggests that coping responses can be clarified by dividing them into three categories:

- **Coping styles**
- **Coping resources**
- **Coping strategies**

Table 9-1: Advisee Coping Skills--Rating Inventory

STUDENT COPING SKILLS: RATING INVENTORY	1	2	3	4	5	6	7	8	9	10
Define the problem and determine the degree of seriousness.										
Three-step process includes: (1) collect information, and (2) determine the cause(s).										
Student problem-focused coping involves the use of realistic strategies that could make a tangible difference in the situation that causes the problem.										
Identify advisee coping strategies.										
The advisee's general attitude is learned helplessness.										
The student's general attitude is learned optimism.										
The advisee has a sense of self-efficacy and believes that they have ability to perform, or the capacity to learn the behaviors necessary to reach their desired goals.										
The advisee psychological thriving includes both enhanced psychological and physical functioning after successful adaptations.										
The advisee is an optimist.										
The advisee exhibits a sense of hardiness.										

Coping styles represent fundamental approaches that learners apply to deal with challenges. Lazarus & Folkman (1984) classify coping styles into three subtypes:

- Attempts to change negative emotions
- Attempts to change the situation that caused the stress
- Seeks to avoid the problem

The related behaviors reflect *emotion-focused coping*, *problem-focused coping*, and *avoidance*. Coping strategies are the more complex behavioral strategies that learners use over time to cope with challenges. According to Lazarus and Folkman (1984), *emotion-focused coping* is "Directed at regulating emotional responses to problems" (p. 150). The goal—to release tension, forget anxiety, eliminate worry—is further divided into two subtypes: (1) cognitive and (2) behavioral. Cognitive emotion-focused coping involves defensive re-appraisals. External resources can help address challenges.

Problem-focused coping involves realistic strategy applications that make a difference in the situation that causes stress. *Problem-focused coping styles* reflect: (1) those directed at changing the situation, (2) those directed at changing self, and (3) coping strategies. The goal of instructional/counseling is to focus on problem-solving solutions.

Seligman (1975) proposes a significant perspective on depression and the *theory of learned helplessness*. Sometimes, when faced with seemingly inescapable stressors, people learn to respond with helplessness and expect defeat. Later, he proposes the opposite response, *learned optimism* (Seligman, 1990). Seligman suggests that those who focus on the positive and the possible can learn to respond to stressors with an attitude of optimism and hope.

Kobasa (1979) examined coping resources by looking at physical illness as an indicator of poor coping. She differentiated a group with high stress and low illness from a group with high stress and high illness. She used the term *hardiness* to describe those in the high stress and low illness group who coped better.

Some learners thrive when confronted with challenge; in fact, they excel. Ickovics (1995) advocated a process defined as *psychological thriving*. Epel, McEwen, & Ickovics (1998) expanded this concept so that thriving includes both enhanced psychological and physical functioning after successful adaptations. As a general statement, we can say that *optimists* tend to have better health outcomes than *pessimists* (Peterson, Seligman, & Vaillant, 1988).

Learners who make positive behavior changes apply a sense of *self-efficacy*. Instructors define performance change requirements and provide pathway destinations. Bandurs (1977) suggests that individuals initiate behavior changes if they have specific beliefs and expectations about effectiveness. *Self-efficacy* is the belief that one has the ability to perform, or the capacity to learn, the behaviors necessary to reach desired goals.

Positive coping strategies vary among learners; a few may need additional support and counseling. Solutions may involve helping others identify the way they view problems and give meaning to events; some exhibit a sense of *hardiness* and *coherence*. Problem identification and causation begins the process, followed by understanding how the learner reacts to stressful events. *Coping skills* improve with the right professional attitude, guidance, and support.

Advisor Attitudes

Instructors adapt attitude behaviors to individual case scenarios. They communicate acceptance, understanding, and sincerity. Body language and facial expressions convey attitudes.

Acceptance describes an essential component of the counseling/advising relationship. Learners experience compassion and understanding. *Acceptance* infers tolerance and encourages a change in behavior—the ultimate goal.

Listen to expressed thoughts and feelings regarding concerns; this serves to gain broader perspectives. Only then will the instructor be in a position to express and reflect the learner's situation correctly—*empathy.*

Empathy is often defined in metaphors: "walking in someone else's shoes," or "seeing something through someone else's eyes." In other words, the advisor has the capacity to understand and acknowledge the emotions of others. Empathy implies compassion and a willingness to help someone in need.

Effective *tending behaviors* include making eye contact that demonstrates acceptance, respect—non-judgmental postures. Responding skills allow communication without relying on overbearing questions. For example, restating the elements of a conversation can help clarify or interpret what the learner said.

Refection techniques assist in clarifying emotional content. For example, the learner's bid for communication might disclose ...

"I just got a call. My father had a heart attack and is being transported to the hospital! I don't know what to do."

"I'm sorry ... and understand the circumstances. You need to meet your family at the hospital, and not worry about class. I'll email the notes to you tonight ... stop by my office if you have questions."

"Thanks!"

"Let me know if there's anything else I can do. I hope all goes well."

The instructor demonstrates that he understands the meaning behind the bid for attention—*he listened.* The bid is addressed quickly—a direct intervention that acknowledges the urgency of the situation. The instructor reflects the learner's concerns; anxiety lessens when needs are addressed and problem-solving solutions unfold.

Countless advisee challenges surface in the learning environment. Diverse personality patterns emerge; however, one predetermined response evades practitioners. Instructional leadership/guidance requires openness, understanding, active listening, and flexibility.

Learner Attitude Patterns

Learner attitudes reveal the presence or absence of enthusiasm for the learning process and may reflect apathy toward the instructor, subject matter, or training program. Instructors respond by conducting personal assessments.

Poor attitudes are destructive to the learning climate and can become contagious—initiating negative collective behaviors. Instructor virtues embrace patience and understanding. They must find the root cause of the behaviors and initiate the motivation to change. Learner frustrations may facilitate angry outbursts—remain calm in the midst of emotional storms—*listen.* Emotional climates often require sustained endurance and calm reassurance.

Starting points for resolving learning problems include—*assessment and feedback.* This requires understanding attitudes that affect learner/instructor relationships. Universal advisee behaviors patterns emerge; however, combinations, exceptions, and specific situations unfold.

Problem learners bring emotional issues to the instructional process. They have unresolved emotional problems that interfere with their ability to identify with authority figures. Their problems may stem from unsolved emotional trauma or former teachers. They resist the learning process and may try to sabotage instructors and learning environments—requiring further attention, supervision, coaching, and counseling.

Disability learners do not always acknowledge personal limitations in the training environment for fear of discrimination and peer acceptance. Disabilities may be mild to moderate; however, they can cause performance problems in training or field situations. Generally, some form of accommodation or compensation may overcome limitations.

Dependent learners require direction, guidance, and appreciate structure in the learning process. They generally expend minimum effort and learn only the basic requirements, often passive—allowing others to lead the way in study groups. Instructors initiate close supervision to achieve optimal training abilities.

Independent learners function best without interference from instructors or other learners. They are self-motivated and have a preference to control the learning process – offer opportunities that allow independent learners to find self-prescribed learning pathways.

Creative learners enjoy the education journey process. They are lifetime learners and future instructors. Their incentive is the discovery of new information in a sincere quest to engage training content. They exceed instructional requirements and impose self-regulation and personal assessment.

Informal learners are cooperative and solicit interaction with group members, achieving considerable influence over peers, companionship is important. Their incentive is to gain instructor and peer admiration and establish rapport with leaders early on. They have the potential to influence others; an adversarial relationship could result in negative consequences.

Learning behavior styles affect group dynamics and instructor interventions. Learners may vacillate from independent to dependent behaviors, depending on lesson expectation. Timely assessments and appropriate interventions offer positive opportunities to address fluid learner behaviors.

Motivation initiates success. Learners do not have to be *great* to start … but they have to *start* to be great. The journey to achieve peak performance is exhausting and demanding. Non-compliance offers comfort and can serve as a reward.

Mistakes often accompany sincere attempts to succeed. Reinforce positive initiatives. Apathy flourishes in environments where participants are not motivated to care about consequences or outcomes. Reinforce positive behaviors that learners are likely to repeat. Negative reinforcement is most helpful when it is non-threatening and addresses a specific behavior.

Resistance to the learning process is a downward spiral that requires immediate remedial action. Readiness to perform tasks influences performance. Therefore, the instructor assessment should include:

- Prior knowledge
- Maturity
- Experience

These factors represent an initial step towards mission achievement. Encourage learners to transfer previous knowledge skills to new situations. Creativity unfolds when learners apply old skills to new skills using a fresh approach or perspective.

Prior knowledge assessment helps avoid "talking down to" or patronizing learners. In addition, instructors devise pathways to address limitations and initiate skill-building activities. Practice enhances feelings of confidence and the motivation to move forward, apply new skills, and learn additional positive behaviors.

Corner 9-1: Learner Case Study Problems

Case Study 1: Jake Moorefield finds the learning task(s) monotonous; there are no consequences for not performing. In addition, instructor feedback does not motivate improved performance.

Solution 1:

- Identify rewarding remedies that motivate enhanced performance.
- Impose consequences that make poor performance less rewarding.
- Offer positive consequences that motivate continued effort.

Case Study 2: Family members constantly remind Helen Jacobs that they feel abandoned by her study time demands. Shift work schedules frequently conflict with class sessions. More re-

cently, she experiences health problems that require hospitaliza-
tion. Family life and job obstacles increase frustration and impact
academic performance.

Solution 2:

- Initiate appropriate and supportive referrals.
- Offer make-up class sessions.
- Active listening and helpful suggestions may initiate
  positive solutions.
- Self-assessment may assist in problem-solving solutions.

Special Note: Refer to Chapter 5: Training Performance
Feedback for information on correcting learner task performance.

Corner 9-1: Problem-Solving Exercise

Analyze the two following case study illustrations. Define the
problem and assess performance using a four-step process:

- **Collect information**
- **Determine the cause**
- **Document performance**
- **Find the correct solution**

How would you improve analysis and recommend solutions to
address performance problems?

Each problem is unique; therefore, selecting one preferred
option or combination of options requires effective instructor judgment. Solutions become apparent in the light of exploratory fact
examinations; instructors are ready to develop corrective plans
for remedial action. Successful interventions offer realistic options and alternatives, support, the hope for success, and flexibility.

Insight into the instructor's own possibility of an error in
judgment is essential to positive learner/advisee outcomes.
Instructor errors are less likely when the mentor is patient,
observant, knowledgeable, compassionate, and has a sense of
integrity and empathy.

Corner 9-2: Case Study Learner Problem

Sandra Wilkins is intelligent and excels in basic Academy Training Center practical exercises. However, she fails a written examination without explaining her poor performance. Prior to that incident, she coached learners that were having academic problems. Wilkins seems to enjoy time spent on practical exercises and mentoring peers.

The instructor comments publicly about her helpfulness and relies on her superior performance abilities during and after class sessions. She defines the helping process as more rewarding and appealing than the mere memorization of facts. Sandra rationalizes that the instructor will "take care of her" as payment for her assistance. She concludes that the instructor will acknowledge her devotion to him and the other trainees by documenting an excellent final grade for the class.

Corner 9-2: Problem-Solving Exercise

Identify the problem, behavior attitude, and possible causes for the learner's performance problem. Does the instructor have a role?

Referral Strategies

The *referral process* includes seeking the support of qualified professionals who help learners with serious emotional problems. Infrequently, instructors/counselors encounter learners who have special needs that are not associated with training objectives or environments. Stress related issues might emerge that include divorce, financial worries, health issues, alcohol abuse, emotional disturbances, and so on. Their plea for help is beyond instructor expertise.

Establish a list of professional referral options before suggesting a course of action, that is, a police psychologist or qualified staff member. Crisis encounters demand an immediate and appropriate response. This is especially the case when addressing possible violence, suicidal ideation, and field-related post-traumatic stress disorders. One very important concept: violence can be turned *inward* or *outward*. Both consequences are dire and demand immediate intervention. Refer to Training Figure 9-3:

Counseling Referral Strategies for an illustration and overview of this process.

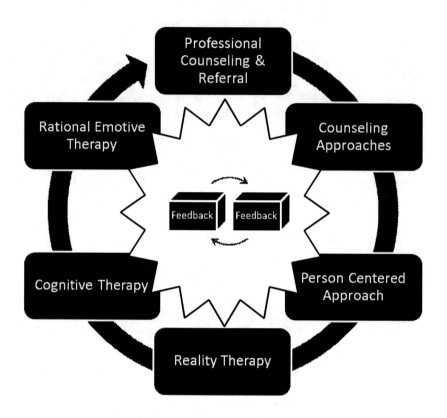

Figure 9-3: Counseling Referral Strategies

Counseling Approaches

Support systems offer guidelines for establishing priorities, goals, and objectives. Counseling theories and applications prove useful when developing an advisory/guidance approach. Collectively, they all stress one common denominator: *relationship*. The helping relationship provides opportunities to initiate positive referral outcomes.

Rogers (1980) recommends the ***"Person Centered Counseling Approach."*** This approach is non-directive and person centered. The focus is on active listening and allows individuals to determine what is important. This thought-reflective style assumes advisees have the ability to solve their problems. The friendly, non-directive approach serves as a rapport builder in the interview process.

The counselor's point of view is not important; the advisee must resolve the conflict. The seemingly logical choice may not necessarily be the correct internal decision. The learner/advisee has the freedom to make a decision without fearing the loss of the counselor's personal regard and relationship. Rogers (1980) suggests three basic tenants or conditions that must be present for improved climate and growth-promoting behaviors:

- The first attitude is genuineness, realness, or congruence. The counselor offers no professional front or façade. There is greater probability that the person will change and grow.
- The second attitude is "unconditional positive regard." The positive acceptance of the person will improve the impetus for change to unfold.
- The third attitude facilitates a relationship that is empathic and understanding. The counselor senses another's feelings and their meaning, providing accurate feedback, clarification, and communicating unconscious meaning. Active listening, on the part of the counselor, is essential to the process.

Client-centered counselors view people as essentially purposeful and self-directed. Positive counseling relationships provide supportive environments that permit self-understanding and self-acceptance. The enhancement of self-concept leads to self-actualization, a higher state of personal development. These outcomes are central to person-centered counseling.

Ellis (1998) pioneered and founded *Rational Emotive Behavior Therapy* (REBT). This form of therapy differs in that it differentiates between healthy behaviors, negative emotions, and unhealthy negative emotions. For example, healthy negative emotions are sorrow, regrets, and frustration. Unhealthy negative emotions include panic, depression, rage, feelings of worthlessness, and self-pity. The latter are particularly dysfunctional, especially for law enforcement personnel.

REBT targets irrational, demanding, and excessive perfectionist belief systems. For example, one self-defeating pattern
is to expect that everyone will love you. Perfectionist behaviors
can produce disturbing mood patterns. The goal is to encourage
learners to substitute rational and less demanding thoughts.

Ellis made significant observations regarding irrational
thinking that relate to effective contemporary interventions. The
ABC theory of emotions has potential impact for law enforcement
learners confronting stressful events. In many cases, the hope-
lessness, helplessness, and haplessness of the law enforcement
personnel represent irrational thinking. The helper must disrupt
irrational thinking and communicate illogical consequences. The
objective is to provide temporary insight that permits an appropriate treatment.

The ABC theory unfolds:

- "A" is the *activating event* (Firearms training)
- "B" represents the *belief system* (I am not going to
  qualify on the firing range)
- "C" represents the *consequence(s)*
- "A" does not cause "C," *irrational beliefs* (IBs) cause:
  "C"

Thus, the activating event does not cause the consequence(s).
The learner's irrational belief system defines activating events
that cause consequences. Therefore, the learner's emotional
perception of an event, not the event itself, can determine an
outcome. Learners who believe they will fail to qualify may
accomplish their self-fulfilling prophesy of failure. Present
evidence that introduces logical methods of disputing irrational
beliefs.

Glasser's (1998) **Reality Therapy** suggests that, in their
unsuccessful efforts to meet and fulfill their needs, people engage
in a variety of unrelated behaviors and dysfunctional symptoms.
Assist the learner in accepting reality and provide support. The
basic concept: people will be successful when they give up denying
the world around them. They must face reality; provide coping
skills for acceptance. "Responsibility, a concept basic to Reality
Therapy, is defined as the ability to fulfill one's needs, and to do

so in a way that does not deprive others of the ability to fulfill their needs," Glasser (1975).

Glasser believes that universal principles guide the decision-making process. He notes commonsense principles:

- We need people in our lives, at least one person who cares for us, and we care for them.
- The more caring people in our lives, the better, especially when the relationships are reciprocal.
- Personal insight is important; people must be in touch with reality and fulfill their own needs within the world.

Counseling Applications

The Person-Centered Approach is especially effective when a learner is struggling with internal conflict. For example, the learner has mixed feelings over course requirements and family illness responsibilities. She is considering withdrawing from the training program.

Some instructors identify with Roger's Person-Centered Approach and view it as an essential mentoring technique. They favor establishing a strong relationship with learners that allows them to resolve their own problems. This approach advocates that counselor attitudes toward learners are more important than counseling techniques. Focus in on the learner, rather than the counselor.

Some instructor/counselors prefer the Rational-Emotive Theory based on illogical or irrational thinking that offers hope. The major foundation for these theories is that emotions control our thinking. Important to this point of view: emotional behaviors stem from self-talk or negative dialogue. A cycle of negativity soon becomes an everyday emotional climate. Assist learners in their journey to control illogical thinking, negative dialogue, and self-destructive emotions.

For example, a trainee may have difficulty on the firing range; negative self-talk persists: *"I'll never qualify ... my hand shakes too much! I know I am going to be dismissed for not passing the shooting range requirement. I'm nothing but a loser."* The trainee continues to imagine the worst possible outcome, creating a cycle of anxiety and poor performance.

Negative self-talk encourages outcomes you are trying to avoid. Focusing on faulty reasoning leads to indentifying what stands in the way of successful performance. Learners modify negative thoughts to positive and learn to control their emotions.

Focus Points

Definitions vary according to experts; however, one theme emerges. Counseling is a helping process directed at establishing successful decision-making and learner performance improvement—*learning is a change in behavior*.

The best indicators for improvement include instructor observations that assess acceptable behavior outcomes. Simply expressing aspirations for change is inadequate; observable evidence is the criteria. Another primary counseling/advising goal: lead advisees toward learner independence. Successful interventions encourage opportunities to recognize personal interests and needs.

A guidance approach suggests service to every learner, not just those who exhibit problems. If the guidance approach focuses only on problem learners, others will avoid the service because of the fear of some stigma or labeling process.

The counseling/guidance component of instructor responsibilities is difficult and time intensive. Focus on successful remedies and learner-assisted solutions. Successful instructors have a genuine interest in helping learners succeed. Key role requirements include knowledge, good judgment, patience, interpersonal skills, and the ability to communicate genuine concern.

The learner must feel free to express feelings and thoughts without retaliation or judgmental comments. Reserve comments until the learner hesitates or experiences emotional blocks. Sometimes, a brief question breaks protracted silence that appears to create an uncomfortable pause in communication.

Avoid becoming involved in problems beyond your range of guidance capabilities and responsibilities. Instructor/counselors are advisors; some intervention solutions may require additional expertise and preparation. Referral is a necessary component of the advising process. It protects *you* as well as a learner who might be in crisis. The use of an appropriate referral does not diminish your competence … it demonstrates strength and good judgment. It is important to remember that the goal is to address learner needs; sometimes that need requires support outside your area of expertise.

Referrals do not imply abandonment. Instructors conduct follow-ups to see if advisee needs are being addressed properly. Instructors who express concern demonstrate continued support. Confidentiality and discreet privacy remain essential requirements that enhance a supportive environment.

Conclusion

The application of appropriate interviewing skills is an important consideration. Positive training climates enhance advisement session rapport. Effective counseling offers a positive impact on learners; therefore, instructors need to prepare for that role. Effective leadership is inclusive—the related positive influence motivates successful trainer interventions and outcomes. Chapter 10: Dynamic Leadership: Pulling it All Together provides a pathway to the synchronization of training advisement and management strategies.

CHAPTER 10

Dynamic Leadership: Pulling it All Together

"One does not become enlightened by imagining the figures of light, but by making the darkness conscious."
— Carl G. Jung

Focus

Instructional strategies offer pathways to mission performance. Training supports the mission; furthermore, it cultivates motivation and morale. The training management process ensures high-quality units of instruction, logical order, and defines learning outcomes. The purpose of this chapter is to explore interpersonal communication and conditions that lead to dynamic training.

Overview

Curriculum managers and instructional leaders monitor lesson progress with learning performance outcomes. Deviations from prescribed objective accomplishments require corrective action. Leadership, mentoring, guidance, and supervision unfold with frequent curriculum assessment. The following topics communicate advanced training skills:

- Training Management Coordination
- Emotional Command Systems
- Johari Window
- Positive Training Program Development

Training Management Coordination

Training leadership and management provide guidance for achieving positive learning outcomes, a significant leadership function. The training program mission: to offer quality programming that promotes law enforcement expertise and field experiences. Dare to aim high!

Lay the proper foundation for successful dynamic training. The first step to successful program management—*train the trainers.* The second step—*prioritize training needs and require-ments.* Practice makes perfect; practice develops skills by experi-ence or practical exercise.

The power that changes the training curriculum remains *thought!* Power grows with use ... the more you think, the more you can think. Believe in your own triumph, then you will become successful. Have the courage to face the truth about limitations and seize the moment to initiate corrective actions. Do the right thing because it is right. Leadership is the compass and planning provides pathways to success. Refer to Figure 10-1 Curriculum Management for an illustration.

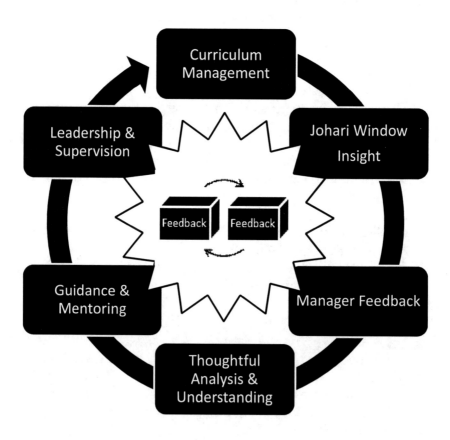

Figure 10-1: Curriculum Management

Inspiration leads to action, the most important component to success. Inspiration can occur spontaneously if you are open to the experience. Law enforcement officers who inspire to achievement overcome obstacles, imagine new pathways, and enter the unknown! Start from a specific destination and forge ahead until you reach your goal.

Coaching Training Staff Members

Dynamic training requires innovative thinking and self-directed coaching behaviors. Positive outcomes emerge when training staff members are properly coached and motivated. Training managers encourage successful coaching behaviors that ultimately motivate staff members. Training managers also identify and define tasks staff trainers must accomplish.

Coaching training staff is an art directly related to mentoring; however, the coach must be discreet, a master of diplomacy. A low profile approach enhances communication, beaks down barriers, and increases openness. The approach may be directive at times, but usually, non-directive. The coached staff member must trust the manager's judgment and experience, whose advice must be competent and concrete.

The most effective coaching method: *use positive* rather than negative motivators. Constructive advice can break down barriers and improve coaching effectiveness, as in the following: "Your job performance in most areas is above average. However, if you made a few changes, you could be one of the top trainers in this law enforcement agency. As an instructor, you have tremendous potential, and if you apply your many talents, opportunities are available. We need you; we must all pull together as a team."

The most common reason for failure: trainers do not fully understand related mission requirements. On many occasions, the trainer will respond, "I did not know *that* is what you wanted." Acknowledge that miscommunication regarding performance expectations may affect a successful outcome.

Good coaching requires a relationship and excellent rapport. Training staff may have difficulty expressing concerns about their performance, so an open-ended question rather than a specific *yes* or *no* question is often the best format. For example, you might ask, "How do you feel about your new training assignment?" This is an excellent opportunity for the training manager (coach) and training instructor to reflect on content and meaning.

Coaches rephrase the question and listen. Coaching requires collecting information that helps interpret motives or foundations that lead to performance discrepancies. Does the trainer/instructor know how to perform the training tasks? Did the trainer think there were other, more important, priorities? One remedy: develop coaching plans that avoid miscommunication. **Coaches generally follow a three-step process:**

The first step in the coaching process: identify behavior(s) that are counterproductive to the achievement of successful training solutions. This requires personal observations and active learning. The coach reviews the trainer's behaviors with objectivity.

The second step: conduct a thorough investigation and analysis of the behaviors that require remedial support. Instill motivation, high achievement, and help them achieve their potential.

The manager/coach must know how to push the motivation button. What is a motivation button? The motivation factor is universal for everyone. To find it you must know what the person wants, what they need, and how you can help them achieve it. Help them synchronize personal goals with agency goals.

The first thing the coach needs to do is to help learners form a quick mental image in their minds for something they do not have and need. Then show them that you have the best way to fill that need. When that need becomes an active wish for the desired performance behaviors, the motivation solution will emerge; pushing the right motivation button will inspire action.

The third step: is a mutual agreement that existing behaviors do not comply with desired outcomes. The training manager encourages agreement on solutions and behavior changes that help solve the problem, and facilitate satisfactory performance. Furthermore, training coaches conduct follow-up inquiries to determine if the desired behaviors have produced positive outcomes. Finally, reward and reinforce preferred performance behaviors that attain success and mission achievement.

In summary: training managers provide appropriate feedback. Accurate feedback is the most essential ingredient in the coaching process. Professional training managers offer information based on evidence, not speculation. Positive coaching feedback enhances dialogue when it is precise and allows staff members time and opportunities to respond.

Training managers do not jump to conclusions; they seek valid evidence and objective problem analysis when evaluating trainer behavior(s) from many sources and directions. Do not take the word of one information source that may be predisposed to employ a biased or personal agenda.

Special Note: Coaching learners is another significant task; however, this is generally by exception and training staff referral. Refer to *Effective Police Leadership: Moving Beyond Management, Positive Police Leadership: Problem-solving Planning* in the Looseleaf Law Publications leadership series for additional leadership, management, and coaching information. In addition, refer to Chapter 5: Performance Training Feedback and Chapter 9: Dynamic Guidance for additional coaching information.

Emotional Command Systems

Successful curriculums move beyond procedural training by engaging personnel relationships. Advanced professional manager/instructors connect with the people around them and interpret *Emotional Command Systems*. Addressing communication bids impacts the training climate. Understanding how emotional brain states vary provides insight into behavior modification. An awareness of Emotional Command Systems improves the ability to respond to staff and learner needs. How do Emotional Command Systems relate to law enforcement training?

Gottman and DeClaire (2001, pp. 89–135) demonstrate how Emotional Command Systems communicate and interact. Emotional command concepts are based on behavioral foundations, that is, frequently appearing emotional brain states. Emotional Command Systems are approximate assessments of modal personality types or most frequently appearing in a series. **These researchers describe several Emotional Command Systems that apply to law enforcement:**

- **The Commander-in-Chief**
- **Explorer**
- **Energy Czar**
- **Nest-Builder**
- **Jester**
- **Sentry**

Special Note: The **sensualists** will not be discussed in the context of this book.

System Descriptions and Self-inventory Scales

Jack Panksepp, (2010) in *The Archaeology of Mind: Neuroevolutionary Origins of Human Emotion* and other publications, identifies brain and behavioral states that coordinate certain functions to preserve survival. Panksepp is the leading original researcher on emotional brain states.

Everyone has their own *comfort zone* by nature and nurture. Environmental experiences such as abandonment and life-threatening events can alter behavioral brain states. The brain may activate one or more combinations based on predisposition or situation.

Understanding that one's *comfort zone* may differ from others is an excellent communication factor, an important issue when connecting with staff and learners. Interpersonal problems emerge when *comfort zones* are mismatched or emotional brain systems are overactive during interpersonal communication.

The following six Self-Inventory Rating Scales are a rough index system that gives readers opportunities to evaluate their Emotional Command System. This scale system represents a nonscientific personal assessment opportunity. Discover your dominant Emotional Command System. Participate in the Self-Rating Inventory that appears after each brain state discussion. Identify strengths and weaknesses that require further analysis. Understating *self* is the first step to understanding *others*. Begin your self-exploration with the Commander-in-Chief Command System.

The Commander-in-Chief System

This emotional command system in everybody's brain coordinates functions related to dominance, control, and power. Individuals are most likely to activate this system when they need to break free from restrictions, take charge of a situation, or force action. You might call upon the Commander-in-Chief inside when you feel physically threatened, when you think you are being treated unfairly, or whenever you feel blocked from achieving a goal.

The Commander-in-Chief is motivated by the need to be self-reliant, strong, and avoid feeling weak or dependent. These individuals may appear overprotective and will fight for justice. When optimally engaged they are protective and these individuals will crusade for causes.

The Commander-in-Chief also has a negative brain state; for example, when overactive the negative consequences will encourage alienating responses from others. This emotional brain state can produce an emotionally driven anger, rage, aggression, and violence to achieve their objectives. When the brain state is under-activated, it causes very passive behaviors such as failing to overcome obstacles, injustice, or personal attacks.

The Emotional Command System may have a positive or negative impact on the learning climate. Building a positive training climate minimizes potential emotional command systems problems. At the interpersonal communication level. The commander-in-chef may create considerable conflict.

Refer to Training Table 10-1: Training Self-Rating Inventory for an assessment of this Emotional Command System. Table 10-1 includes an assessment rating of one to ten: (ten being the *high* and one the *low*).

Table 10-1. **The Commander-in-Chief System—Self-Rating Inventory**

Commander-In-Chief System: Self-Rating Inventory	1	2	3	4	5	6	7	8	9	10
I prefer dominance, control and power.										
I prefer to take charge of a situation, or take action by force if necessary.										
I feel the need to break free from restrictions.										
I am motivated to be self-reliant, strong, and avoid feeling weak or dependent.										
I tend be overprotective and will fight for justice.										
I am inclined to protect others and will crusade for justice causes.										
I need to be self-reliant and strong.										

Commander-In-Chief System: Self-Rating Inventory	1	2	3	4	5	6	7	8	9	10
I react strongly when physically threatened, or when being treated unfairly.										
I am comfortable in the Commander-in-Chief role and being in charge.										
I am relentless in pursing goals and objectives.										

SOURCE: Adapted from Gottman and DeClaire (2001), Commander-in-Chief System.

The Explorer System

The Explorer is the ideal researcher for finding alternative instructional methods. The Explorer is optimistic when seeking information and involved in sorting, planning, learning, and goal setting. When optimally engaged, the Explorer may feel a sense of high expectations, interest, and accomplishment. An overactivated Explorer system is compulsively driven to continue searching even if it results in fatigue and exhaustion. When underactivated the Explorer will experience boredom, restlessness, irritable, and anxiety.

Explorers excel at developing curriculum management, goals, and objectives. Their research methods assure training content accuracy, excellent lesson planning and course development. *Explorers* must motivate their emotional brain state to embrace an instructional mode. Otherwise, they may engage the instructional process with less enthusiasm and prefer research.

The transition will be difficult, but not impossible, if instructional units are sustained for brief intervals from the preferred *comfort zone*. Explorer systems prefer searching, learning, and satisfying one's curiosity. Refer to Training Table 10-2: Training Self-Rating Inventory for an assessment of this Emotional Command System. Table 10-2 includes an assessment rating of one to ten: (ten being the *high* and one the *low*).

Table 10-2. The Explorer System—Self-Rating Inventory

Explorer System: Self-Rating Inventory	1	2	3	4	5	6	7	8	9	10
I am the ideal researcher for finding alternative methods and solutions.										
I am most effective when seeking information.										
When fully engaged, I feel a sense of high expectations, interest and accomplishment.										
I function best when involved in sorting, planning, learning and goal setting.										
I am compulsively driven to continue searching, even if it results in fatigue and exhaustion.										
I prefer searching, learning, and curiosity pursuits.										
When under-activated, I experience boredom, restlessness, irritability and anxiety.										
I enjoy learning and new growth opportunities.										
I dislike predictable routines and enjoy change.										
I am curious about the future and have a sense of vision.										

SOURCE: Adapted from Gottman and DeClaire (2001), The Explorer System.

The Energy Czar System

The Energy Czar System is responsible for making sure that the body gets the rest and care it needs to stay healthy. When you work or play too long, the Energy Czar sends you a signal that it is time to stop and rejuvenate yourself. Mild signals may include feelings of fatigue or boredom. Ignore them for a while and you are likely to become drowsy or irritable. Ignore them for a long time and you may develop serious problems, such as a weakened immune system or chronic illness.

The Energy Czar is operating at an optimal level, when we remain physically and emotionally comfortable without a lot of extra stress and effort. When the Energy Czar is overactivated, we may become obsessed with issues like fatigue, stress, diet, and exercise or weight control. When the Energy Czar is underactivated, we may pay little attention to our need for rest, stress relief, and physical effort.

The *Energy Czar* system is important to everyone, especially law enforcement personnel who engage in shift work. This system tells the body when it is tired, hungry, thirsty, or otherwise physically under attack. When the *Energy Czar* is working properly, individuals can maintain physical and emotional fitness. Conversely, some individuals may not pay attention to stress and disregard signs of exhaustion; this can lead to many other health issues.

Law enforcement training should address stress management, nutrition, and lifetime fitness. Instructors with a high *Energy Czar* system are ideally suited to the task. Refer to Training Table 10-3: Training Self-Rating Inventory for an assessment of this Emotional Command System. Table 10-3 includes an assessment rating of one to ten: (ten being the *high* and one the *low*).

Table 10-3. Energy Czar System—Self-Rating Inventory

The Energy Czar System: Self-rating Inventory	1	2	3	4	5	6	7	8	9	10
I monitor my body so that it gets the proper relaxation and rest.										
I take responsibility and address precautions to stay healthy.										
I respond to body signals that it's time to stop and get rejuvenated.										
When I ignore body signals, I am likely to become drowsy or irritable.										

The Energy Czar System: Self-rating Inventory	1	2	3	4	5	6	7	8	9	10
When I experience mild signals, it may include feelings of fatigue or boredom.										
I have experienced serious problems, such as a weakened immune system or chronic illness.										
I tend to take time to rest and improve my energy levels.										
I rarely experience exhaustion and excessive stress.										
I am able to get enough sleep most nights.										
I find my life exciting and have considerable drive to accomplish goals and objectives.										

SOURCE: Adapted from Gottman and DeClaire (2001), The Energy Czar System.

The Nest-Builder System

The Nest-Builder System coordinates functions related to affiliation, bonding, and attachment. We engage this system when we form other types of relationships as well, including friendships. You feel a sense of belonging and bonding when the Nest-Builder System is functioning optimally.

The Nest-Builder System may also come into play as we become attached to work teams, jobs, clubs, schools, and other people. This emotional brain system organizes our activities when we nurture another's growth, care for another's needs, and express affection. The Nest-Builder System is what drives you to make new friends; it encourages relationships that serve as a source of comfort and support in your life.

Overactivated individuals have problems with crossing boundaries in personal relationships. A chronically under-activated system will experience isolation and loneliness, which can produce feelings of sadness and anxiety.

Overactivated Nest Builders may result in boundary crossing dilemmas and relationship issues. Sharing excessive sensitive personal information may facilitate uncomfortable situations for Nest-Builder instructors and affect the learning environment.

Underactivated Nest-Builder Systems may experience panic at the thought of separation. Relationships often crumble under the burden of irritation, resentment, and martyrdom.

Nest Builders excel in training environments. Learners experience attachment and identification with their trainer. Learning climates offer strong bonding opportunities. Excellent rapport initiates interpersonal relationships and feedback communication skills. Refer to Training Table 10-4: Training Self-Rating Inventory for an assessment of this Emotional Command System. Table 10-4 includes an assessment rating of one to ten: (ten being the *high* and one the *low*).

Table 10-4. **The Nest-Builder System—Self-Rating Inventory**

The Nest-Builder System: Self-rating Inventory	1	2	3	4	5	6	7	8	9	10
I tend to coordinate functions related to affiliation, bonding, and attachment.										
I enjoy forming work relationships and other types of relationships as well, including friendship.										
I tend to become attached to work teams, jobs, clubs, schools, and other people.										
I find that personal relationships serve as a source of comfort and support in my life.										
I enjoy making new friends; it encourages a positive life experience.										

The Nest-Builder System: Self-rating Inventory	1	2	3	4	5	6	7	8	9	10
I seek activities to mentor or nurture another's growth; care for another's needs, and express affection.										
Sometimes, I feel that comfort zones may result in having problems with establishing personal boundaries.										
I get lonely when not in a close relationship.										
I make it a priority to spend time with friends.										
I like to listen to my friends' problems.										

SOURCE: Adapted from Gottman and DeClaire (2001), The Nest Builder System.

The Jester System

The Jester System demonstrates the following attributes: (1) play, (2) recreation, and (3) diversion. Behaviors associated with the Jester include playing games, seeking entertainment, telling jokes, engaging in make-believe, and simply "fooling around."

They function best in brainstorming sessions where group members feel free to say whatever comes to mind. Wacky notions surface, but together you also devise novel ideas. This is the Jester at work—helping people to both relax and renew.

When Jesters are in full expression, they feel a sense of relaxed stimulation, peace, and enjoyment. Jesters can become overactivated and so "wound-up" that they need to calm down. When underactivated, Jesters can feel inhibited, lethargic, or emotionally down.

Jesters have the potential to become entertaining instructors if they offer balanced presentations. They make excellent hosts who introduce speakers with contagious enthusiasm. *Jesters* may find it difficult to organize training content and maintain con-

sistent lectures. They can be great motivators and improve staff
and learner morale.

An overactive disadvantage: a *Jester's* sense of humor
directed at staff and learners with negative results. When the
Jester is hyperexcited, his audience becomes disenchanted. Refer
to Training Table 10-5: Training Self-Rating Inventory for an
assessment of this Emotional Command System. Table 10-5 includes an assessment rating of one to ten: (ten being the *high* and
one the *low*).

Table 10-5. The Jester System—Self-Rating Inventory

The Jester System: Self-rating Inventory	1	2	3	4	5	6	7	8	9	10
Sometimes, I experience being appreciated, but often undervalued by many.										
I enjoy playing games, seeking entertainment, telling jokes, engaging in make-believe, and simply "fooling around."										
I function best in a brainstorming session where the group feels free to say whatever comes to mind.										
I take pleasure in helping people to both relax and renew.										
When I am in full expression, people feel a sense of relaxed stimulation, and combination of peace, and enjoyment.										
When I am hyper-excited; my fooling around can cause the audience some displeasure.										
When I am in an under-activated state; I may feel inhibited lethargic or emotionally depressed.										
I poke fun at pretentious people.										
I like the role of the clown.										
I take pleasure in slapstick comedy.										

SOURCE: Adapted from Gottman and DeClaire (2001), The Jester System.

The Sentry System

The Sentry emotional command system relates to survival. The Sentry System coordinates functions in the body and mind related to worry, fear, vigilance, and defense. When activated, the Sentry helps you regulate fear and avoid danger.

When facing life-threatening situations, for example, an armed robbery or burglary, the Sentry System goes into a hyperalert mode. The survival approach takes precedent; you take necessary action to survive. However, when the Sentry is underactive, the person may not focus their watchfulness to stay safe. An example might be someone who lives on the edge, enjoys "cheating death," and engages in thrill-seeking pursuits.

The Sentry may rally the Commander-in Chief system to engage rage and attack in the pursuit of defending self and others. On the other hand, the overactivated person may experience unnecessary fears that interfere in a normal and productive life.

The *Sentry* system likely performs as a crime prevention or street survival instructor and prevails in community safety presentations. Refer to Training Table 10-6: Training Self-Rating Inventory for an assessment of this Emotional Command System. Table 10-6 includes an assessment rating of one to ten: (ten being the *high* and one the *low*).

Table 10-6.   The Sentry System—Self-Rating Inventory

The Sentry System: Self-rating Inventory	1	2	3	4	5	6	7	8	9	10
I am interested in safety and survival issues.										
I can focus on issues related to fear, vigilance, defense, and avoiding danger.										
When I face a threatening situation, my attentiveness goes into hyper-alert action.										

The Sentry System: Self-rating Inventory	1	2	3	4	5	6	7	8	9	10
I can sense and anticipate trouble before others can.										
Sometimes I am a person who lives on the edge, enjoys "cheating death," and engages in thrill-seeking pursuits.										
Becoming a victim is easy, if one does not stay alert and vigilant.										
I view the world as a dangerous place.										
I believe that forethought and prevention can avoid danger.										
I view myself as a protector of others.										
I tend to look for danger in ordinary situations.										

SOURCE: Adapted from Gottman and DeClaire (2001), The Sentry System.

Corner 10-1: Case Study Application

The *Commander-in Chief* System may have excellent training management and podium lecture skills. Lieutenant Steve Burt, a law enforcement commander, is respected by his chain of command—subordinates have a different and negative point of view. His arrogant and over controlling behaviors create a climate of fear.

The Lieutenant serves as temporary Training Commander. His overactivated *Commander-in-Chief* System emphasizes negative consequences and minimizes the positive. He experiences relationship difficulties as a temporary substitute instructor for reassigned trainers. Poor indicators include sabotage, alienation, and disrespect. His fast-track career aspirations may diminish if he does not modify an overactive emotional brain state.

Corner 10-1: Critical Thinking Exercise

What does the *Commander* need to do to correct his emotional brain state? What other Emotional Command Systems would improve staff and learner relationships? Compare and contrast Emotional Command Systems to the Enneagram personality Types in Chapter 2: Group Dynamics.

Corner 10-2: Case Study Application

Sergeant Wingfoot is everything he appears to be. The Sergeant is concerned with doing a good job; however, he is genuinely modest, benevolent, and accepts his limitations. Furthermore, he focuses on the welfare of officers; strong bonding pulls shift members together. He is alert to burnout and always approaches those at risk.

The old American Indian Sergeant approaches an officer in a locker-room that is in need of renovation. His sun-wrinkled face appears grimaced with concern for the young officer's stressful and driven demeanor. He leans against an adjoining rusty locker ...

"There's an old Indian story about a grandfather who offers advice to his grandson. He tells the young warrior that there is a war between two wolves inside all of us ... one is *good* and the other is *bad*. The grandson is curious to learn which wolf survives. The grandfather responds ... *the one you feed*."

"Feeding the good wolf is not always easy, and may come thwarted with costly consequences. You have to be strong in your convictions when you feed the good wolf—honor, compassion, and courage remain steadfast.

"Life offers many opportunities to nourish the bad wolf. The bad wolf lies, deceives, and does everything possible to destroy peaceful human existence. He plays on limitations and fears, waiting for momentary lapses in judgment."

"... so, Tom, which wolf do you feed?"

Tom lowers his eyes. "I think I might be feeding the bad wolf."

"You have the power to feed the good wolf. Allow yourself to enter a peaceful and forgiving place in your heart and stop blaming *yourself* for all the bad things that happen on the job."

Tom smiles, "I'm going to work on changing that ... *starting now.*"

Corner 10-2: Critical Thinking Exercise

The case study description in Corner 10-2 best describes which of these described the Emotional Command System? Compare and contrast Emotional Command Systems to the Enneagram personality Types in Chapter 2: Group Dynamics.

Training Leadership: Johari Window

Why is the Johari Window an excellent approach to critical thinking and emotional command systems? The answer: communication is the very substance of training and relating to instructional staff. The Johari solution enhances human communication strategies and eliminates major feedback impediments.

The Johari Window Model offers opportunities to examine leadership, training, and the social climate from communication and feedback perspectives. Two psychologists, Joseph Luft and Harry Ingham, conceived a "window model" for giving and receiving information feedback. This model offers law enforcement applications in management, leadership, and training. Refer to Training Figure 10-2 for examples and a Johari Window Overview.

The Johari Window encourages the expansion of shared curriculum training and achieving accurate feedback, but it requires personal risk for leaders. Curriculum management and leadership require candid leaders who establish trust and mutual respect. Suggest information exchanges rather than one-way dialogues that do not offer feedback.

Feedback provides information concerning leadership behaviors. Open training managers encourage opportunities that assess how others feel about their leadership. Unapproachable leaders deny opportunities to disclose feelings by maintaining their façade and offering little feedback.

The Johari Window offers training managers and instructors the possibility of expanding personal power. Feedback is the reaction of trainers and learners (feelings and perceptions), thereby informing training managers about how his/her behaviors affect them. Managers/instructors equipped with crucial feedback are in the best position to be effective decision-makers. Candid managers/instructors amplify communication and feedback, enhancing follower information and training support.

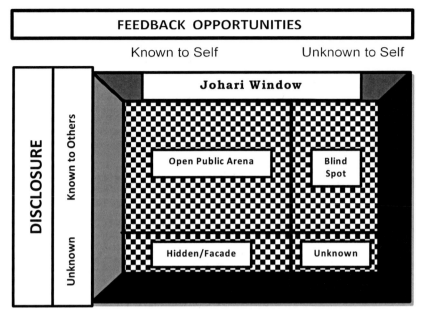

Figure 10-2. Johari Window Overview

The lack of feedback is a statement in itself; it is a silent announcement about the manager's effectiveness. Poor reciprocal communication isolates and places the manager/instructor outside the informal communication loop. Managers/instructors, who hide behind their façade, or remain silent and do not take risks, fail to communicate and remain isolated. Open managers/instructors who ask for feedback and disclose information about self, position themselves to influence others.

Self-disclosure affects relationships and training situations. However, communication techniques do not require disclosing the intimate details of one's life. Avoid over disclosure that damages respect or status. Sharing essential information is target specific; opportunities may unfold for expressing personal feelings.

The goal is to obtain information *not known* to self, but *known* to others. The opportunity to gain information from the *blind spot,* and *unknown* portions of the four Johari quadrants, proves essential to successful decision-making. Sharing information from the *hidden area* (sometimes referred to as the façade) provides greater understanding for following and sharing feedback. Manager self-disclosure encourages rapport and trust relationships with individual training staff, informal groups, and the learner participants.

Peering into the Johari Window allows law-training managers/instructors to expose the façade or the *hidden area* (the issues others do not know about). The purpose is to gain sufficient knowledge about the *blind spot and unknown* (the issues the managers/instructors do not know about, for example, Emotional Command Systems).

Thus, shrinking the windowpanes or quadrants around the *blind spot* ultimately offers insight into the *unknown area* and related issues. Insight provides opportunities to communicate initiatives and problem-solve with appropriate curriculum and instructional remedies.

The *open space* is the key to personal power, the quadrant, or windowpane, where managers/instructors have opportunities to be authentic and open. Openness allows for the exchange of what one knows about self and what others know. This form of personal leadership interaction and risk-taking invites the necessary feedback for effective training decision-making. Managers/instructors unwilling to share the *hidden* or *façade* windowpane that keep secrets do not receive proper training feedback.

The return flow of information helps shrink the blind area and unknown. Curriculum and learner instructional opportunities result when the *blind spot* and *unknown* panes shrink, creating new vision requirements. Vision requirements are particularly important in curriculum construction, technology applications, and future operations.

Managers/leaders assess Emotional Command Systems and determine comfort zones. In addition, astute training managers assist instructors by acknowledging alternate command systems. More important, training managers can initiate proactive steps by creating opportunities to avoid negative traits that accompany over or underactivated command systems.

Improving instructor bids for connection avoids emotional stress. When managers/instructors establish real-time feedback and communication, learning takes place in an efficient and effective manner. The applications are endless if leadership remains open to information sharing.

Training Applications

The Johari Window introduces new instructional strategies. Law enforcement training requirements are determined by needs assessment, task analysis, and participant performance requirements. Peering through the four quadrants or windowpanes provides a telescope for training management systems.

Manager/instructor participation in instructional operations is the deciding factor in the equation of communication and learner outcomes. Instructor evaluations at the end of training are behind schedule to influence the currently affected audience. Therefore, training feedback (reaction from learners) needs to occur during the learning process. In addition, the impact is substantial once instructors obtain learner assessments.

The logical extension to critical and analytical thinking requires applying Johari Window observations to training staff and field operations. Training management and the Johari Window are consistent with excellent communication, practice, and training applications. Numerous unknown learner factors and important considerations may unfold.

The Johari Window turned externally can assist in obtaining accurate training information. Johari Window and training curriculum requirements have overlapping connections to program evaluation requirements in pursuit of feedback and training content confirmation.

Basic program evaluation information provides the raw data for collection, planning, and direction. Curriculum transformations are served by examining unknown factors and building excellent training climates. The feedback may prove essential to manager/instructor learning opportunities, and may lead to effective analysis and curriculum lesson planning.

Feedback: Bid-Busting Behavior

Managers determine perceptions through the feedback process. Personal disclosure bids assist in modifying the feedback process. Communication feedback involves verbal or nonverbal cues and learner perceptions. The instructional staff has opportunities to express their feelings about the training process. Refer to communication bids in Chapter One for additional feedback information.

Learning assessment requires observations and opinions concerning content and instructional methods. Avoid overacting to negative responses; neutralize provocative behaviors. Occasionally, behavior bids are simply attention seeking. Listen and avoid bid busters. Refer to Training Table 10-7: Training Self-Rating Inventory for an illustration of Bid Buster behaviors. Rating Inventory Scale Table 10-7 includes an assessment rating of one to ten: (ten being the *high* and one the *low*):

Table 10-7. Bid Busters Behaviors—Self-Rating Inventory

Bid Busters: How to Avoid Them	1	2	3	4	5	6	7	8	9	10
Being Mindless, Rather than Mindful: But if you don't pay attention, you don't connect. And, if you don't connect, you wind up operating on the principle that your partner, your friend, or your coworker is not going to be there for you. This also applies to training staff and students.										
Starting on a Sour Note: Instead, our exchange was a classic example of what I call "harsh startup." You want to connect with somebody, so you make a bid for their connection. But because your bid begins in such a negative, blaming, or critical way, you get just the opposite of what you're after. You drive the person, trainer or student away.										
Using Harmful Criticism, Instead of Helpful Complaints: Here's the basic rule of thumb: Complain when you must, but don't criticize. What's the difference? A complaint focuses on a specific problem, addressing the other person's behavior, not his or her perceived character flaws. Criticism, on the other hand, is more judgmental and global; it										

Bid Busters: How to Avoid Them	1	2	3	4	5	6	7	8	9	10
frequently includes such phrases as "You always ..." or "You never..." Criticism attacks the other person's character, often with negative labels or name-calling. It often assigns blame.										
Practicing a Crabby State of Mind, by Habit of Mind: Everybody feels irritable on occasion, but when you have a crabby habit of mind, you feel this way just about all the time. You constantly scan the world for evidence to justify your feelings. And, in this imperfect world, that evidence is not hard to find.										
Avoiding the Conversation You Need to Have: When things go wrong in a relationship, people often ask, "Was it something that I said?" Well, maybe. But, more often it's the things people don't say that harm their relationships with staff, students, and others.										
Flooding: In troubled relationships, discussions of conflict can trigger intense emotions that sometimes lead to "flooding." This means you feel so stressed that you become emotionally and physically overwhelmed. You're no longer able to think clearly, or to participate in the conversation in a fruitful way. You would rather be anywhere else than right here with this person, instructor, or student.										

Source: Adapted from Gottman and DeClaire (2001), pp. 65-82.

In Summary

The conscious versus the unconscious mind is an integral part of the learning process. Training managers and instructors are capable of processing information on both levels. When others inquire into your mind, they are probing for attention on both levels. Intellectual emotional bid messages can ramble down many paths. Motivation is not always obvious, especially when the unconscious mind is bidding for attention.

Emotional bids are difficult to decipher. Active listeners are capable of reading hidden emotional messages or bids for attention. Instructors who cannot dismiss listening obstacles or distractions fail to see subtle bids. The ability to be open and candid improves the training and learning process.

Focus Points

Emotional Command Systems, Enneagrams, and Johari Window applications offer insight into human behavior. These strategies offer opportunities for improved understanding and bidding communication. The result is dynamic law enforcement training.

Training curriculum management includes three unrelated components:

- Curriculum design
- Learning climate
- Instructional strategies

Training curriculum provides learners with the knowledge, skills, and abilities to perform successfully in the field.

Training mission accomplishment improves when Emotional Command Systems and Johari Window opportunities unfold. Identifying Emotional Command Systems facilitates trainer capacities to avert conflict and enhance learning climates.

Trainers identify individual Command Systems and include self-assessment:

- Commander-in-Chief
- Explorer
- Energy Czar
- Nest-Builder

- Jester
- Sentry

Clarification helps facilitate change and positive interpersonal relationships.

Overactive command systems are not receptive to bids for communication. Mismatches in Emotional Command Systems lead to interpersonal conflict. Anticipate mismatches and compensate during social interactions.

Four Johari Window quadrants help analyze emotional command systems and interpret learner behaviors. Managers/instructors encourage meaningful communication with learners. Suggest techniques that challenge, not overwhelm, trainees.

***Pulling it all together* requires thinking in four dimensions:**

- Training management/instructional staff
- Trainers
- Learners
- Social climates

Connecting training dots and pathways assures requirement achievement, and opening the door to the fifth dimension—*training vision* and *future applications.*

The synchronization of curriculum strategies is not the perfect solution; however, it offers another important dimension to proactive training delivery systems. Predicting the future is not without risk; however, much of what happens is determined by attempting to envision the hope for successful training strategies. A clear sense of vision enables training managers to understand the importance of specialized training methods and visualize learning opportunities.

Conclusion

Excellent managers/instructors maximize learner potential. They apply inductive and deductive reasoning skills and think "outside the box." Even better, they create a new box. Drive, focus, persistence, and motivation generate successful outcomes. Special note: Why not reread this chapter again! You may see things you missed during the former read.

Innovation and learning opportunities unfold in multiple dimensions and pathway directions; the pathway to success starts when you are inspired to make the professional effort. Inspiration starts when you are motivated to dissatisfaction with leaving things as they stand. Refer to the Epilogue: Self-Assessment Review for pathways to assess your training strength and weaknesses.

EPILOGUE

Self-Assessment Review

"Genius is 1 percent inspiration and 99 percent perspiration. Success is based on imagination plus ambition and the willingness to work."

— Thomas Edison

Focus

The purpose of the **Epilogue** is to engage in self-assessment and determine one's final appraisal of training knowledge, expertise, and competencies. Instructional strategies emerge from *pathway* skills. The previous *ten pathway chapters* provide essential training foundations.

How do you get training foundations knowledge? You do not get it; you accumulate knowledge. The process originates from direct training action, experience, and learning applications ... it comes to you in that struggle. When you have it, you will know its power. *Eventful journeys offer meaningful endings!*

Overview

There are many *pathways* to trainer destinations. *Pathways* that lead to an ultimate selection of dynamic training strategies: twist, turn, and intersect along the way. Optimal decision-making or the formulation of training strategies depend on curriculum, lesson planning, and underpinning *pathways*. Excellent trainers navigate through fog and discover true north. This Epilogue reviews training focus points, appropriate applications, and offers personal assessments. What does the phrase "self-assessment" mean to you? Formulate your thoughts by answering the questions that follow. Your endeavor might offer new personal insights.

Self-Assessment and Arrival

Training Self-Rating Inventories are non-scientific personal assessment opportunities. Scales are rated 1 to 10, with ten being the *high* and one the *low*. Results provide opportunities to evaluate the learning process.

The fill-in questions supplement the self-assessment process; score them in the same manner. Compare those scores with the Training Self-Rating Inventories. In addition, take the opportunity to compare those results with the multiple-choice examination after the Epilogue Conclusion (Appendix A). Those three scores should provide an index for follow-up; identify strengths and weaknesses that require further review and study.

Special Note: Fill-in questions are more difficult than multiple-choice questions because they require direct recall. Multiple-choice questions require recognition. However, fill-in questions stimulate retention and future application. Check the answer solutions in Appendix E and G.

The purpose of the inventory is to allow readers opportunities to rate themselves using a 10-point general scale. Scores that range:

- below 70% (require additional study and training)
- 70 – 79% = average
- 80 – 89% = above average
- 90% – 100% = positive training skills

Enjoy the self-exploration process. Only you, the reader, know the results of your self-assessments.

Written Exercise

Critical thinking requires focusing on dynamic curriculum strategies and lesson planning. Compare and contrast what is important. Which pathway needs improvement to enhance training outcomes? Refer to the Training Rating Inventories and self-assessment opportunities. Reflect on your Self-Inventory Rating Scale results and determine how they might affect future role requirements.

Leadership Destination Arrival

Successful training outcomes depend on the pathways that follow. Once you truly understand what they mean, you are on the way to an excellent career future. Inspiration to action is the most important road to success in any training activity. However, the best source of inspiration and imagination originates from opening your mind and looking for the intuitive meaning. The remaining Epilogue pathways in this book provide that final destination.

Successful training programs empower learners to reach their potential. Primary to that objective are effective communication and competent decision-making skills. Managers/instructors apply curriculum content; propose performance objectives and dynamic learning strategies. Professional efforts enhance technical skills and field methods.

Accomplished learners appreciate the justice process and ethical concerns that envelop practitioners. In addition, training programs prepare learners for professional investigative endeavors and challenging careers. The need for competent law enforcement personnel is imperative in an increasingly complex and dangerous society. Training programs require specific pathways for successful programming:

- Excellence
- Imagination
- Creativity

Pathway One—Role Modeling: Dynamic Lecture Strategies

Instructors are responsible for establishing a personal philosophy and skills that support training missions. Thoughtful positioning provides a *center of gravity* for communicating values and attitudes. Defining the following pathways and applying them to instructional endeavors provides navigational direction to the correct destination.

Self-candor opens the door for becoming an effective instructor, engaging the future, and achieving self-understanding. Superior instructors self-monitor behaviors that derail progress.

Positive self-control and the ability to delay gratification demand patience and thoroughness. The instructor makes the transition from *average* to *superior* because they have insight into their own behavior. Self-assessment helps to focus and concentrate on maximizing personal strengths and addressing weaknesses.

Self-assessment procedures provide insight into what trainers need to understand about themselves. This requires introspection and self-criticism to achieve the aptitude for superior training maneuvers. Self-assessment is no easy task because it requires being honest with *self*; however, the effort is worth positive instructional results.

The mandate for superior instructors requires building on strengths. Identifying personal strengths requires:

- Introspection
- Identifying self-assessment
- Self-candor

This means taking time to (1) appraise the training situation and (2) identify new directions.

Content and Self-Inventory Questions

Refer to the following fill-in questions to formulate a general assessment of your training content knowledge:

1. _____ helps establish positive training methods and instructor success.

2. _____ is a life-controlling mechanism that regulates_____, persistence, and dedication.

3. Successful instructors are capable of positive _____, an asset that creates an aura of confidence and a willingness to try another approach.

4. Instructors who practice positive_____ envision success. They stay on the cutting edge and position themselves to enter the instructional arena, while charting the course for arriving at their destination.

5. Positive_____ and aspirations are powerful motivating forces.

6. Another important instructor quality is positive _____. This requires the ability to step back and appraise one's personal impact on the instructional process. The skill demands examining strengths, weaknesses, and potential limitations.

7. Effective instructors engage in positive _____ and concentrate on what they desire to achieve. There are limitations; however, fear of failure is not one of them.

8. Superior instructors own positive _____. They have insight into overcoming instructional barriers and insulators. This self-fulfilling prophesy offers powerful learner enticements. Anticipate successful instructional solutions and prompt them to unfold.

9. Instructors with positive _____ take responsibility for their actions and do not rationalize mistakes.

10. Gottman and Declare (2001), in *The Relationship Cure*, describe excellent solutions for resolving instructor communication conflict. The authors divulge the need to respond to social bidding effectively. These researchers identified three basic bid communication responses: (1) _____, (2) _____, and an extreme form of turning away is the (3) _____.

Special Note: Refer to Appendix E: Fill-in question solutions. In addition, refer to Table E-1: Self-Rating Inventory for an assessment of these skills. Rating Inventory Scale Table E-1 includes an assessment rating of one to ten (ten being the *high* and one being the *low*).

Table E-1. Self-Rating Inventory

Pathway One: Training Skills	1	2	3	4	5	6	7	8	9	10
Identify instructor attributes.										
Appraise lecture fundamentals.										
Cite main lecture speaking points.										
Appraise rational for questioning.										
Define lecture questioning feedback.										
Distinguish between the purposes of communication bidding.										

Pathway One: Training Skills	1	2	3	4	5	6	7	8	9	10
Describe reflection technique qualities.										
List purpose of lecture's central idea.										
Identify the principle of the rhetorical question.										
Illustrate the related terms: turning toward, turning away, and unrequited responses.										

Instructor Applications

Excellent instructors are aware of the learner "bidding" process and recognize the need to respond appropriately. Superior instructors seize bid opportunities to communicate and establish rapport. Instructors drop what they are doing, make direct eye contact, and listen to bids for attention.

Learner facial expression interpretation is important. Clarify questions and respond appropriately without deflecting or faking answers. If necessary, admit the need for additional research. Clarification unfolds in the next class session. Quality responses require insight, understanding, and sincere answers.

Practical Exercise Application: Make specific efforts to read individual bids in your next classroom session or social encounter. Try to assess learner needs and underlying motivation. Read learner facial expressions for emotional reactions. Refer to Chapter 1: Dynamic Lecture Strategies for bidding and facial expression assessment tools.

Pathway Two — Group Leadership Dynamics

The application of group dynamics extends instructor influence outside the classroom. Active group instructional methods address the potential to influence learning outcomes. Three key training elements assist problem-solving projects:

- **Supplemental passive learning techniques**
- **Small group work**
- **Flexible class time**

Active learning instructional strategies create multiple opportunities to evaluate performance.

Content and Self-Inventory Questions

Refer to the following fill-in questions to formulate a general assessment of your training content knowledge:

1. Individual behaviors are unpredictable; however, group behaviors have three predictable stages of development. The predictable stages are: (1) _____*stage*, (2) _____*stage*, and (3) _____ *or*_____ *stage*.

2. The Enneagram _____ is principled, purposeful, self-controlled, and a perfectionist.

3. The Enneagram _____ is generous, demonstrative, people pleasing, and possessive.

4. The Enneagram _____ is adaptable, ambitious, image conscious, and driven.

5. The Enneagram _____ is expressive, romantic, and can be withholding and temperamental.

6. The Enneagram _____ is innovative, cerebral, detached, and provocative.

7. The Enneagram _____ is reliable and committed; however, they can be defensive and suspicious.

8. The Enneagram _____ is spontaneous, versatile, distractible, and excessive.

9. The Enneagram _____ is self-confident, decisive, dominating, and confrontational.

10. The Enneagram_____ is reassuring, agreeable, and can be disengaged and stubborn.

Special Note: Refer to Appendix E: Fill-in question solutions. In addition, refer to Table E-2: Self-Rating Inventory for an assessment of these skills. Rating Inventory Scale Table E-2 includes an assessment rating of one to ten (ten being the *high* and one being the *low*).

Table E-2. Self-Rating Inventory

Pathway Two: Training Skills	1	2	3	4	5	6	7	8	9	10
Appraise the group dynamics approach.										
Identify group feedback.										
Appraise the active learning process.										
Describe three stages of group development.										
Appraise the group content dimension.										
Distinguish the group development dimension.										
Define group cohesion.										
Apply rules of the feedback process.										
Apply the case study method.										
Define group critique.										

Instructor Applications

The case study method requires critical thinking and develops problem-solving skills. Gantt (1996) concludes that case studies facilitate critical thinking by requiring learners to identify principles and theories present in actual situations, thereby building analytical skills. Case studies participation occurs in cooperative exploration and constructive disagreement, while moving toward the solution of a problem. In addition, participants may learn respect for conflicting positions and opinions.

Holkeboer (1993) suggests that when learners work as a team, a three-step critical thinking process develops where individuals:

- **Identify the core problem**
- **Brainstorm possible solutions**
- **Agree on the best solution**

In addition, case studies require learners to identify theories and concepts in authentic situations, thereby building analytical skills.

Practical Exercise Application: Instructors supplement participant presentations by offering related comments and compliments, but do not duplicate efforts. Problem-solving questions accompany follow-up discussions. Refer to Chapter 2: Group Dynamics; Case Study Example: The Cult; and Appendix B: The Expanded Version and Support Document for the Cult Case Study. Write an after-action Summary Sheet addressing conclusions of the case study and potential learner follow-up questions.

Pathway Three—Dynamic Curriculum Management

The need to analyze, construct curriculum, and improve instruction involves effort. Philosophical foundations that include attitudes and values serve as foundations for course curriculum— a navigational system for learners. The philosophy is action-oriented, involves critical thinking, and problem-solving activities. Philosophy offers a motivation and direction compass for academic excellence and quality instruction.

Content and Self-inventory Questions

Refer to the following fill-in questions to formulate a general assessment of your training content knowledge:

1. Curriculum management provides the "_____" and pathway to practical training solutions.

2. A _____ is a collection of organizing principles, belief systems, or creative models that shape understanding.

3. The _____ domain refers to (recall or recognition of knowledge).

4. The _____ domain refers to (feelings or emotions; changes in interest, attitudes, values, and appreciations).

5. The _____ domain refers to (reflexes, fundamental, perceptual, and complex motor patterns).

6. Dynamic _____ training methods involve real world multidimensional situations.

7. _____ learning requires participants to learn not only from the instructor, but also from each other, while participating in the problem-solving process.

8. The_____ motivates instructors because it offers direction, enhances evaluation in response to specific performance, and meets task linkage requirements.

9. Specific participant_____ function on the operational field level.

10. _____ evaluation focuses on the global nature of instruction.

Special Note: Refer to Appendix E: Fill-in question solutions. In addition, refer to Table E-3: Self-Rating Inventory for an assessment of these skills. Rating Inventory Scale Table E-3 includes an assessment rating of one to ten (ten being the *high* and one being the *low*).

Table E-3. Self-Rating Inventory

Pathway Three: Training Skills	1	2	3	4	5	6	7	8	9	10
Define curriculum paradigm.										
List three parts of a performance objective.										
Appraise concept of curriculum philosophy.										

Pathway Three: Training Skills	1	2	3	4	5	6	7	8	9	10
Describe critical thinking foundations.										
Distinguish elements of active learning strategies.										
List elements of an organizing center.										
Define requirements of training goals.										
Apply Systematic Design of Instruction (SDI).										
Appraise role of learner assessment process.										
Identify elements of summative evaluation planning.										

Instructor Applications

Several researchers outline a framework for teaching *critical thinking* that may prove useful in defining instructor philosophy. Marzano (1992) outlines five dimensions that support critical thinking:

- **The need to acquire and integrate thinking**
- **Thinking needed to extend and define knowledge**
- **Thinking needed to make meaningful use of knowledge**
- **Thinking needed to develop favorable habits of the mind**
- **Thinking needed to develop attitudes and perceptions that create a positive classroom climate**

Practical Exercise Application: Refer to Chapter 3: Dynamic Curriculum, Corner 1: Training Case Study-Terrorist First Responder Curriculum for lesson planning modifications. Analyze the case study and try to improve and modify the facts of this Summary Sheet. Review the content materials and write at least three questions or comments on the case study. Develop constructive information for improving the case study:

- **Critical thinking**
- **Problem-solving**
- **Decision-making applications**

Select training environments that develop desired goals and objectives. If performance objectives require field components, move to appropriate learning environments. When you set out to accomplish the training mission, do not come back until it is accomplished. The training system works *if* you work the system. For continuous success, it is necessary to get ready for tomorrow. To get ready for tomorrow, you must prepare today.

Pathway Four—Dynamic Lesson Planning

The lesson plan is a blueprint for planning instructional content and defining instructor destination. It assists in determining how to proceed and determines timely arrival. Lesson planning defines administrative instructional support, instructor, and learner activities. Specifically, the planning process outlines theories, concepts, main points, and illustrative support materials.

Content and Self-Inventory Questions

Refer to the following fill-in questions to formulate a general assessment of your training content knowledge:

1. _____ defines the *what, when,* and *how* performance task(s) standards timeline.

2. Knowledgeable trainers apply the "_____ planning" sequence.

3. A clustering of_____ refers to phases, levels, or sections.

4. Each unit includes designated performance _____ and related tasks.

5. Generally, begin the lesson plan by presenting the "big _____ picture," then restate it.

6. Lesson plans start with basic _____ and continue to build the groundwork for difficult requirements.

7. Outline a distinct_____ of learning progressions.

8. Learning that offers _____ steps requires arranging them in the sequence in which they logically occur.

9. Lesson planning requires selecting appropriate _____ methods. Performance objectives match teaching method(s).

10. The _____ of the lesson determines instructional method selection.

Special Note: Refer to Appendix E: Fill-in question solutions. In addition, refer to Table E-4: Self-Rating Inventory for an assessment of these skills. Rating Inventory Scale Table E-4 includes an assessment rating of one to ten (ten being the *high* and one being the *low*).

Table E-4. Self-Rating Inventory

Pathway Four: Training Skills	1	2	3	4	5	6	7	8	9	10
Describe the purpose of lesson plan check points.										
Appraise the elements of back-step lesson planning.										
Define the "lesson hook."										
List elements of the overview training plan.										
Illustrate the purpose or instructional units.										
Describe the application of learning progression.										
Describe the elements of developing a course.										
Cite principal teaching points.										

Pathway Four: Training Skills	1	2	3	4	5	6	7	8	9	10
Apply the body of supporting knowledge.										
Appraise elements of the final review.										

Instructor Applications

Instructors may need to revise lesson plans. Decisions to modify plans revolve around meeting learner needs and improving performance objectives. Generally, revisions unfold during instructional assessment observations. Recommendations result from identifying necessary modifications and the motivation to improve the quality of instruction.

Modifications improve learning opportunities and further efficient instruction delivery systems. The first reason for revision is to make the lesson content suitable for target audiences. The second reason is to implement instructional methods that facilitate performance objectives. Finally, the third reason is to make lessons more interesting.

Practical Exercise Application: Modifications include enhancing lessons with additional background or introductory content. The addition or modification of instructor examples may prove helpful when they correspond with learner experiences. Increasing practice sessions or incorporating practical exercises enhance retention and understanding.

Refer to Chapter 4: Dynamic Lesson Planning, Corner 4-1: Introduction: Terrorist Lesson Plan and the section concerning the Introduction and Learner Orientation for direction.

- Describe icebreaker activities that enhance participant relationships, communication, and rapport.
- How would you implement paired introductions and the one-minute biography?
- Identify essential learner orientation objectives.
- What would you include in your Orientation Summary Sheet?

Pathway Five—Leadership Feedback

Learners assess and select their preferred instructional style in response to varied learning opportunities. Everyone has a mix of learning styles. However, combinations differ and dominant preferences emerge. How does cognitive learning style influence learning and retention? Some learn best by listening (auditory learners), meaning they rely on hearing information from others. However, additional learners depend on visual presentations such as PowerPoint. Evidence suggests that learners retain more information when multiple senses are involved. Innovative instructors understand learner preferences; they initiate appropriate activities that support differences.

The combination of auditory, visual, and kinesthetic experiences reinforces the learning process even when there is a preference for one learning modality. For example, tactile or psychomotor learners prefer the "hands-on approach." These learners define practical exercises and learning simulations as being exciting and stimulating.

Content and Self-Inventory Questions

Refer to the following fill-in questions to formulate a general assessment of your training content knowledge:

1. The word_____ defines learner knowledge and results.

2. Effective instructors recognize the role of _____ in the learning process.

3. Training performance objectives have three parts: (1) _____, (2) _____, and (3) _____.

4. Some performance objectives are _____ and do not require sequencing hierarchies.

5. The _____ provides direction, defines learner performance and activity completion.

6. Training_____ may include specific learning criteria and describe the conditions under which the learner performs the task(s).

7. Training _____ describe measurable criteria for assessment and a system for achieving accountability.

8. _____ provides a systematic understanding of information. Moreover, it allows self-paced advancement. This format provides immediate feedback, reinforcement, and learner involvement.

9. Training _____ serve as learner-centered guidance.

10. The _____ offers venues for problem-solving applications.

   Special Note: Refer to Appendix E: Fill-in question solutions. In addition, refer to Table E-5: Self-Rating Inventory for an assessment of these skills. Rating Inventory Scale Table E-5 includes an assessment rating of one to ten (ten being the *high* and one being the *low*).

Table E-5. Self-Rating Inventory

Pathway Five: Training Skills	1	2	3	4	5	6	7	8	9	10
Appraise three preferred learning styles.										
List four basic feedback steps.										
Describe student performance objectives.										
Illustrate the application of the elements of learner feedback.										
Name elements of the practical exercise model.										
List four goals of the Field Training Program.										
Identify basic components of the practical exercise feedback process.										
Distinguish elements of task analysis.										
List basic performance assessment standards.										
Outline the rational for field performance training development.										

Instructor Applications

Law enforcement practical exercises prepare learners for emergency responses that demand problem solving under stressful conditions. Personnel require active learning opportunities in:

- Homeland security
- Anti-terrorism
- Counter-terrorism planning
- Hostage negotiations
- Disaster response planning

Dynamic learning improves planning, performance, and successful mission execution.

Practical Exercise Application: Refer to Chapter 5: Performance Feedback, Performance Objectives, and Task Analysis. Write a Summary Sheet on a field training exercise:

- **Define Exercise:** service weapon sight alignment.
- **Write:** performance objective(s) or statements of what learners must accomplish as a result of the service weapon alignment instructional unit.
- **Define:** conditions under which learners must perform service weapon alignment task(s).
- **Define:** performance standards describing how well learners must perform service weapon sight alignment task(s).

Pathway Six—Organizing the Practical Exercise

Why are the gravesite practical exercise stations important lessons for criminal investigation? The practical exercise facilitates the learning process and specifies investigative learning outcomes. The practical exercise approach requires the Systematic Design of Instruction. Learner opportunities address foundation requirements throughout the course of instruction in preparation for the gravesite practical exercise.

Content and Self-Inventory Questions

Refer to the following fill-in questions to formulate a general assessment of your training content knowledge.

1. _____ is an acronym that describes *Plan, Rehearse, Early Intervention, Proceed, Active Learning, Review, and Evaluate.*

2. Trainers pose a basic question: "Where are we going?" The answer determines goals, _____, and defines appropriate performance objectives.

3. The second question: "How will you get there?" is answered by developing *goals* and the derived _____ objectives.

4. The gravesite excavation exercise appeals to multiple _____ styles.

5. _____ enhance the learning design through the articulation and sequencing of related goals and performance objectives.

6. The _____ (gravesite practical exercise) is a goal frame of reference.

7. _____ originate from specific goals and inform participants regarding standards and learning progressions.

8. Trainers understand the "_____" principle. Trainers train up to the required level of proficiency, in the minimum amount of time.

9. Every "learning curve" contains a "_____," a quantitative curve that leads to decline in the learning process.

10. Conduct an "_____" during the final classroom instruction and at the beginning of the field training practical exercise.

Special Note: Refer to Appendix E: Fill-in question solutions. In addition, refer to Table E-6: Self-Rating Inventory for an assessment of these skills. Rating Inventory Scale

Table E-6 includes an assessment rating of one to ten (ten being the *high* and one being the *low*).

Table E-6. Self-Rating Inventory

Pathway Six: Training Skills	1	2	3	4	5	6	7	8	9	10
Appraise three essential elements of this organizing center.										
Identify three essential elements of the gravesite practical exercise.										
Identify gravesite practical exercise goals.										
List elements of the PREPARE training model acronym.										
Distinguish principles of comparison and victim identification.										
Explain gravesite practical exercise coordination procedures.										
Identify gravesite practical exercise support measures.										
Describe gravesite excavation check-points.										
Appraise elements of the monitoring and feedback process.										
Appraise gravesite coordination requirements.										

Instructor Applications

Instruction involves systematic planning procedures and effective logistical response efforts. Law enforcement training requires active learning practical exercises that ensure field applications. Dynamic training models require individuals who reason, know how to coordinate, and support field operations. Practical exercises provide opportunities to approximate realistic lesson planning strategies and case scenario applications. Preparation is vital to successful implementation. Learning station development requires attention to performance objective details.

Practical Exercise Application: Refer to Chapter 6: Gravesite Practical Exercise, Demonstration and Check Points, and Appendix A.

- **Select:** one training station and assess how *you* would conduct the practical exercise.
- **Develop** a related worksheet.
- **Prepare** a brief, oral introduction and content application for the exercise.
- **Reflect** training skills applied during the onsite gravesite simulation.

The introduction and demonstration explains the station process. For example, the chain of custody station should clarify the purpose and exercise procedure. Practical exercise demonstrations explain the criteria for successful chain of custody accomplishment. Instructors may initiate questions to assess comprehension and provide feedback in response to learner questions.

Pathway Seven—Organizing the Learning Simulation

The mock trial simulation involves extensive role-play that allows learners to act out realistic courtroom scenarios. Players understand the storyline and have access to a role script Summary Sheet. They interact with each other and analyze performance requirements.

The role-play experience allows related skill(s) practice. Prosecution and defense roles promote an understanding of differing perspectives and diverse professional roles. The mock trial experience often provides an unexpected realization of unexploited personal qualities.

Content and Self-Inventory Questions

Refer to the following fill-in questions to formulate a general assessment of your training content knowledge.

1. The main argument for advocating simulation technique revolves around _____.

2. _____ refers to player problem solving that enables learners to explore field situations.

3. _____ demands rules, regulations, authentic settings, and hypothetical situations.

4. The intersection of the horizontal and vertical axes locates the _____.

5. The following behaviors emerge on the _____ axis of the mock trial simulation: cooperation, self-control, due process, and respect for the rights of others.

6. The _____ axis documents content and learning objectives: evidence collection and preservation, chain of custody/scientific laboratory procedures, interview strategy models and courtroom testimony, and so on.

7. The evidence trail and "_____" will hopefully prove one of them guilty beyond a reasonable doubt in the mock trial simulation.

8. The ideal time for _____ is during the suppression hearing, before the courthouse mock trial.

9. The main purpose of the _____ simulation is to challenge evidence concerning chain of custody.

10. In summary, mock trial _____ strategies encourage: (1) problem solving, (2) decision-making, and (3) critical thinking skill applications.

Special Note: Refer to Appendix E: Fill-in question solutions. In addition, refer to Table E-7: Self-Rating Inventory for an assessment of these skills. Rating Inventory Scale Table E-7 includes an assessment rating of one to ten (ten being the *high* and one being the *low*).

Table E-7. Self-Rating Inventory

Pathway Seven: Training Skills	1	2	3	4	5	6	7	8	9	10
Appraise the mock trial learning simulation strategies.										
List the five basic learning progressions for the mock trial.										
List the witness development progressions in mock trial simulation.										
Appraise Suppression Hearing rehearsal strategies.										
Identify mock trial active learning strategies.										
List learning benefits when students are engaged in role playing.										
Describe requirements for rules and procedures during the simulation.										
Describe role requirements for the judge and magistrate (district Justice) during the mock trial simulation.										
Define the need for practice exercises and case study applications.										
Appraise the necessity for an evaluation survey questionnaire.										

Instructor Applications

The mock trial offers opportunities to excel beyond traditional tests. Instructional applications build confidence and assist in the assessment process. Professional role-play changes learner perspectives and offers insight into career opportunities.

- **Practical Exercise Application:** Refer to Chapter 7: The Mock Trial.
- **Write:** a case study Summary Sheet.
- **Write:** a witness role script.
- **Describe:** the witness's emotional climate.
- **Outline:** the dialogue and facts witnesses can contribute.
- **Anticipate:** the basic facts investigators and prosecution team will need at trial.
- **Outline:** the best information for the follow-up interview.

Pathway Eight—Training for Peak Performance

Training for *peak performance* requires learning opportunities. Instructors and learners striving for a peak performance may achieve excellence in the training experience. Furthermore, the struggle for excellence increases the possibility of achieving flow and finding a peak experience.

This book represents a training opportunity for brainstorming and peak performance. If you incorporate its lessons, it can start you on the approach to a successful training career. Take advantage of the training pathways and techniques, which arm you for the future. This knowledge maximizes successful training outcomes that will eventually come your way.

Content and Self-Inventory Questions

Refer to the following fill-in questions to formulate a general assessment of your training content knowledge.

1. Privette defines _____ as "behavior that transcends or goes beyond predictable functioning to use a person's potential more fully than could be reasonably expected."

2. Striving for *peak performance* facilitates a sense of creative
   _____.

3. There are two basic levels of the *peak experience*. The first
   level is the _____ *peak performance*.

4. _____ and _____ experiences are more likely to occur during
   practical exercises or simulations.

5. _____ defines extreme personal performance efforts
   that demand practiced expertise and the application of
   related skills.

6. _____ requires "dreaming the dream" in pursuance of
   positive images.

7. Creativity generally takes time; however, insight gleaned
   from _____ can jump-start the dynamic instructor approach.

8. The criteria for _____ evaluation includes: (1) creative
   solutions to the problem; (2) participation of all group members; (3) novel solutions; (4) valuable ideas; and (5) a trusting
   social climate.

9. *Peak performances* and *flow* experiences are more likely to
   occur during _____ or _____.

10. The _____ model states that "Six resources need to work
    together in creativity: intellectual abilities, knowledge,
    personality traits, motivational style, thinking styles, and an
    environment that is supportive of the creative process and
    creative output."

**Special Note: Refer to Appendix E: Fill-in question solu-
tions. In addition, refer to Table E-8: Self-Rating Inventory
for an assessment of these skills. Rating Inventory Scale
Table E-8 includes an assessment rating of one to ten (ten
being the *high* and one being the *low*).**

Table E-8. Self-Rating Inventory

Pathway Eight: Training Skills	1	2	3	4	5	6	7	8	9	10
Define peak performance.										
List four parameters of peak performance.										
Illustrate level one peak performance.										
Illustrate level two peak performance.										
Appraise peak performance training applications.										
Distinguish the elements of "flow."										
Appraise the elements of creativity.										
Identify the criteria for the Resonance Performance Model (RPM).										
Define the brainstorming problem-solving process.										
Appraise the main argument for peak performance training.										

Instructor Applications

Chapter 8: Peak Performance Training addressed a number of topics associated with creativity. This optimal experience connects flow and peak performance. This requires movement beyond the individual's comfort zone. These are the moments when the individual excels beyond his or her normal functioning and establishes a clear focus on the task(s). The peak performance can occur in any realm of human activity: *intellectual functioning, emotional response,* or *psychomotor.*

Practical Exercise Application: Refer to Chapter 8: Peak Performance Training and Corner 8-3: Level Two: Case Study Briefing. Analyze the dialogue for peak performance attributes and connect the principles of peak performance training. How might these approaches apply to the Case Study Briefing? Was the speaker in flow with her presentation? How would you apply brainstorming strategies to the detective audience?

Pathway Nine—Leadership Counseling

The instructor/counselor assumes responsibility for personal leadership and demonstrates enthusiasm for counseling and advisement. Instructor feedback reinforces learning outcomes. Advisee counseling is problem solving rather than punitive, providing ongoing feedback concerning the instructor/ learner process.

For example, the learner is failing examinations because of anxiety. Subsequent counseling sessions motivate considerable improvement, less anxiety, and renewed self-confidence. One cannot say absolutely that the intervention had a cause and effect result. However, there is at least probable cause evidence that counseling might have contributed.

Content and Self-Inventory Questions

Refer to the following fill-in questions to formulate a general assessment of your training content knowledge.

1. Instructors help learners gain self-understanding once relationship foundations are in place – no easy task. Two factors affect the process: (1) _____, and (2) _____ *or* _____.

2. The counseling interview process has three overlapping phases: (1) _____, (2) _____ (self-exploration, self-understanding, commitment), and (3) _____.

3. Assess _____ skills as soon as possible, accurate behavioral analysis determines positive outcomes.

4. _____ infers tolerance and encourages a change in behavior—the ultimate goal.

5. _____ defined in form of metaphors: "walking in someone else's shoes," or "seeing something through someone else's eyes."

6. _____ *learners* bring emotional issues to the instructional process.

7. _____ *learners* do not always acknowledge personal limitations in the training environment for fear of discrimination and peer acceptance.

8. _____ *learners* require direction, guidance, and appreciate structure in the learning process.

9. _____ *learners* function best without interference from instructors or other learners. They are self-motivated and have a preference to control the learning process—offer opportunities that allow independent learners to find self-prescribed learning pathways.

10. The _____ *process* includes seeking the support of qualified professionals who help learners with serious emotional problems.

Special Note: Refer to Appendix E: Fill-in question solutions. In addition, refer to Table E-9: Self-Rating Inventory for an assessment of these skills. Rating Inventory Scale Table E-9 includes an assessment rating of one to ten (ten being the *high* and one being the *low*).

Table E-9. Self-Rating Inventory

Pathway Nine: Training Skills	1	2	3	4	5	6	7	8	9	10
List three basic components of the counseling/advising process.										
Identify the basic phases of the counseling process.										
Appraise ideal instructor/counseling attitudes.										
Identify basic student attitude patterns.										
Describe the foundation for helping the student gain self-understanding.										
Appraise student confidentiality factors.										

Pathway Nine: Training Skills	1	2	3	4	5	6	7	8	9	10
List the counseling three overlapping phases.										
Cite basic counseling advising skills.										
Appraise four counseling theories.										
Identify the basic criteria for a professional referral.										

Instructor Applications

Learners may look for clarification, understanding, or involvement; they are seeking a helping relationship. Instructors recognize assistance-seeking behaviors, even when not expressed verbally. Learners are reluctant to express needs; remain alert to address nonverbal clues. Embrace the helping relationship and support learner concerns.

Practical Exercise Application: Refer to Chapter 9: Dynamic Guidance and Referrals and Corner 9-2: Case Study Learner Problem.

- **Prepare** to conduct a counseling session with Sandra Wilkins.
- **Select** a counseling approach and appropriate content.
- **Offer** appropriate advisor attitudes.
- **Identify** interview stages.
- **Assess** coping skills.
- **Define** the problem.
- **Determine** the cause(s).
- **Identify** possible solutions.
- **Implement** solution(s).
- **Describe** required performance tasks.
- **Describe** lower level behavior changes that make-up those tasks.

Pathway Ten—Dynamic Leadership: Pulling it All Together

Positive motivation enhances learning climates and motivates mutual understanding, acceptance, approval, and respect. Training managers reduce learner stress and anxiety by applying Johari Window principles. Identify Emotional Command Systems and clarify training methods.

Content and Self-inventory Questions

Refer to the following fill-in questions to formulate a general assessment of your training content knowledge.

1. The first step to successful program management is to train the _____.

2. The second step is _____ training needs and requirements.

3. _____ training staff is an art directly related to mentoring.

4. Advanced professional manager/instructors connect with the people around them and interpret _____ Systems.

5. The _____ is motivated by the need to be self-reliant, strong, and avoid feeling weak or dependant.

6. The _____ emotional command system relates to survival.

7. The _____ System coordinates functions related to affiliation, bonding, and attachment.

8. When the _____ System is working properly, individuals can maintain physical and emotional fitness.

9. When the _____ System is in full expression, they feel a sense of relaxed stimulation, combination of peace, and enjoyment.

10. The _____ Model offers opportunities to examine leadership, training, and the social climate from communication and feedback perspectives.

Special Note: Refer to Appendix E: Fill-in question solutions. In addition, refer to Table E-10: Self-Rating Inventory for an assessment of these skills. Rating Inventory
Scale Table E-10 includes an assessment rating of one to
ten (ten being the *high* and one being the *low*).

Table E-10. Self-Rating Inventory

Pathway Ten: Training Skills	1	2	3	4	5	6	7	8	9	10
Distinguish elements of curriculum leadership/management.										
Appraise the emotional command systems.										
Define the Commander-Chief System.										
Define the Explorer System.										
Define the Energy Czar System.										
Define the elements of the Nest-Builder System.										
Define the elements of the Jester System.										
Define the elements of the Sentry System.										
Describe the Universal Design for Instruction curriculum model.										
Distinguish the elements of the Johari Window.										

Instructor Applications

The art of ending the training process successfully requires
finding the final destination. *Pulling it all together* demands:

- Curriculum planning
- Learner feedback
- Instructor feedback
- Positive training management and leadership

The *training grand strategy* is to perceive the strategic picture
through the Johari Window and define the vision for the future.

Practical Exercise Application

1. Purpose: This written exercise encourages readers to reflect on, formalize, and define their personal training philosophy. Effective training strategies assist in preparation for selection and promotion to training leadership positions. Recording your training vision clarifies the goals, objectives, and direction for successful outcomes. Refer to *Pathway One* in Chapter One for additional guidance.

2. Recommendation: This exercise is important because if leadership does not know where they are going, how can they expect others to follow? Refer to the *training pathways* to formulate your personal assessment.

3. Introduction: Focus on your personal training philosophy:

- Phrase comments in the "first person," that is, "When I become a training manager/instructor ..."
- Create a hypothetical scenario if you do not serve in a training capacity.
- Compare and contrast what is important to **YOU!**
- Establish your central idea or theme in the Introduction.

4. Paragraphs, Themes, and General Instructions: Your personal training assessment answers the following questions concerning training vision:

- Where am I going?
- How will I get there?
- How will I know when I have arrived?
- Where do I go next?
- How can I influence training staff and learners?

5. Summary and Conclusion: Reflect on your rank or training position. Include your personal philosophy, goals, objectives, and training leadership approach. Include a summary of important issues that affect your situation. In addition, address:

- **Vision**
- **Training climate**
- **Direction**
- **Values**

The conclusion reaffirms important observations, restates controlling ideas or themes, and offers summary statements. **This exercise enhances your endeavors to connect the training pathways and *pull it all together.***

Conclusion

Arriving at this stage presupposes that former pathways set the foundation for positive learning climates. This requires successful completion of the ***ten basic pathways*** by applying quality instructional methods. **Instructors initiate activities that have positive outcomes:**

- **Dynamic training**
- **Dynamic management**
- **Dynamic leadership**

At the end of the Epilogue, you should know exactly what your strengths and weakness are. At this point, are you aware of your true potential? If not, take another inventory of yourself. To know where you are going and how to get there, you must first know yourself. Every training advantage has an equivalent disadvantage; however, you must take the time to find it. Be a lifetime learner; it is never too late to learn—do not stop learning. ***The Journey ends, or is it just beginning?***

Multiple-Choice - Final Personal Assessment

Chapter 1: Multiple-Choice Questions

1. You have recently been assigned to train the trainers. The first lecture concerns the attributes of superior instructors. Which of the following choice(s) offer the best solution?

    a. Positive self-expectancy
    b. Positive self-control
    c. Choices a and b
    d. Content mastery
    e. All of the above

2. You are preparing your first lecture and applying the fundamentals. The basic principles of organization apply. Which of the following choice(s) offer the best solution?

    a. Central ideas
    b. Lecture points
    c. Lecture continuity
    d. All of the above
    e. None of the above

3. You are speaking before a large group of trainees. Powerful speech is a combination of several factors. Which of the following choice(s) offer the best solution?

    a. Volume
    b. Effective modulation
    c. Projection
    d. All of the above
    e. None of the above

4. In the case of Robinson v. Ewell, the defense attorney conducted a lecture. The main point of the lecture is stated below. Which of the following choice(s) offer the best solution?

    a. The courts have faults
    b. The Supreme Court of the United States
    c. The Justice of the Peace Court Decision
    d. Equality before the law
    e. None of the above

5. Gottman and Declare describe social bonding and the bidding process. Which of the following choice(s) offer the best solution?

    a. Turning toward
    b. Turning away
    c. Unrequited response
    d. All of the above
    e. None of the above

Chapter 2: Multiple-Choice Questions

1. You serve as an instructor for the training academy and apply group dynamic strategies to facilitate group transitions to the highest level. Which of the following choice(s) offer the best solution?

    a. Achieve the adjustment phase
    b. Achieve the cooperation phase
    c. All of the above
    d. None of the above

2. The word "enneagram" refers to a model. The word description is twofold. Ennea means_____, Gram is Greek for model. Which of the following choice(s) offer the best solution?

    a. Six   c. Eight
    b. Seven   d. Nine
          e. None of the above

3. The_____ is innovative, cerebral, and provocative. Which of the following choice(s) offer the best solution?

    a. Investigator
    b. Reformist
    c. Enthusiast
    d. None of the above

4. The_____ is self-confident, decisive, dominating, and confrontational. Which of the following choice(s) offer the best solution?

    a. Investigator
    b. Reformist
    c. Leader
    d. None of the above

5. The_____ is adaptable, ambitious, image conscious, and driven. Which of the following choice(s) offer the best solution?

    a. Investigator
    b. Reformist
    c. Motivator
    d. None of the above

Chapter 3: Multiple-Choice Questions

1. A _____is a collection organizing principles, belief systems, or creative models that shape understanding. Which of the following choice(s) offer the best solution?

    a. Training paradigm
    b. Bloom's System
    c. Performance objectives
    d. None of the above

2. _____ is a search of reality, truth, and professional conduct. Which of the following choice(s) offer the best solution?

    a. Goal
    b. Performance
    c. Philosophy
    d. None of the above

3. Dynamic _____ training methods involve real world multidimensional situations. Which of the following choice(s) offer the best solution?

    a. Training paradigm
    b. Bloom's System
    c. Performance of objectives
    d. Virtual reality
    e. None of the above

4. _____ requires participants to learn not only from the instructor, but also from each other, while participating in the problem solving process. Which of the following choice(s) offer the best solution?

    a. Virtual reality
    b. Training paradigm
    c. Active learning
    d. None of the above

5. _____ provides a linkage basis for vertical and horizontal content articulation and sequencing. Which of the following choice(s) offer the best solution?

    a. Training paradigm
    b. Organizing center
    c. Active learning
    d. None of the above

Chapter 4: Multiple-Choice Questions

1. Knowledgeable trainers apply the _____ planning process. The planning process provides an overview of training plans, such as long-range, short-range, and near-term plans. Which of the following choice(s) offer the best solution?

    a. Back-step
    b. Chronological steps
    c. None of the above
    d. All of the above

2. _____is the primary means of getting trainee attention in the beginning of the lecture. Which of the following choice(s) offer the best solution?

    a. Learning hook
    b. Learner orientation
    c. Training objectives
    d. None of the above

3. The content of the lesion plan determines the instructional method. Which of the following choice(s) offer the best solution?

    a. Lecture
    b. Demonstration
    c. Role-play/small group
    d. All of the above

4. The body of supporting knowledge is the most important part of the lesson plan. Which of the following choice(s) offer the best solution?

    a. Dominates time factor
    b. Drives the learning process
    c. Drives the performance objectives
    d. All of the above

5. The summary and closing statement offer the last opportunity to capture the learner's attention and imagination. Which of the following choice(s) offer the best solution?

   a. Summarizes instructional points
   b. Emphasizes performance objectives
   c. Practical exercise points
   d. Last learning hook
   e. All of the above

Chapter 5: Multiple-Choice Questions

1. You are about to conduct the feedback process with a specific learner. Feedback communication is related to learning style. Therefore, you remember that most learners acquire what percentage from seeing. Which of the following choice(s) offer the best solution?

   a. 53%
   b. 62%
   c. 73%
   d. 83%

2. Feedback is a communication process that assesses _____. Which of the following choice(s) offer the best solution?

   a. Learning style
   b. Task readiness
   c. Performance appraisal
   d. Instructor response
   e. All of the above

3. The common feedback response is correcting _____. Which of the following choice(s) offer the best solution?

   a. Praise
   b. Errors
   c. Rapport
   d. None of the above

4. Program standards state the degree of correctness the learner must demonstrate during the task(s). What are you looking for as an instructor from the learner? Which of the following choice(s) offer the best solution?

    a. Accuracy
    b. Speed of the response
    c. Both a and b
    d. None of the above

5. Programmed instruction is a highly structured form of _____. Which of the following choice(s) offer the best solution?

    a. Self-study
    b. Independent learning
    c. Immediate feedback
    d. None of the above
    e. All of the above

Chapter 6: Multiple-Choice Questions

1. Every "learning curve" contains a "_____." Which of the following choice(s) offer the best solution?

    a. Rehearsal appraisal
    b. Feedback appraisal
    c. Evaluation appraisal
    d. None of the above

2. Directions in the form of a _____ offer special written directions. Which of the following choice(s) offer the best solution?

    a. Summary Sheet
    b. Group dynamics
    c. PREPARE MODEL
    d. None of the above

3. Successful trainers pose a question: Where are we going? Which of the following choice(s) offer the best solution?

   a. Goals
   b. Organizing centers
   c. Performance objectives
   d. All of the above
   e. None of the above

4. Organizing centers enhance learning design through the_____ and sequencing of goals and objectives. Which of the following choice(s) offer the best solution?

   a. Description
   b. Articulation
   c. Standards
   d. All of the above
   e. None of the above

5. Evaluation is necessary to_____ the curriculum and helps the planning process. Which of the following choice(s) offer the best solution?

   a. Redirect
   b. Formulate
   c. Guide
   d. None of the above

Chapter 7: Multiple-Choice Questions

1. The main argument of advocating the learning simulation revolves around _____. Which of the following choice(s) offer the best solution?

   a. Reproduction
   b. Motivation
   c. Participation
   d. None of the above

2. **Role play refers to player problem solving that enables learners to explore _____. Which of the following choice(s) offer the best solution?**

    a. Field situations
    b. Creative elements
    c. Internalization of content
    d. All of the above

3. **The organizing center horizontal axis of the mock trial incorporates articulation. Which of the following choice(s) offer the best solution?**

    a. Evidence collection
    b. Chain of custody
    c. Courtroom testimony
    d. All of the above
    e. None of the above

4. **The organizing center vertical axis of the mock trial incorporates articulation. Which of the following offer the best solution?**

    a. Cooperation
    b. Self-control
    c. All of the above
    d. None of the above

5. **The ideal time for coaching for the mock trial is during _____. Which of the following choice(s) offer the best solution?**

    a. Preliminary investigation
    b. Follow-up investigation
    c. Suppression Hearing
    d. None of the above

Chapter 8: Multiple-Choice Questions

1. A peak performance definition includes which of the following choice(s):

   a. Peak performance is superior behavior at a task(s)
   b. Represents an intrinsic value to the person
   c. Direct, active engagement with the valued subject
   d. All of the above
   e. None of the above

2. A citizen stumbles on an airliner crash and saves passenger lives. Which of the following choice(s) offer the best solution?

   a. Level one peak performance
   b. Level two peak performance
   c. None of the above
   d. All of the above

3. The law enforcement trainer work tirelessly for years before experiencing a peak performance while speaking before the Police Academy graduating class. Which of the following choice(s) offer the best solution?

   a. Level one peak performance
   b. Level two peak performance
   c. None of the above
   d. All of the above

4. _____denotes the holistic sensation present when we act with total involvement. It is the state in which action follows upon action according to an internal logic, which seems to need no conscious intervention on our part. Which of the following offers the best solution?

   a. Performance
   b. Flow
   c. Intrinsic
   d. None of the above

5. A four-stage model that begins with (1) "The dream or the feelings a person seeks when engaged in an activity. This is not a goal for the future, but a sense of what the person wishes to feel like in the present. (2) The person must be involved intensely and engage in preparation." Which of the following offers the best solution?

> a. Creativity Model
> b. Confluence Model
> c. All of the above
> d. None of the above

Chapter 9: Multiple Choice Questions

1. Instructors help learners gain self-understanding once relationship foundations are in place—no easy task. What blocks the process? Which of the following offers the best solution?

> a. Defensive behaviors
> b. Denial
> c. Both a and b
> d. None of the above

2. The emphasis of the interviewing process is on rapport. Interviews begin with neutral topics—attempts to encourage understanding with open and friendly dialogue. Provide positive feedback. Be attentive to learner needs and demonstrate genuine interest in their concerns, demonstrating sincerity and enthusiasm. Which of the following offers the best solution?

> a. Development phase
> b. Conclusion phase
> c. Opening phase
> d. All of the above

3. Defining the problem provides a systematic approach for performance assessment. Analyze deficits and poor performance motivation. Which of the following offers the best solution?

   a. Collecting information
   b. Determining the cause(s)
   c. Both a and b
   d. None of the above

4. The "Person's Centered Counseling Approach" is non-directive and person centered. The focus is on active listening and allows individuals to determine what is important. This thought-reflective style assumes advisees have the ability to solve their problems. The friendly, non-directive approach serves as a rapport builder in the interview process. Which of the following offers the best solution?

   a. Glasser
   b. Ellis
   c. Rogers
   d. None of the above

5. ABC theory unfolds: "A" is the activating event/ firearms training event, "B" represents the belief system (I am not going to qualify on the firing range), and "C" represents the consequence(s). A does not cause C—irrational beliefs (IBs) cause C. Thus, the activating event does not cause the consequence(s). The learner's irrational belief system defines activating events that cause consequences.

   Which of the following offers the best solution?

   a. Glasser
   b. Ellis
   c. Rogers
   d. None of the above

Chapter 10: Multiple Choice Questions

1. Lay the proper foundation for successful dynamic training. The first step to successful program management. Which of the following offers the best solution?

   a. Prioritize training needs and requirements
   b. Train the trainers
   c. Practice makes perfect
   d. None of the above

2. The_____ is motivated by the need to be self-reliant, strong, and avoid feeling weak or dependent. They have the tendency to be over protective and will fight for justice. Which of the following offers the best solution?

   a. Sentry System
   b. Explorer System
   c. Commander-in-Chief System
   d. None of the above

3. The_____ is the ideal researcher for finding alternative instructional methods. They are optimistic when seeking information and involved in sorting, planning, learning, and goal setting. Which of the following offers the best solution?

   a. Sentry System
   b. Explorer System
   c. Commander-in-Chief System
   d. None of the above

4. They function best in brainstorming sessions where group members feel free to say whatever comes to mind. Wacky notions surface, but together you also devise novel ideas. Which of the following offers the best solution?

   a. Sentry System
   b. Explorer System
   c. Jester System
   d. None of the above

5. The _____ encourages the expansion of shared
   curriculum training and achieving accurate feedback;
   however, it requires personal risk for leaders. Curriculum management and leadership require candid leaders who establish trust and mutual respect. Suggest
   information exchanges rather than one-way dialogues
   that do not offer feedback. Which of the following
   offers the best solution?

       a. Explorer System
       b. Best-Builder
       c. Johari Window
       d. None of the above

Special Note: Refer to Appendix F for the Multiple-Choice
Question Solutions.

Appendices

Gravesite Practical Exercise

Advanced Summary Sheet

A jogger finds several bones near a remote park area. Numerous investigative questions quickly emerge: (1) Are they human bones? (2) Can the person's identity be established? (3) What was the cause of death? (4) What other details will the crime scene reveal? At this point, the learners require basic knowledge concerning crime scene processing and understand the need to coordinate with scientific experts, that is, forensic archeologists, forensic anthropologists, forensic entomologists, and forensic odontology specialists.

The responding officer preserves the scene and notifies police headquarters. The learning coordinator dispatches the investigative and evidence teams to the site. Twenty-six learners are assigned to one of five investigative teams and rotate through five learning stations: (1) main gravesite, (2) scattered bones, (4) dried bloodstains, and (5) chain of custody. In addition, stations 1 to 4 require evidence collection, note taking, photographing, and sketching.

Initially, the teams conduct a walk-through preliminary search. This involves finding all associated evidence, such as missing body segments, clothing, weapons, shell casings, hair, blood, and other related items. The search focuses on the skeletal remains and surrounding gravesite. Visual inspection involves moving outward from the center to related sites until all body parts are recovered. Thus, the search starts at the site, moving away in the cardinal directions and fanning out *away* from the body (Byers, 2002).

Designated leader participants assume command, supervise other participants, and coordinate the learning stations. In addition, they arrive early and rotate through the learning stations before the simulation begins. Ultimately, everyone plays the role of evidence technician when collecting their own evidence samples and taking crime scene photographs.

The instructor evaluates practical exercise stations for the successful completion of all requirements. Particular attention is devoted to appropriate evidence collection and chain of custody procedures. The primary assessment tools include the preliminary, supplemental, and related laboratory reports submitted by participants.

The primary purpose of this field project is to follow-through on protecting the crime scene. In addition, write preliminary and follow-up reports and coordinate with the scientific lab and related experts.

Basic Supporting Learning Goals

➢ Describe the four steps in the excavation of human remains.
➢ Identify the elements of organizing a walking ground search.
➢ Identify the need to follow the proper procedures after human remains have been located.
➢ Describe the use of flags and wooden posts to protect the crime scene.
➢ Appraise the requirements of the marked remains and their relationship to grid square and datum point.
➢ Identify the suitable containers for transporting human remains and biologically associated materials to the proper facility.
➢ Identify the elements of chain of custody that are maintained throughout the recovery process.

Supporting Outline and Learning Objectives

Forensic Anthropology

• Introduction to Forensic Anthropology
• Crime Scene Processing
• Examining Remains
• Biological Profile
• Forensic Anthropology Documentation

Supporting Learning Objectives

• Define forensic anthropology.
• List the elements of a biological profile.
• Define physical anthropology.

- Describe the role of scavengers in the movement, alteration, and scattering of human remains.
- Identify the need to utilize remote sensing methods to locate human remains.
- Identify and name some skills of the forensic anthropologist.
- List clues that can lead to the identification of male or female skeletal remains.
- List clues that identify the approximate age of the skeletal remains.
- Identify the legal issues when a forensic anthropologist testifies as an expert witness.

Related Case Studies

Forensic Taphonomy

- Defining Forensic Taphonomy
- Determining Premortem and Postmortem Intervals
- Estimating the Time of Death
- Distinguishing Animal and Human Remains
- Human Remains in Water
- Buried Remains
- Insect Cycles

Supporting Learning Objectives

- Define forensic taphonomy.
- Identify the role of paleontology and connection to forensic taphonomy.
- List the contributions, methods, and theories or related description to forensic taphonomy.
- Identify the taphonomic factors in the premortem and postmortem intervals.
- List the elements that temperature plays in decomposition of the human body.
- Identify the role of insects and scavengers in body decomposition and damage to soft body tissues.
- Identify the decomposition influence on buried remains.

Related Case Studies

Phase 11: Evaluation of the Crime Scene
Crime Scene Investigation

- Defining the Crime Scene
- Information and Physical Evidence
- General Crime Scene Procedures
- Crime Scene Management
- First Responding Officer
- Securing the Crime Scene
- Crime Scene Survey
- Crime Scene Documentation

Supporting Learning Objectives

- List and describe the primary and secondary crime scene classifications.
- List the basic stages of crime scene investigation.
- List the eight types of information that can be obtained from the examination of physical evidence found at crime scenes.
- Identify the four elements of crime scene management.
- Describe the five crime scene models.
- List the duties of the first responder to the crime scene.
- List the elements of the multilevel approach to crime scene security.
- Describe the components of crime scene documentation.
- List the basic elements of crime scene photography.
- List the two basic types of crime scene sketches.

Related Case Studies

General: This practical exercise project at the rotation level is team oriented. However, the report writing and evidence procedures that follow are not team efforts. Each participant is responsible for his or her own evidence and reports. Individual stations serve as the foundation, the remaining reports constructed from the facts of the case.

INSTRUCTIONS: Bring the following items to the learning simulation:
☐ Camera (Participants are responsible for their own photographs)
☐ Notebook and paper (Notes are essential for writing the preliminary, follow-up, and laboratory reports)
☐ Ruler
☐ Rubber gloves
☐ Pencils and pens
☐ Textbook

Searching and Mapping Remains: Initially, the teams conduct a walk-through preliminary search. This involves finding all associated materials, such as missing body segments, clothing, weapons, shell casings, and other related items. The focus of the search remains (the body, and the gravesite). Visual inspection involves moving outward from the center to related sites until all body parts are discovered. Thus, the search starts at the site, moving away in the cardinal directions and fanning out *away* from the body.

What techniques could be applied to determine the age, sex, height, and facial features of the victim? Note this information in your follow-up report and laboratory analysis.

Mapping Remains:

➤ The first step in the mapping process is to set up a datum point close to the remains.
➤ This should be placed on permanent structures or objects that are not likely to be obliterated with the passage of time.

> In uninhabited areas, a large tree or rock can be used, whereas the corner of a building will suffice in populated areas.
> After this point has been fixed, its position on a large map should be indicated.
> In towns, a city map is ideal (if it is detailed enough); outside of metropolitan areas, a USGS quadrangle (a map developed by the U.S. Geological Survey Office that depicts geographic features in a 1-square-mile area) is preferred.
> When using a quadrangle, the datum point can be located by triangulation with a compass to other visible permanent structures or by using the Global Positioning System (GPS) (Byers, 2002).

After Datum Point Is Established:

> The area immediately surrounding the body must be marked using a grid square to provide a framework for mapping relevant findings.
> The area usually entails setting up a 10 to 15 foot square, constructed of four wooden posts (one is each corner) connected with string.
> The investigator or crime technician orients sides along north-south and east-west axes for ease of understanding by law enforcement and other persons.
> Once established, the grid is depicted on a map and the compass direction and distance to the datum point of its nearest corner should be noted.
> A tape measure is used to locate bones and other items in relation to the grid square.
> For associated material located more than 100 feet away, pacing off distances may be sufficiently accurate.

Station #1

Main Gravesite Performance Objectives:

Use checkmark to indicate task is completed:

☐ Conduct a ground search to locate the human remains.
☐ After the remains have been located, establish an access barricade and command post.

☐ First, photographs are taken before anything is touched, moved, or altered. The essential photographs are: (1) an overview long-range shot, (2) mid-range shot, (3) 360-degree body coverage, (4) overhead body shot, and (5) related pieces of evidence.

☐ Biological and associated "evidence finds" (**at other learning stations**) must be marked and placed using flags or wooden posts.

☐ Using a permanent structure, locate a datum point at the gravesite.

☐ Establish a grid square from 10 – 15 feet on the side.

☐ The grid should be established around the area where the major parts of the remains are located.

☐ Distance and compass direction of the datum point are connected to other pieces of evidence.

☐ Conduct essential measurements with a 50 ft. tape.

☐ Complete a rough sketch of the main site using graph paper.

RECOVERY OF HUMAN REMAINS FOUR STEPS:

➤ **Location**

➤ **Mapping**

➤ **Excavation**

➤ **Retrieval**

List of Tools for Body Recovery:

☐ Shovel	☐ Square and pointed trowels
☐ Pruning shears and saws	☐ Screens (1/4 and 1/8 inch)
☐ Wooden and metal stakes	☐ Paint brushes
☐ Toothbrushes	☐ Dental picks
☐ Flags on wooden posts	☐ Wooden digging instruments
☐ Buckets for moving dirt	☐ Evidence gags and wrapping
☐ Notebook and pencils	☐ Graph paper
☐ Protractor	☐ String or twine
☐ Cameras	☐ Metal detector
☐ Tape measure	☐ Compass
☐ Line level	☐ Transit and stadia rod
☐ Insect collection jars	☐ Entomologist's net

Station #2 (Second Skeletal Remains: Hair Dna Evidence) Performance Objectives: Use checkmark to indicate task is completed:

☐ First, photographs are taken before anything is touched, moved, or altered. The essential photographs are: (1) an overview long-range shot, (2) mid-range shot, (3) 360-degree body coverage, (4) overhead body shot, and (5) related pieces of evidence.

☐ Collect hair samples found near the femur, patella, tibia, fibula, tarsus, metatarsals, and phalanges.

☐ Use the **druggist fold** to secure your sample.

☐ Place your **initial, time, and date** on the outside of the druggist fold.

☐ Do not handle the hairs directly with your hands.

☐ Wear rubber gloves!

☐ The importance of screening: Locating trace evidence.

☐ As the soil is moved out of the grave, it should be placed in buckets and taken to a location where it can be sifted through a one-quarter inch of fine screen.

Station #3 (Third Skeletal Remains: Entomology Site) Performance Objectives: Use checkmark to indicate task is completed:

Data Collected at the Scene:

☐ First, photographs are taken before anything is touched, moved, or altered. The essential photographs are: (1) an overview long-range shot, (2) mid-range shot, (3) 360-degree body coverage, (4) overhead body shot, and (5) related pieces of evidence.

☐ Take ambient air temperature at chest height. Use a thermometer with known accuracy taken in the shade.

☐ Temperature of any maggot mass (place the thermometer directly in center of mass).

☐ Ground surface temperature.

☐ Temperature at the interface of the body and ground (place the thermometer between the body surface and ground).

☐ Temperature of soil under the body after removal.

☐ Weather data for a period of two weeks *before discovering* the body and 3-4 hours *after discovery*.

Insect Collection:

☐ First, photographs are taken before anything is touched, moved, or altered. The essential photographs are: (1) an overview long-range shot, (2) mid-range shot, (3) 360-degree body coverage, (4) overhead body shot, and (5) related pieces of evidence.

☐ Collect adult insects with a net.

☐ Kill adult insects by placing them in a jar containing ethyl acetate or common fingernail polish remover.

☐ Place the adult insects into jars partially filled with 70 percent ethyl alcohol.

☐ Label the jars and lid labels with pencil (labels should have standard identification data as for all other types of physical evidence).

☐ Larvae may be placed directly into a solution of 70 percent ethyl alcohol, label, and seal the jars as for adult specimens. Some samples should be kept alive with liver and paper cover so oxygen can enter.

☐ Place labeled and sealed jars in shipping container to prevent breakage during transport.

☐ *Refer to entomology handout.*

Station #4 (Clothing and Related Blood Splatter) Performance Objectives: Use checkmark to indicate task is completed:

☐ Wear gloves and avoid cross-contamination.

☐ Generally, bloodstain evidence should be dried and frozen to preserve the genetic markers and stains.

☐ Do not package bloodstain evidence in plastic bags, because plastic bags promote the growth of microorganisms by retaining moisture.

☐ Obtain a control swab from the unstained area.

☐ Use the same type of swab and same liquid as used for the bloodstains.

☐ Allow swabs to air dry.

☐ Package in appropriate marked paper envelopes or druggist folds.

☐ Large objects with hard, porous surfaces (brick wall, concrete, pavement, etc.).

☐ Scrape the stain into a piece of clean paper, fold the paper into a packet bindle or,

☐ Collect the stain by using a slightly dampened (with distilled water) sterile cotton swab as for hard, nonporous surfaces. Allow to air dry and package in paper.

☐ A background control swab of an unstained area of the surface must be obtained.

Station #5 (Chain of Custody) Performance Objectives: Use checkmark to indicate task is completed:

Evidence Control System
Characteristics of Good Evidence Control System
☐ Prevents loss or unauthorized release of evidence
☐ Establishes and maintains continuous chain of custody
☐ Establishes custodial responsibility for evidence
☐ Lists, identifies, and indicates location of items
Evidence Control System: Performance Objectives
☐ Requires supervisor's approval before evidence is released
☐ Identifies individual to whom evidence is released
☐ Indicates reasons surrounding release of evidence
☐ Documented proof that release is authorized and indicates final disposition of evidence
Marking Evidence
☐ Date
☐ Time
☐ Personal Identifications
Basic Evidence Tag Information
☐ Report number
☐ Location of evidence
☐ Person taken from
☐ Address where found
☐ Description of article
☐ Alleged owner
☐ Property received by
☐ Special Disposition
☐ Evidence log number and item number
Chain of Custody Form
☐ Relinquished by
☐ Received by
☐ Purpose of change of custody
☐ Date and Time
Purpose of Evidence Ledger
☐ Serves as a cross-reference to the chain of custody documents and evidence tags
Advantages of Clear Plastic Evidence Pouch over Gum-sealed Evidence Envelope
☐ Clear plastic evidence pouches are heat sealed
☐ Evidence can be viewed without opening the pouch
☐ Any tampering with the evidence is immediately apparent

Evidence Control System
Advantages of Paper Transmittal Envelopes:
☐ Blood
☐ Hair
☐ Semen
☐ Or any other biological evidence that is subject to mold or decomposition by moisture
Evidence Submitted to a Lab
☐ Evidence may be transmitted by:
☐ Courier
☐ Air Express
☐ Registered Mail
☐ Railway Express
Method of Transmittal Is Determined by Two Factors
Nature of the Evidence
Urgency with Which Results must Be Obtained

Conclusion: The purpose of this practical exercise is to allow the learner to experience directly the investigative process and its relationship to criminalistics. The investigation does not stop in a day; the reporting process will take place over the course of training cycle. The preliminary and follow-up reports set the foundation for the forensic reports. This investigation is the learner's responsibility from beginning to end.

Sources: The Gravesite Excavation Simulation was adapted from:

Byers, S. (2002). *Introduction to forensic anthropology: A textbook.* Boston, Massachusetts: Allyn and Bacon.
R.R. Ogle, Jr. (2007). *Crime scene investigation and reconstruction.* Upper Saddle River, New Jersey: Pearson Education, Inc.
Stuart H. James, Jon J. Nordby, Suzanne Bell (2014). *Forensic science: An introduction to scientific and investigative techniques.* Roca Raton, Florida: CRC Press.

Appendix B: Chapter 2

CRIMINAL CULT CASE STUDY

I. Criminal Cult

Attention Hook: The human mind presents a huge challenge for law enforcement personnel. Reading behavioral cues can save your life. Your professional responsibility is to learn how to read the cues and anticipate the offender's danger to you and others.

Learner Objectives

- Appraise appropriate law enforcement responses.
- Illustrate cult leadership strategies.
- Identify possible law enforcement responses.
- Cite possible law enforcement solutions.
- Appraise the cult involved in the case study.
- Select superior response solutions for case studies.

II. The Law Enforcement Responses:

- Law enforcement officers should try to arrest cult leaders away from the group and avoid unfriendly terrain.
- If arrested in front of followers, group solidarity will form and this will result in civil unrest and collective behavior.
- The external threat only forces the leaders into a powerful position.
- Avoid using deception in the negotiation process.
- Provide for and take care of all human needs: health, safety, food, water, and shelter.
- Attempt to provide medical attention to the injured.
- Use the opposite gender in the negotiation process, there may be less resistance in the interviewing process.
- Above all, avoid all harassment and threats of violence in barricade incidents. This will add to the panic reaction.

- Law enforcement officers should understand that this kind of mind is capable of planning advanced tactical and security procedures to include booby traps.
- The cult leadership should not be allowed to manipulate the media.
- However, media information should flow to the cult followers. This will increase accurate information that will facilitate appropriate decision-making.

III. Attack the Cult Leader's Center of Gravity:

- Allow the membership to slowly disaffect and leave the siege situation gradually.
- When accurate information is provided by every means possible, the truthful information will help circumvent the leadership propaganda.
- Isolate, contain, and communicate with truthful information to the cult followers.
- The cult's deceptions, manipulations, and delusions must be exposed.
- These paranoid leaders see membership in a cult as an opportunity to participate in violent behavior.
- Avoid giving leaders the opportunity and excuse for violence.

IV. Finding Solutions:

- Use think-tank teams for developing strategy and tactics. This informal group may prove useful in barricade/siege incidents.
- These teams can conduct brainstorming sessions to develop possible courses of action to resolve a conflict situation.
- Generally, teams are composed of a mixture of experts from selected areas.
- These innovative thinkers are noted for attacking problems in unconventional ways.
- The solutions are advisory in nature; the law enforcement official-in-charge at the scene will make the final decision.
- Receive, analyze, use, and disseminate intelligence information from all levels. Act on accurate information that can be verified.

- Avoid speculation, false assumptions, and hasty planning.
- The special reaction teams should be used as a last resort and their actions based on accurate intelligence.
- They should be used when serious charges are pending and when force is essential.
- Law enforcement officers should be a part of the solution —peacemaker's first and using force only when necessary.

V. Underlying Strategy:

- Negotiation may find the solution with patience and time on the side of negotiators.
- The tactical solution should be used only when necessary.
- In most cases, the solution may be found in nonviolent, not violent procedures.
- However, examining the psychological factors may provide some possible insight by way of inductive/deductive reasoning that will support the negotiation process and avoid a self-fulfilling apocalyptic ending.

VI. Teaching Points:
Lesson linkage – Instructional Units:

- First Responder Unit
- Crisis Manage Unit
- Hostage Negotiation Unit

Personality Profiling

- The development and use of the psychological profile is just one more technique used to develop courses of action.
- The psychological makeup of the offender should not be overlooked.
- A psychological profile should include background, attitudes, values, motivations, and idiosyncrasies.
- The key trademark core and signature behaviors exhibited while committing the offenses must be carefully defined.
- It is from the core and offender profile information that the investigator will be able to identify the offender's underlying motivation.

Psychological Personality Profiling

- At the present state of development, profiling is considered an art and not a science.
- "Criminal personality assessment helps investigators identify those patterns of behavior and personality." Ressler, Burgess, and Douglas (1988, p. 11)
- Personality assessment should be directed at profiling the cult leaders, key subordinates, and the followers when possible.
- The Stockholm Syndrome and follower behaviors should be evaluated for identification with the kidnapper(s) and cooperation.

Signature and Core Behaviors

- "Modus Operandi—MO is learned behavior. It is what the perpetrator does to commit the crime. It is dynamic—that is, it can change. Signature is a term I coined to distinguish from MO, is what the perpetrator has to do to fulfill him. It is static; it does not change." Douglas (1995)
- Negotiators have a number of possible ways to profile all hostage takers. These categories may be useful in developing negotiating styles and decision-making purposes.

Stratton (1978) has identified three basic categories

• **The mentally ill hostage-taker**
• **The criminal hostage-taker**
• **The social, political, religious, or ethnic crusader hostage-taker**

- The mentally ill hostage-taker has considerable power over law enforcement officials.

This problem is compounded when the mentally ill person is suicidal.

- This scenario is the most unstable for law enforcement officials to isolate and control.
- The mentally ill individual is the most difficult to negotiate with because their behavior is irrational and often unpredictable. Negotiating with an emotionally disturbed individual requires a great deal of patience with a downplay of tactical power authority.
- The incident is more complicated when a hostage/barrier scenario is comprised of followers who have adopted suicidal ideation.
- For example, negotiating with a suicidal individual charged with a weapon violation as opposed to a non-suicidal individual.
- Because of the overlapping nature of the classification of typology systems, it is quite possible for law enforcement officials to misread the situation.
- The criminal hostage-takers in the barrier situation are generally the most rational and predictable.
- These incidents have a higher success rate in the area of hostage negotiations, but not when suicide is part of the equation.

VII. Body of Knowledge

Paranoid: Suicidal Cults

- At the risk of adding more confusion to the hostage negotiation process, it appears there is a need to define a revised sub-typology that is based on the former models.

This paranoid sub-typology is related to:

- The mentally ill
- Psychic
- Fanatical religious beliefs
- Has suicidal tenets
- Survivalist themes
- Has an unconscious or conscious death wish

- Apocalyptic philosophy
- Based on the armed conflict approach

Motivation

- Quite often, the needs of paranoid cult leadership will include money, power, and sex.
- The leader claims direct power from God or convinces his following that he is in fact, God!
- Once the converts believe that he is God-like, the logic of absolute obedience follows.
- He must achieve total control of his own immediate social world.

Method of Operation

- According to many experts, members do not join the cult.
- Unsuspecting victims are psychologically seduced into membership status.
- The typical modus operandi is that recruits meet a friendly person who has targeted them.
- The preferred subject is young, talented, and intelligent.

Method of Operation

- Paranoid cult leaders will attempt to isolate, control information and use group pressure to engage in intense indoctrination.
- The combination of psychological factors with inadequate diet and fatigue will eventually destroy critical thinking skills.
- In addition, new members are given a great deal of attention and positive rewards.

Controlling Behaviors

- The paranoid cult leader will establish the elements of command control.
- When absolute dedication to the leader is established, the mind-controlling teachings will follow in order to establish supreme power.

- At this stage of development the potential for abuse will be exploited
- The primary tool is the use of fear.
- Investigators will find them difficult to deal with and resistant to compromise.
- These cult leaders will be hostile, stubborn, defensive, and rigid.
- Expect them to be suspicious and continually on the lookout for possible signs of trickery.

VIII. Part Three: Threat Assessment

Crime Analysis and Threat Assessment

- They may also read hidden messages and signs into any event.
- At all cost, they must maintain power and control over events.
- They must have it their own way.
- The underlying theme of everything the paranoid personality does is power, manipulation, domination, and control.
- Avoid adding to the stress in the immediate environment.
- It could cause violence during a paranoid transient psychotic reaction.
- Generally, the paranoid cult leader has knowledge and considerable expertise in group psychology.
- The cult leader understands how people think, feel, and act in group situations.
- The delusional beliefs are induced and transmitted to the group through personal influence and group manipulated dynamics.
- In fact, group members must totally accept the cult leader's delusions in order to gain trust and acceptance.

The learner will be able to apply the following 10 objectives:

- Appraise the role of personality profiling.
- Define the term modus operandi.
- List the behavioral elements of the mentally ill cult leader.
- Describe the paranoid cult leader's motivation.

- Distinguish the paranoid cult leader's controlling behavior strategy.
- Apply the threat assessment procedures.
- Describe the law enforcement response options.
- Appraise the element of attacking the cult's center of gravity.
- List the role of think-tank strategies.
- Identify the purpose of brainstorming strategies.

Lesson Linkage: Instructional Units

- First Responder Unit
- Crisis Manage Unit
- Hostage Negotiation Unit

IX. Case Study: Problem-solving Groups

The instructor tasks the learners to describe the following content on the blackboard. Learners explain the implications of the case study scenario. The solution will require group blackboard presentations during class discussions. Assign the relevant chapter readings and specific chapter graphics or concepts to specific groups for classroom presentations.

- **Group One** will be responsible for presenting a personality profile of the Prophet's psychological behavior and case study solution.
- **Group Two** will be responsible for discussing the Prophets use of fear tactics and case study solution.
- **Group Three** will be responsible for presenting paranoid cult assessment applications and case study solution.
- **Group Four** will be responsible for presenting threat assessment strategies and case study solution.
- **Group Five** will be responsible for discussing law enforcement strategies and case study solution.
- **Group Six** will be responsible for discussing the cult leader's center of gravity and case study solution.

General Instructions

Trainee groups brief solutions on the blackboard—then compare, contrast, and explore solutions. In addition, they offer brief agency descriptions and Task Force code name. This exercise serves as a warm-up to further group endeavors.

Group One	Police Psychologist Role
Group Two	Special Reaction Team Role
Group Three	Local Law Enforcement
Group Four	State Police
Group Five	Federal Law Enforcement
Group Six	Command Element

Special Note: Maintain learners in groups and apply remote viewer strategies from different locations. Respond to questions within the group. Caution learners when it is their time to brief the class and provide time to organize presentations.

Groups are responsible for assigned topics and provide think-tank solutions. Members vote on law enforcement solutions after discussing relevant social and tactical issues. Instructors complement learners regarding positive participation and cooperation.

Corner 2-2 Critical Thinking

Finally, instructors conclude lecture segments with a critique or formalized follow-up activity. After presenting individual group solutions on the blackboard, learners select the best applications to develop a class consensus on how to solve the case study. Instructors serve as guides during this process; all recommendations are worthy and should not be criticized. Tact and diplomacy are applied when addressing technical errors.

Critiques can be effective procedures that pose issues not previously discussed and serve the purpose of informing learners of their training progress. Critiques also assess solutions and provide constructive feedback. Ultimately, critiques clarify, emphasize, or reinforce performance objectives, critical thinking, and problem-solving strategies. How would you insert critical thinking points learners might overlook?

X. Case Study Summary and Conclusion

Case studies and practical group scenarios encourage learner activities that enhance the learning process. Group dynamics and active learning case studies offer opportunities for learner involvement, expression, and development. The emphasis is on the integration of concepts, analysis, and problem solving related to law enforcement interventions and response tactics.

Training References

- Baker, T. (2007). teaching public safety administration: Active learning simulations. *Journal of Police Crisis Negotiations: An International Journal*, 7, (2), 85 – 106.
- Strentz, T. (1986). Negotiating with the hostage-taker exhibiting paranoid-schizophrenic symptoms. *Journal of Police Science and Administration*, 14, 12 – 17.
- Vecchi, G. M. (2002). Hostage/barricade management: A hidden conflict within law enforcement. *FBI Law Enforcement Bulletin*, 71, 1 – 6.

APPENDIX C: CHAPTER 3

Building the Training Climate

The Universal Design for Instruction offers an instructional model for building a positive learning climate. Why is the Universal Design for Instruction (UDI) important to law enforcement training? UDI facilitates the learning process and specifies learning outcomes. Therefore, the UDI philosophy and goals are important and related to specific foundation learning outcomes. Moreover, the UDI approach meets the needs of learners with diverse learning styles. The UDI approach requires the systematic design of instruction, diverse active learning strategies, critical thinking, and problem solving. Learners are offered opportunities to address these requirements throughout the training course.

The principles of UDI are applicable to training learners. A more systematic method of meeting the needs of diverse learners is required. UDI offers such a model (Scott, McGuire, and Shaw, 2001). The quality of instructor effectiveness is a critical requirement of learning environments (Scott and Gregg, 2000). The following paragraphs are examples of the UDI system approach. The framework of the nine principles of UDI has been adapted from the Center for Universal Design (Shaw and Dukes, 2001) and illustrated by Scott, McGuire, and Shaw (2001). This guide assists trainers in contemplating and developing instruction for a broad range of learners. The author has modified and adapted the UDI system to teaching an **Investigative Process** course.

Instructional Climate

Instructional design should be welcoming, encouraging high expectations for all learners. **UDI system example:** The instructor writes a statement in the syllabus affirming the need for learners to respect diversity, underscoring the expectation of tolerance, and encouraging learners to discuss any special learning needs with the instructor. **Investigative Process course example:** The instructor provides a learning contract that specifies course requirements, encourages respect for others, and offers referral information for learners with disabilities.

The UDI system provides a systematic process to meet the needs of diverse learners. An increase in participants with learning disabilities requires accommodations and modifications in pedagogical methods, imagination, and curriculum expertise. Moreover, this inclusive approach improves the quality of instruction, communication, and learning climate for all learners.

UDI applies to lectures, classroom discussions, group work, and related supplementary support materials in the learning climate. Internet-based instruction, case studies, fieldwork, and other academic activities and materials complement the UDI approach. Inclusive methods provide learners with meaningful access to the curriculum by assuring access to the learning environment. The combination makes course content and activities accessible to people with a wide range of abilities, disabilities, ethnic backgrounds, language skills, and learning styles (Scott, McGuire and Foley, 2001).

Equitable Use

Instruction should be useful to and accessible by people with diverse abilities. It provides the same means of use for all learners, identical whenever possible, equivalent when not. **UDI system example:** Using web-based courseware products with links to on-line resources so all learners can access materials, regardless of varying academic preparation, distance from campus, and so on. **Investigative Process course example:** The instructor developed various teaching modalities, that is, Angel or Blackboard websites. In addition, publisher websites that include online practice tests are available for learners. Classroom activities include instructor lectures and case studies that encourage group decision-making and problem solving.

Flexibility

Instruction seeks to accommodate a wide range of individual abilities. It provides choice in methods of use. **UDI system example:** The instructor provides varied instructional methods (lecture with a visual outline, group activities, use of case studies, or web-based discussions) to support different ways of learning. **Investigative Process course example:** The instructor allows additional time for examination completion. Learners receive advanced notice concerning report or warrant submission requirements. In addition, the instructor provides samples of reports that assist participants in the documentation and report writing process.

Simple and Intuitive Instruction

Organized and predictable instructional design facilitates the learning process. Diverse learner populations benefit from planned curriculum. It eliminates unnecessary complexity. **UDI system example:** The instructor provides a grading scheme for papers or projects that clearly states performance expectations for learners. **Investigative Process course example:** The instructor provides models for written assignments and lists specific requirements for witness presentations. In addition, investigative process course goals and task(s) related training objectives stated in the course outline provide additional guidance.

Perceptible Information

Instructional design offers the necessary information and communicates effectively, regardless of ambient conditions or the learner's sensory abilities. **UDI system example:** Selecting textbooks, reading material, and other instructional supports in digital format so participants with diverse needs can access materials through print or by using technological supports (e.g., screen reader, text enlarger). **Investigative Process course example:** The instructor adopts textbooks that offer supplementary support items.

Tolerance for Error

Instruction anticipates variation in individual participant learning pace and requisite skills. **UDI system example:** The instructor allows long-term course projects with the flexible option of turning in individual project components separately for analysis and provides constructive feedback for integration into the final product. **Investigative Process course example:** The instructor provides lead-up and practice case study exercises, which assist participants in developing investigative skills for the mock trial; that is, he or she dismisses classes early and coaches individual participant on role requirements.

Low Physical Effort

Instructional design minimizes nonessential physical effort to allow maximum attention to learning. Note: This principle does not apply when physical effort is integral to essential requirements of a course. **UDI system example:** Allowing participants to use a computer for writing and editing papers or essay exams provides additional support. **Investigative Process course example:** The instructor posts PowerPoint lecture notes online prior to class. This practice offers opportunities to concentrate on classroom activities. The class notes support the learning process and help move participants forward in their preparation for the mock trial.

Size and Space

Instructional design with consideration for appropriate size and space for approach, reach, manipulations, and use regardless of a participant's body size, posture, mobility, and communication needs. **UDI system example:** Using a circular seating arrangement in small class settings to allow participants to see and face speakers during discussion is important for learners with attention problems. **Investigative Process course example:** The instructor divides learners into groups of 4 – 5. Participants provide interactive solutions to case study activities and related case assignments in preparation for the mock trial.

A Community of Learners

The instructional environment promotes interaction and communication among participants and training staff members. **UDI system example:** The instructor fosters communication among learners in and out of class by structuring study and discussion groups, e-mail lists, or chat rooms. **Investigative Process course example:** The instructor provides the opportunity to participate in e-mail and Internet website communications with other participants. E-mail correspondence is essential to pretrial communication and trial rehearsal. Learners exchange email addresses and often meet independently and as a group in preparation for the trial.

Chapter 3: Case Study References

- Clifford O. (2010). *Catastrophic disaster planning and response.* Florida: CRC Press.
- Dyson, W. (2001). *Terrorism: An investigator's handbook.* Cincinnati, Ohio: Anderson Publishing Company.
- Lindell, M. & Prater, C. & R. Perry. (2006). *Emergency management.* New Jersey: Wiley.
- McEntire, D. (2006). *Disaster response and recovery.* New Jersey: Wiley.
- Phelan, T. D. (2008). *Emergency management and tactical response.* United Kingdom: Elsevier Butterworth-Heinemann.
- Poland, J. *Understanding terrorism: Groups, strategies and responses.* Englewood Cliffs: Prentice-Hall, Publisher, 2005.
- Reich, W. (1998). *Origins of terrorism: Psychologies, ideologies, theologies, states of mind.* Washington, DC: Woodrow Wilson Center Press.

APPENDIX D: CHAPTER 4

Body of Supporting Knowledge

Trainee Presentations

Group One: Hostage Negotiations: Basic Techniques

Techniques for developing trust and rapport between negotiator and hostage-takers:

- Self-disclosure
- Empathy
- Being a good listener
- Being understanding
- Showing personal interest in hostage negotiations
- Apply hostage negotiations procedures
- Address hostage-taker problems
- Reflect on hostage-taker feelings
- Avoid rejecting outright all demands
- Primary role is to establish favorable and supportive climate with the hostage-takers

Group Two: Hostage Negotiations:

Three Styles of Negotiation Observed:

• **Win/Lose or Agitation**
• **Harmony**
• **Mutual Concession**

- If hostage taker likes negotiator or finds similarities, negotiator is more likely to be successful in resolving situation.
- Stockholm Syndrome (the victims' identification and cooperation with the kidnappers)
- "Scarcity Principle": offering solutions and putting limit on solutions
- Example: trading hostages for food

Group Three: Power or Violence Potential of Hostage-Takers:

- Certain items universally accepted as nonnegotiable
- Would not want to negotiate for new weapons, explosives, or more ammunition
- Nonnegotiable policies
- Procedures commonly adhered to by law enforcement:
- No exchange of hostages
- No concessions without something in return
- Nonnegotiable Items: Drugs, Narcotics, and Alcohol
- Unpredictable Situation:
- Unduly dangerous when intoxication substances are introduced
- Negotiator should stall for time

Group Four: Time, Trust, and the Stockholm Syndrome:

- Standing Operating Procedures
- Possible Reasons for Failure
- Negotiators should be lower or middle-ranking officers
- Report to a decision-maker
- Buying time
- Negotiator must always consult with superiors before decision is made

Additional Advantages:

- Unfavorable decisions accepted as coming from higher-ups
- Not the negotiator
- Will not influence trust that has developed
- Hopefully between negotiator and hostage-taker:
- Bargain for time
- Time is on your side

Establish the Relationship:

- Negotiate the release of hostages
- Watch for the Stockholm Syndrome
- Trade the hostages for needs of terrorists

- For example: food and items you can provide to reduce tension and stress
- Stabilize and contain

Group Five: Time-Phase Model for Hostage Negotiation:

- Introduction – 15%
- Demands made and demands met or refused – 50 %
- Impasse – 10 %
- Suicide – 10 %
- Surrender – 15 %

Introduction Phase (1.5 Hours):

- "Getting to know each other" phase
- Build rapport
- Create positive emotional bond
- Provides information used in planning and refining negotiating strategies
- Flexible time boundaries
- Next phase begins in cooperative atmosphere
- Most of negotiation work is done
- Two parts: demands made and demands met or refused
- Demands made: "just go away" discounted

Demands Phase (6 Hours):
"Go to the boss" demands: money for escape vehicle, food, private conversation with a loved one or friend before going to jail:

- Time-consuming phase
- Usually positive tone
- Demands Phase (6 Hours)
- Negotiators make list of demands and delay tactics before taking action
- First time suspect is told "no"
- Frustration and anger build

Demands Phase (6 Hours):
Anger focused on situation and negotiator in particular:

- Suspect becomes more and more upset
- Bonding with negotiator starts to break down
- Breakdown of communication indicates next stage of negotiations
- Impasse Phase (1+ Hours)
- Suspect breaks off communication
- Refuses to talk to negotiator
- Long silence
- Tense period for negotiators

Impasse Phase (1+ Hours):

- Decision: Bring suspect back to the phone by intruding on his area?
- Alternatively, let the suspect sit in silence to rest or regroup?
- No clear-cut indicators
- Pressure on negotiators from tactical
- "Get things moving again"
- Impasse Phase (1+ Hours)
- Literature indicates keep suspect awake
- Command level decision
- Suspect realizes that situation is hopeless
- No further demands or compromises to be gained
- Depression sets in and begins to grow
- Suspect becomes hopeless
- Suicide Phase (1+ Hours)
- Sometimes passing, half-hearted feeling
- Most often serious
- Skillful handling of suspect important
- Negotiator attempts to dissuade suspect
- Phase usually brought to successful resolution

Group Six: Surrender Phase (1.5 Hours):

- Suspect must understand all steps in surrender process
- Suspect's mental state deescalated from high levels of anger and frustration

- Surrender Phase (1.5 Hours)
- Replaced with feelings of calmness and relief
- Moderate levels of anxiety felt by negotiators and tactical officers over surrender being accomplished without incident
- Dividing lines between phases can be clear or obscure
- Key statements may help indicate end or beginning of phase
- Summary – Key Statements

Demand Phase:

- Negotiator: "What do you want?"
- Suspect: "I want ..."
- Summary – Key Statements

Impasse Phase:

- Suspect: "I don't want to talk to you anymore" or "You can't help me. I'm through talking"
- Summary – Key Statements

Suicidal Phase:

- Suspect: Negative comments
- Obvious depression
- Suspect makes suicidal statements
- Summary – Key Statements

Surrender Phase:

- Increasing return of cooperative attitude
- Suspect's acceptance surrender as inevitable
- Key statements vary
- Phases can be lengthened or shortened
- Provides yardstick of progress in negotiations
- Must remain flexible
- Allows negotiators to anticipate what might happen next
- Operations manager can estimate how much more time will be required to complete operation
- How to allocate resources
- Request additional resources?

Chapter 4: Case Study References

- Hammer, M. R., and Rogan, R. G. (1997). "Negotiation models in crisis situations: The value of a communication-based approach." In R. G. Rogan, M. R. Hammer, and C. R. Van Zandt (Eds.), *Dynamic processes of crisis negotiation: Theory, research, and practice* (9–23). Westport, CT, Praeger.
- Kaiser, N. F. (1990). "The tactical incident: A total police response." *FBI Law Enforcement Bulletin*, 59, 14–18.
- McMains, M. J., and Mullins, W. C. (2001). *Crisis negotiations: Managing critical incidents and hostage situations in law enforcement and corrections* (2nd Ed.). Cincinnati, OH, Foundation Press.
- Romano, S. J., and McMann, M. F. (Eds.) (1997). *Crisis negotiations: A compendium. Crisis Negotiation Unit, Critical Incident Response Group.* Quantico, VA, FBI Academy. (1), 35–46.
- Womack, D. F., and Walsh, K. (1997). "A three-dimensional model of relationship development in hostage negotiations." In R. G. Rogan, M. R. Hammer, and C. R. Van Zandt (Eds.), *Dynamic processes of crisis negotiation: Theory, research, and practice.* Westport, CT, Praeger.

Epilogue Solution Sheet for Fill-in Questions

Chapter 1: Answer Key

Refer to the following fill-in questions to formulate a general assessment of your training content knowledge:

1. *Self-image* helps establish positive training methods and instructor success.
2. *Self-concept* is a life-controlling mechanism that regulates *self-discipline*, persistence, and dedication.
3. Successful instructors are capable of positive *self-projection*, an asset that creates an aura of confidence and a willingness to try another approach.
4. Instructors who practice positive *self-direction* envision success. They stay on the cutting edge and position themselves to enter the instructional arena, while charting the course for arriving at their destination.
5. Positive *self-discipline* and aspirations are powerful motivating forces.
6. Another important instructor quality is positive *self-awareness*. This requires the ability to step back and appraise one's personal impact on the instructional process. The skill demands examining strengths, weaknesses, and potential limitations.
7. Effective instructors engage in positive *self-motivation* and concentrate on what they desire to achieve. There are limitations; however, fear of failure is not one of them.
8. Superior instructors own positive *self-expectancy*. They have insight into overcoming instructional barriers and insulators. This self-fulfilling prophesy offers powerful learner enticements. Anticipate successful instructional solutions and prompt them to unfold.
9. Instructors with positive *self-control* take responsibility for their actions and do not rationalize mistakes.
10. Gottman and Declare (2001), in *The Relationship Cure*, describe excellent solutions for resolving instructor communication conflict. The authors divulge the need to respond to social bidding effectively. These researchers identified three

basic bid communication responses: (1) *turning toward*, (2) *turning away,* and an extreme form of turning away is the (3) *unrequited response.*

Chapter 2:

Refer to the following fill-in questions to formulate a general assessment of your training content knowledge:

1. Individual behaviors are unpredictable; however, group behaviors have three predictable stages of development. The predictable stages are: (1) *disorganized stage*, (2) *adjustment stage*, and (3) *cooperation or performance stage*.
2. The Enneagram *Reformer* is principled, purposeful, self-controlled, and a perfectionist.
3. The Enneagram *Helper* is generous, demonstrative, people-pleasing, and possessive.
4. The Enneagram *Motivator* is adaptable, ambitious, image-conscious, and driven.
5. The Enneagram *Individualist* is expressive, romantic, and can be withholding and temperamental.
6. The Enneagram *Investigator* is innovative, cerebral, detached, and provocative.
7. The Enneagram *Loyalist* is reliable and committed; however, he or she can be defensive and suspicious.
8. The Enneagram *Enthusiast* is spontaneous, versatile, distractible, and excessive.
9. The Enneagram *Leader* is self-confident, decisive, dominating, and confrontational.
10. The Enneagram *Peacemaker* is reassuring, agreeable, and can be disengaged and stubborn.

Chapter 3: Answer Key

Refer to the following fill-in questions to formulate a general assessment of your training content knowledge:

1. Curriculum management provides the *strategic big picture* and pathway to practical training solutions.

2. A *training paradigm* is a collection of organizing principles, belief systems, or creative models that shape understanding.
3. The *cognitive* domain refers to (recall or recognition of knowledge).
4. The *affective* domain refers to (feelings or emotions; changes in interest, attitudes, and values; appreciations).
5. The *psychomotor* domain refers to (reflexes, fundamental, perceptual, and complex motor patterns).
6. Dynamic *virtual reality* training methods involve real world multi-dimensional situations.
7. *Active* learning requires participants to learn not only from the instructor, but also from each other, while participating in the problem-solving process.
8. The *goals approach* motivates instructors because it offers direction, enhances evaluation in response to specific performance, and meets task-linkage requirements.
9. Specific participant *performance objectives* function on the operational field level.
10. *Summative* evaluation focuses on the global nature of instruction.

Chapter 4: Answer Key

Refer to the following fill-in questions to formulate a general assessment of your training content knowledge:

1. *Lesson planning* defines the *what, when,* and *how* performance task(s) standards timeline.
2. Knowledgeable trainers apply the *back-step* planning sequence.
3. A clustering of *units* refers to phases, levels, or sections.
4. Each unit includes designated performance *objectives* and related tasks.
5. Generally, begin the lesson plan by presenting the big *strategic* picture, then restate it again.
6. Lesson plans start with basic *definitions* and continue to build the groundwork for difficult requirements.
7. Outline a distinct *hierarchy* of learning progressions.
8. Learning that offers *chronological* steps requires arranging them in the sequence in which they logically occur.

9. Lesson planning requires selecting appropriate *instructional methods*. Performance objectives match teaching method(s).
10. The *content* of the lesson determines instructional method selection.

Chapter 5: Answer Key

Refer to the following fill-in questions to formulate a general assessment of your training content knowledge:

1. The word *feedback* defines learner knowledge and results.
2. Effective instructors recognize the role of *feedback* in the learning process.
3. Training performance objectives have three parts: (1) *action verb*, (2) *content area,* and (3) *measurable criteria.*
4. Some performance objectives are *terminal* and do not require sequencing hierarchies.
5. The *action verb* provides direction, defines learner performance and activity completion.
6. Training *objectives* may include specific learning criteria and describe the conditions under which the learner performs the task(s).
7. Training *standards* describe measurable criteria for assessment and a system for achieving accountability.
8. *Programmed instruction* provides a systematic understanding of information. Moreover, it allows self-paced advancement. This format provides immediate feedback, reinforcement, and learner involvement.
9. Training *objectives* serve as learner-centered guidance.
10. The *practical exercise* offers venues for problem-solving applications.

Chapter 6: Answer Key

Refer to the following fill-in questions to formulate a general assessment of your training content knowledge:

1. *PREPARE* is an acronym that describes *Plan, Rehearse, Early Intervention, Proceed, Active Learning, Review, and Evaluate.*

2. Trainers pose a basic question: "Where are we going?" The answer determines goals, *organizing centers,* and defines appropriate performance objectives.

3. The second question: "How will you get there?" is answered by developing *goals* and the derived *performance* objectives.

4. The gravesite excavation exercise appeals to multiple *learning* styles.

5. *Organizing centers* enhance the learning design through the articulation and sequencing of related goals and performance objectives.

6. The *organizing center* (gravesite practical exercise) is a goal frame of reference.

7. *Performance objectives* originate from specific goals and inform participants regarding standards and learning progressions.

8. Trainers understand the *learning curve* principle. Trainers train-up to the required level of proficiency, in the minimum amount of time.

9. Every "learning curve" contains a *forgetting curve*, a quantitative curve that leads to decline in the learning process.

10. Conduct an *exercise review* during the final classroom instruction and at the beginning of the field training practical exercise.

Chapter 7: Answer Key

Refer to the following fill-in questions to formulate a general assessment of your training content knowledge.

1. The main argument for advocating simulation technique revolves around *motivation.*

2. *Role-playing* refers to player problem solving that enables learners to explore field situations.

3. *Role-playing* demands rules, regulations, authentic settings, and hypothetical situations.

4. The intersection of the horizontal and vertical axes locates the *organizing center.*

5. The following behaviors emerge on the *horizontal axis* of the mock trial simulation: cooperation, self-control, due process, and respect for the rights of others.

6. The *vertical axis* documents content and learning objectives: evidence collection and preservation, chain of custody/ scientific laboratory procedures, interview strategy models, and courtroom testimony, and so on.
7. The evidence trail and *theory of transfer* will hopefully prove one of them guilty beyond a reasonable doubt in the mock trial simulation.
8. The ideal time for *coaching* is during the suppression hearing, before the courthouse mock trial.
9. The main purpose of the *suppression hearing* simulation is to challenge evidence concerning chain of custody.
10. In summary, mock trial *active learning* strategies encourage: (1) problem-solving, (2) decision-making, and (3) critical thinking skill applications.

Chapter 8: Answer Key

Refer to the following fill-in questions to formulate a general assessment of your training content knowledge:

1. Privette defines *peak performance* as "behavior that transcends or goes beyond predictable functioning to use a person's potential more fully than could be reasonably expected."
2. Striving for *peak performance* facilitates a sense of creative *flow*.
3. There are two basic levels of the *peak experience*. The first level is the *novice* peak *performance*.
4. *Peak performances* and *flow* experiences are more likely to occur during practical exercises or simulations.
5. *Excellence* defines extreme personal performance efforts that demand practiced expertise and the application of related skills.
6. *Creativity* requires "dreaming the dream" in pursuance of positive images.
7. Creativity generally takes time; however, insight gleaned from *experiences* can jump-start the dynamic instructor approach.
8. The criteria for *brainstorming* evaluation includes: (1) creative solutions to the problem; (2) participation of all group

members; (3) novel solutions; (4) valuable ideas; and (5) a trusting social climate.

9. *Peak performances* and *flow* experiences are more likely to occur during *practical exercises* or *simulations*.

10. The *confluence* model states that "Six resources need to work together in creativity: intellectual abilities, knowledge, personality traits, motivational style, thinking styles, and an environment that is supportive of the creative process and creative output.

Chapter 9: Answer Key

Refer to the following fill-in questions to formulate a general assessment of your training content knowledge.

1. Instructors help learners gain self-understanding once relationship foundations are in place—no easy task. Two factors affect the process: (1) *defensive behaviors*, and (2) *denial or blockage*.

2. The counseling interview process has three overlapping phases: (1) *opening*, (2) *development* (self-exploration, self-understanding, commitment), and (3) *conclusion*.

3. Assess *coping skills* as soon as possible, accurate behavioral analysis determines positive outcomes.

4. *Acceptance* infers tolerance and encourages a change in behavior—the ultimate goal.

5. *Empathy* defined in form of metaphors: "walking in someone else's shoes," or "seeing something through someone else's eyes."

6. *Problem learners* bring emotional issues to the instructional process.

7. *Disability* learners do not always acknowledge personal limitations in the training environment for fear of discrimination and peer acceptance.

8. *Dependent* learners require direction, guidance, and appreciate structure in the learning process.

9. *Independent* learners function best without interference from instructors or other learners. They are self-motivated and have a preference to control the learning process—offer opportunities that allow independent learners to find self-prescribed learning pathways.

10. The *referral process* includes seeking the support of qualified professionals who help learners with serious emotional problems.

Chapter 10: Answer Key

Refer to the following fill-in questions to formulate a general assessment of your training content knowledge.

1. The first step to successful program management is to train the *trainers*.
2. The second step is *prioritize* training needs and requirements.
3. *Coaching* training staff is an art directly related to mentoring.
4. Advanced professional manager/instructors connect with the people around them and interpret *Emotional Command* Systems.
5. The *Commander-in-Chief* is motivated by the need to be self-reliant, strong, and avoid feeling weak or dependent.
6. The *Sentry* emotional command system relates to survival.
7. The *Nest-Builder* System coordinates functions related to affiliation, bonding, and attachment.
8. When the *Energy Czar* System is working properly, individuals can maintain physical and emotional fitness.
9. When the *Jester* System is in full expression, they feel a sense of relaxed stimulation, peace, and enjoyment.
10. The *Johari Window* Model offers opportunities to examine leadership, training, and the social climate from communication and feedback perspectives.

Appendix F: Multiple-Choice Answer Key

Multiple-Choice
Final Personal Assessment

Chapter 1: Multiple-Choice Questions

1. c. Choices a and b

2. d. All of the above

3. d. All of the above

4. d. Equality before the law

5. d. All of the above

Chapter 2: Multiple-Choice Questions

1. b. Achieve the cooperation phase

2. d. Nine

3. a. Investigator

4. c. Leader

5. c. Motivator

Chapter 3: Multiple-Choice Questions

1. a. Training paradigm

2. c. Philosophy

3. d. Virtual reality

4. c. Active learning

5. b. Organizing center

Chapter 4: Multiple-Choice Questions

1. a. Back-step

2. a. Learning hook

3. d. All of the above

4. d. All of the above

5. e. All of the above

Chapter 5: Multiple-Choice Questions

1. d. 83%

2. e. All of the above

3. b. Errors

4. c. Both a and b

5. e. All of the above

Chapter 6: Multiple-Choice Questions

1. d. None of the above

2. a. Summary Sheet

3. d. All of the above

4. b. Articulation

5. a. Redirect

Chapter 7: Multiple-Choice Questions

1. b. Motivation

2. d. All of the above

3. e. None of the above

4. d. None of the above

5. c. Suppression Hearing

Chapter 8: Multiple-Choice Questions

1. d. All of the above

2. a. Level one peak performance

3. b.   Level two peak performance

4. b.   Flow

5. b.   Resonance Performance Model

Chapter 9: Multiple Choice Questions

1. c.   Both a and b

2. c.   Opening phase

3. c.   Both a and b

4. c.   Rogers

5. b.   Ellis

Chapter 10: Multiple Choice Questions

1. b.   Train the trainers

2. c.   Commander-in-Chief System

3. b.   Explorer System

4. c.   Jester System

5. c.   Johari Window

References and Recommended Readings

Anderson, Lorin W. and Krathwohl, David R. (Eds.) with Airasian, Peter W., Cruikshank, Kathleen A., Mayer, Richard E., Pintrich, Paul R., Raths, James, and Wittrock, Merlin C., A taxonomy for learning, teaching, and assessing: A revision of Bloom's taxonomy of educational objectives. Addison Wesley Longman, Inc. 2001.

Baker, T. E. (1996). Teaching criminal investigation: A critical thinking approach. *Journal of Police and Criminal Psychology*, 11 (1): 19 – 26.

Baker, T. E. (2007). Teaching public safety administration: Active learning simulations. *Journal of Police Crisis Negotiations: An International Journa*l, 7 (2): 85-106.

Baker, T. E. (2008). Integrated automated fingerprint identification system. In R. K. Rasmussen, (Ed), *Encyclopedia of Forensic Science* (636-638). California: Salem Press.

Baker, T. E. (2008). Integrated ballistics identification system. In R. K. Rasmussen, (Ed.), *Encyclopedia of Forensic Science* (638-640). California: Salem Press.

Baker, T. E. (2007). Police litigation: Citizen complaints on the use of force. *The Chief of Police.* 21 (1): 25-30.

Baker, T. E. (2004). Police criminalistics: Gravesite excavation training. *The Chief of Police*, 18 (1): 20-26.

Baker, T. E. (2009). Police criminalistics: Learning modalities and evaluation. *Forensic Examiner*, 18 (3): 50-55.

Baker, T. E., and Thomas, G. (2008). Criminal analysis: A synergistic and consolidated curriculum model. *International Association of Law Enforcement Intelligence Analysts Journal*, spring, 1, 44-68.

Baker, T. E., Cimini, J. & Cleveland C. (2010). Mock trial journey: An assessment. *Forensic Examiner*, 20 (3): 32-43.

Beck, A. T. (1976). *Cognitive therapy and the emotional disorders*. New York: International Universities Press.

Benjamin, L. (1991). Personalization and active learning in large introductory psychology classes. *Teaching of Psychology*, 18: 68-74.

Bloom, B. S., Englehart, M. B., Furst, E. J., Hill, W. H., & Krathwohl, D. R. (1956). *Taxonomy of educational objectives, the classification of educational goals*, Handbook I: Cognitive Domain. New York: McKay.

Bonwell, C. & Eison, J. (1991). *Active Learning: Creating Excitement in the Classroom.* ASHE-ERIC Higher Education Report #1, Washington, D.C.: George Washington University.

Bonwell, C. *The enhanced lecture: A resource book for faculty.* Cape Girardeau, MO, Southeast Missouri State University, Center for Teaching and Learning, 1991.

Bonwell, D., & Sutherland T. (1996). The active learning continuum: Choosing activities to engage students in the classroom. *New Directions for Teaching and Learning,* 67: 3.

Brinckerhoff, L. C., McGuire, J. M., & Shaw, S. F. (2002). *Postsecondary education and transition for students with learning disabilities.* Austin, TX: PRO-ED.

Brookfield, S. (1990). *The skillful teacher: on technique, trust, and responsiveness in the classroom.* San Francisco: Jossey-Bass Publishers.

Byers, S. N. (2004). *Introduction to forensic anthropology.* Boston, Massachusetts: Allyn & Bacon.

Cannon, R. & Newble, D. (2000). *A handbook for teachers in universities and colleges: A guide to improving teaching methods.* Sterling, Virginia: Stylus Publishing.

Chatterji, M. (2003). *Designing and using tools for educational assessment.* Boston, Massachusetts: Allyn and Bacon.

Clynes, M. & Panksepp, J. (1988). *Emotions and psychopathology.* New York: Plenum Press.

Compas, B. (1987). Coping with stress in childhood and adolescence. *Psychological Bulletin,* 101(3): 393-403.

Costa, A. L., & O'Leary, P. J. (1992). *Co-cognition.* In N. Davidson & T. Worsham (Eds.), *Enhancing thinking through cooperative learning* (41 – 65). New York: Teachers College Press.

Csikszentmihalyi, M. (1975). Play and intrinsic rewards. *Journal of Humanistic Psychology,* 15 (3): 41 – 63.

Csikszentmihalyi, M. (1988) Society, culture, person: A systems view of creativity. In R. J. Sternberg (Ed.), *The nature of creativity.* Cambridge: Cambridge University Press (325 – 339).

Davis, B. G (2009). *Tools for teaching.* San Francisco, CA: Jossey-Bass Publishers.

Dick, W. & Carey, L. (1990). *The systematic design of instruction.* Glenview, Illinois: Scott, Foresmen Company.

Dressel, P. L., & Mayhew, L. B. (1954). *General education explorations in evaluation*. Washington, DC: American Council on Education.

Eble, E., McEwen, B, & Ickovics, J. (1998). Embodying psychological thriving: Physical response in response to stress. *Journal of Social Issues*, 54 (2): 301 – 322.

Eble, K. E. (1988) *The craft of teaching; a guide to mastering the professor's art*. San Francisco: Jossey-. Bass.

Ellis, A. (1998). *How to control your anxiety before it controls you*. Secaucus, NJ: Carol Publishing Group.

Emerson, J. D., & Mosteller, F. (1998). *An interactive multimedia in college teaching. Part II: Lessons from research in the sciences*. Educational Media and Technology Yearbook 23, 59 – 75.

Ennis, R. (1985). A logical basis for measuring critical thinking skills. *Educational Leadership*, 43 (2): 44 – 48.

Ferrett, S. K. (1994). *Peak performance*. Burr Ridge, IL: Irwin Mirror Press.

Flavell, J. H. (1976). *Metacognitive aspects of problem solving*. In L. Resnick (Ed.), The nature of intelligence (231 – 236).

Gantt, V. The case method in teaching critical thinking. In Freeman, A., Pretzer, J., Fleming, B. & Simon, K. (2004). *Clinical Applications of Cognitive Therapy*, second edition. New York: Plenum Press.

Garlief, C., & Bennett, H. (1984). *Peak performance: Mental training techniques of the world's greatest athletes*. Los Angeles: California. Presented at the Annual Meeting of the Southern States Communication Association (Memphis, TN, March 27 – 31, 1996).

Geberth, V. (1996). *Practical homicide investigation: tactics, procedures, and forensic techniques*. Boca Raton, Fla.: CRC Press.

Girard, J. (2008). *Criminalistics: forensic science and crime*. Sudbury, MA: Jones and Bartlett Publishers.

Glasser, W. (1999). *Choice theory: a new psychology of personal freedom*. New York: Harper Collins Publishers.

Glasser, W. (2000). *Reality therapy in action*. New York: Harper Collins Publishers.

Gottman, J. M., & DeClaire, J. (2001). *The relationship cure: a five-step guide to strengthening your marriage, family, and friendships*. New York: Three Rivers Press.

Greek, C. (1995). Using active learning strategies in teaching criminology: A personal account. *Journal of Criminal Justice Education*, 6: 152 – 62.

Gronlund, N. E., & Gronlund, N. E. (1998). *Assessment of student achievement* (6th Ed.). Boston: Allyn & Bacon.

Hamil, J. &. Janssen, S. (1987). Active learning in large introductory sociology classes. *Teaching Sociology*, 15: 45 – 54.

Herrington, A. & Cadman, D. (1991). Peer review and revising in an anthropology course: Lessons in learning. *College Composition and Communication*, 42: 184 – 89.

Holkeboer, R. (1993). *Right from the start: Managing your way to college success.* Belmont, California: Wadsworth.

Hunt, T. (1982). Raising the issues of ethics through the use of scenarios. *Journalism Educator*, 37: 55 – 58.

J. Panksepp (Ed.) (1995). *Advances in Biological Psychiatry*, Vol. 1, Greenwich, Connecticut. JAI Press.

Jackson, S. A., & Csikszentmihalyi, M. (1999). *Flow in sports.* Champaign, IL: Human Kinetics.

James, S. H. (2005). *Forensic science: An introduction to scientific and investigative techniques* (2nd Ed.). Boca Raton, Fla.: CRC Press.

Knight, C. (1989). *Teaching for thinking in history and the social sciences.* Pre-conference Workshop, What Current Curricular Trends Tell Us about General Education, held prior to the Annual Convention of the Virginia Community College Association (7th, Roanoke, VA, October 12-14 1989).

Kobasa, S. (1979). Stress life events, personality, and health: An inquiry into hardiness. *Journal of Personality and Social Psychology*, 37, 1 – 11.

Lazarus, R. & Folkman, S. (1984). *Coping and adaptation.* In W. Doyle Gentry (Ed.) *Handbook of behavioral medicine* (282 – 325). New York: Guilford Press.

Lowman, J. (1984). *Mastering the techniques of teaching.* San Francisco: Jossey-Bass.

Luft, J. (1970). *Group processes: an introduction to group dynamics.* Palo Alto, Calif.: National Press Books.

Marzano, R. (1992). The many faces of cooperation across the dimension of learning. In N. Davidson & T. Worsham (Eds), *Enhancing thinking through cooperative learning.* New York: Teachers College Press.

McCormick, G. M. The application of cognitive learning theory to criminal justice education. *Journal of Criminal Justice Education*, 5 – 14.

McGuire, J. & Scott, S. (2006). Universal design for instruction: Extending the universal design paradigm to college instruction. *Journal of Postsecondary Educational Disability*, 19 (2): 124 – 134.

McGuire, J., & Scott, S. (2002). Universal Design for Instruction: A promising new paradigm for higher education. *Perspectives*, 28 (2): 27 – 29.

McGuire, J., & Scott, S. (2006). An approach to inclusive college instruction: Universal design for instruction. *Learning Disabilities: A Multidisciplinary Journal*, 14, 21 – 31.

McKeachie, W. J. (1986). *Teaching tips: a guidebook for the beginning college teacher.* Lexington, Massachusetts: D.C. Heath and Company.

McKinney, M. K. (1997). Assessing criminal justice student learning styles for multimedia instruction. *Journal of Criminal Justice Education*, 8 (1): 1 – 18.

Model, H. & Carroll, R. (1993). *Promoting active learning in the life science classroom.* Seattle, Washington: National Resource for Computers in Life Science Education.

Moenssens, A., Starrs, J, Henderson, C., & Inbau, F. (1995). *Scientific evidence in civil and criminal cases* (4th Edition). Foundation Press, New York.

Molden, J. (1996). The FTO troubleshooter. *The Trainer.* 4(1): 34 – 37.

Nance, J. & Nance, C. (1990). Does learning occur in the classroom? *College Student Journal*, 24 (4): 338-340.

Nanda, S. (1985). Active learning in the introductory cultural anthropology course. *Anthropology and Education Quarterly*, 16: 271 – 275.

Newburg, D., Kimieck, J., Durand-Bush, N. & Doell, K. (2010). The role of resonance in performance excellent and life engagement. *The Journal of Applied Sport Psychology*, 14, 249 – 267.

Nierenberg, D. W. (1998). The challenge of teaching large groups of learners: Strategies to increase active participation and learning. *The International Journal of Psychiatry in Medicine*, 28 (1): 115 – 122.

O'Leary, V. & Ickovics, J. (1995). Resilience and thriving in response to challenge: An opportunity for a paradigm shift in women's health. *Women's Health: Research on Gender, Behavior, and Policy*, 1, 121 – 142.

Ogle, R. R. (2004). *Crime scene investigation and reconstruction: With guidelines for crime scene search and physical evidence collection.* Upper Saddle River, N.J.: Pearson Education.

Olliphant, J. (1990). *From research to reality: Activities and strategies that work.* Paper presented at the Annual Meeting of the Pacific Northwest Council on Foreign Languages (Portland, OR, May 3 – 5 1990).

Osborne, R. (1996). *The costs and benefits of critical thinking.* In Proceedings of the Annual Conference on Undergraduate Teaching of Psychology (March 20 – 22).

Osterman, D. (1982). Classroom lecture management: Increasing individual involvement and learning in the lecture style. *Journal of College Science Teaching*, 12: 22 – 23.

Panksepp, J (Ed.) (1996). *Advances in biological psychiatry,* Vol. 2, Greenwich, Connecticut: JAI Press.

Panksepp, J. (2001). The Neuro-evolutionary cusp between emotions and cognitions: Implications for understanding consciousness and the emergence of a unified mind science. *Consciousness & Emotion*, 7 (1): 15 – 54.

Panksepp, J., & Biven, L. (2012). *The archaeology of mind: Neuro-evolutionary origins of human emotions.* New York: W. W Norton.

Paul, R. (1992). *Critical thinking: What every person needs to survive in a rapidly changing world.* Santa Rosa, CA: Foundation for Critical Thinking.

Pennebaker, J. W. Health complaints, stress, and distress: Exploring the central role of negative affectivity. *Psychological Review*, 234 – 254.

Peterson, C. Seligman, M. & Vaillant, G (1988) Pessimistic explanatory style is a risk factor for physical illness: A thirty-five-year longitudinal study. *Journal of Personality and Social Psychology*, 55 (1): 23 – 27.

Privette, G. & Landsman, T. (1983) Factor analysis of peak performance: The full use of potential. *Journal of Personality and Social Psychology*, 44 (1): 195 – 200.

Privette, G. (1965). Transcendent functioning. *The Teacher College Record*, 66: 733 – 739.

Privette, G. (1981). Dynamics of peak performance. *Journal of Humanistic Psychology,* 21(1): 57 – 67.

Riso, D. R. (1987). *Personality types: Using the enneagram for self-discovery.* Boston, Massachusetts: Houghton Mifflin.

Riso, D. R. (2000). *Understanding enneagrams: The practical guide to personality types.* Boston, Massachusetts: Houghton Mifflin.

Robinson, M. B. (2000). Using active learning in criminal justice: Twenty-five examples. *Journal of Criminal Justice Education,* 22 (1): 65 – 78.

Rogers, C. (1980). *A way of being.* Boston, Massachusetts: Houghton Mifflin.

Ross, D. (2000). Emerging trends in police failure-to-train liability. *Policing: An International Journal of Police Strategies & Management,* 23 (2): 169 – 193.

Saferstein, R. (2011). *Criminalistics: an introduction to forensic science* (10 Ed.). Boston: Pearson.

Scott, S. & Gregg, N. (2000). Meeting the evolving needs of faculty in providing access for college students with LD. *Journal of Learning Disabilities,* 33, 158 – 167.

Scott, S., McGuire, J.M., & Foley, T. E. (2001). *Universal design for instruction: An exploration of principles for anticipating and responding to student diversity in the classroom.* Storrs, CT: Center on Postsecondary Education and Disability.

Scott, S., McGuire, J.M., & Shaw, S. (2001). *Principles of universal design for instruction.* Storrs, CT: Center on Postsecondary Education and Disability.

Seligman, M. E. (1975). *Helplessness: on depression, development, and death.* San Francisco: W.H. Freeman.

Seligman, M. E. (1998). *Learned Optimism.* New York: Pocket Books (Simon and Schuster).

Shaw, S., & Dukes, L. (2001). Program standards for disability services in Higher education. *Journal of Postsecondary Education and Disability,* 14 (2): 81 – 90.

Silverman, R., & Welty, W. (1992). *Case studies for teacher problem solving.* New York: McGraw-Hill.

Simonton, D. (2000). Creativity: cognitive personal development and social aspects. *The American Psychologist,* 55 (1): 151 – 158.

Smith, S. & Benscoter, A. (2000). Student technology skills and attitudes towards Internet-based courses: The potential benefits of an internet tutorial. *Journal of Criminal Justice Education*, 22 (1): 97 – 109.

Smith, S. & Benscoter, A. (2000). Student technology skills and attitudes toward internet based courses: The potential benefits of an internet tutorial. *Journal of Criminal Justice Education*, 22 (1): 97 – 109.

Snyder, C. R., & Dinoff, B. L. (1999). *Coping: Where have you been?* In C. R., Snyder, (Ed.) (1999). Coping: The psychology of what works (3-19). New York: Oxford University Press.

Stalheim-Smith, A., (1998). *Focusing on active, meaningful learning,* IDEA paper, No. 34, IDEA Center, Kansas State University

Stetson, N. (1993). Professional development for two-way teaching and learning. *Leadership Abstracts* 6: 2 – 3.

Strickland, B. (1978). Internal-external expectancies and health-related behaviors. *Journal of Counseling & Clinical Psychology*, 46(6), 1192 – 1211.

Tardif, T. & Sternberg, R. (1988). What do we know about creativity? In R. Sternberg (Ed.) *The nature of creativity* (429 – 440) New York: Cambridge Press.

Wassermann, S. (1993). *Getting down to cases: learning teaching with case studies.* New York: Teachers College Press.

Watson, D. & Pennebaker, J. (1989). Health complaints, stress, and distress: Exploring the central role of negative affectivity. *Psychological Review*, 96, 234 – 254.

Watson, D.L., Kessler, D.A., Kalla, S., Kam C.M., & Ueki, K. (1996). Active learning exercises are more motivating than quizzes for underachieving college students. *Psychological Reports,* 78, 131 – 134.

Weast, D. (1996). Alternative teaching strategies: the case for critical thinking. *Teaching Sociology.* 24 (2): 189 – 194.

Wells, J. & McKinney, M. (1997). Assessing criminal justice student learning styles for multimedia instruction. *Journal of Criminal Justice Education*, 8 (1): 1 – 18.

Wile, D. B. (1993). *After the fight: using your disagreements to build a stronger relationship.* New York: Guilford Press.

Wilkins, D. F. (1996). Are we using the wrong teaching method in our criminal justice classes? *Journal of Criminal Justice Education*, 7 (1): 23 – 34.

Williams, J. M. (2005). *Applied sport psychology: personal growth to peak performance.* McGraw-Hill Humanities/Social Sciences/Languages; 5 edition.

Yin, R. K. (1994). *Case study research: design and methods.* Thousand Oaks: Sage Publications.

Young, D., & McCormick G. (1991). The application of cognitive learning theory to criminal justice education. *Journal of Criminal Justice Education,* 2 (1): 5 – 14.

INDEX

Improving Motivation and Morale
A Police Leader's Guide
by Jody Kasper

Progressive Police Supervision
A Simple & Effective Approach for Managing a Police Agency
by Jody Kasper

Crucial Elements of Police Firearms Training
by Brian R. Johnson

Law Enforcement Management
What Works and What Doesn't
by Michael Carpenter & Roger Fulton

The Path of the Warrior – *2nd Edition*
*An Ethical Guide to Personal & Professional Development in
the Field of Criminal Justice*
by Larry F. Jetmore, Ph.D., Capt., Hartford, CT PD (Ret.)

Path of the Hunter
Entering and Excelling in the Field of Criminal Investigation
by Larry F. Jetmore, Ph.D., Capt., Hartford, CT PD (Ret.)

The Verbal Judo Way of Leadership
Empowering the Thin Blue Line from the Inside Up
by Dr. George Thompson & Gregory A. Walker

(800) 647-5547   www.LooseleafLaw.com